Satan's Underground

Lauren Stratford's moving account of prolonged and treacherous exploitation by the occult is A WORK OF NATIONAL IMPORTANCE. Her experiences and insights provide the missing links in an evil power movement that is spreading across the American landscape.

This personal story is more than a book. It is A TRIUMPHANT EPIC OF COURAGE AND HOPE conquering hatred and death.

—Kenneth Wooden
Former Special Investigative Reporter
for ABC News' "20/20"

THIS BOOK IS WORTHY OF YOUR READING. The story is absolutely incredible and true. I rarely recommend other people's books; however, this one needs to be put before the public.

—Hal Lindsey

Based on my knowledge of the staggering increase of child sexual abuse and of the escalating brutality of that abuse, LAUREN STRATFORD'S STORY IS ONLY TOO CREDIBLE.

When you talk about a child who is able to emerge with a clear voice out of the abusive circumstances in which she has been demeaned, degraded, and lost, that is a miracle of God. IT IS ABSOLUTELY CRUCIAL THAT LAUREN, AS ONE OF THESE PRECIOUS FEW, SPEAK OUT. BUT IT IS EVEN MORE CRUCIAL THAT WE LISTEN TO HER STORY.

—Judith Reisman, Ph.D.
Principal Investigator for the
Department of Justice on Child
Abuse/Pornography

Satan's Underground

A noted psychologist recently stated that it does not matter if you believe in God, or the devil. There is something evil out there—and it wants our children!

> —CNN, Turner Broadcasting Network
> From a report on satanic ritualistic
> abuse, November 11, 1987

LAUREN STRATFORD'S STORY IS ONE THAT NEEDS TO BE TOLD. The world needs to hear that there is hope and victory for those who have been held captive by the bonds of the enemy.

> —Mike Warnke
> Author of *The Satan Seller*

LAUREN'S BOOK IS LITERALLY A GODSEND, whether the reader is a policeman, psychotherapist, parent, dabbling teen, Christian counselor, trapped victim, or adult survivor. WE HAVE NEEDED SUCH A TOOL DESPERATELY! Thank you so much for publishing this book. THERE IS NONE OTHER QUITE LIKE IT.

> —Larry M. Jones
> Director,
> Cult Crime Impact Network, Inc.

SATAN'S UNDERGROUND

LAUREN STRATFORD

HARVEST HOUSE PUBLISHERS
Eugene, Oregon 97402

The story contained in this book is true. However, names of certain persons have been changed in order to protect the privacy of the individuals involved.

SATAN'S UNDERGROUND

Copyright © 1988 by Harvest House Publishers
Eugene, Oregon 97402

Library of Congress Catalog Card Number 87-081660
ISBN 0-89081-630-1

Printed in the United States of America.

With deep love
to my brother and sister
Randolph and Johanna
who loved me to my healing.

And to the many others throughout my life
whose faithful prayers
gave me the will to survive.

ACKNOWLEDGEMENTS

My forever thanks

. . . to my home church and shepherds, who learned all about me but still accepted me, loved me, and stood behind me.

. . . to my typists, Dorothy W. and Val, both of whom have earned medals for bravery as they tackled stacks of rough drafts that at first glance looked like instructions to World War III!

. . . to Hal and Kimmie, who have opened their hearts and their home to me. (Hal, I'm still trying to appreciate the wonderful world of cappuccino coffee!)

. . . to Debbie S., my generic prayer intercessor, and to the many other prayer warriors. Your unceasing prayers gave me the strength to persevere during the 13 months it took to write this book.

. . . to my dear friend in law enforcement, for your invaluable insight and support.

. . . to Caryl, my "pre-editor," who gave me the courage to share the real me with the rest of the world.

. . . to Al and Eileen, my editors, for their commitment in helping this book convey the message of God's love and hope. No two editors could have given this project more TLC.

. . . to Harvest House, for their dedication to publishing books that minister to hurting people and for their courage in accepting *Satan's Underground* as one of those books.

. . . to the Lord Jesus Christ for doing the impossible.

I have been blessed!

FOREWORD

by Johanna Michaelsen

This will not be an easy book for you to read. The story of Lauren's abuse, of the years of horrors and tortures she experienced, of the satanic rituals and murders she witnessed, will prove more than many of you can bear. Some of you will be tempted to dismiss this book altogether, comforting yourselves with the thought that the whole story is so beyond belief that it simply cannot be true . . . that she must have made the whole thing up . . . that things like this simply don't happen in today's civilized world . . . and that even if they do, they probably involve an insignificant minority of people, so we don't want to know about the happenings!

That attitude is precisely what satanists are counting on. They're depending on our disbelief and fear and ignorance—on our out-of-hand rejection of cases like Lauren's. Yet victims across the country are telling stories very much like hers. In virtually every city and town I've traveled to during the last three years, at least one person has come to me after my lecture to tell me, often weeping and in frightened whispers, of rituals, abuse, and human sacrifice. Hundreds of children in preschools and kindergartens across the country are talking about grown-ups in robes, chanting in a strange guttural language while they perform dark ceremonies that include sexual abuse. They tell about watching animals and little babies being tortured and killed with knives. At least 70 preschools in the Los Angeles area have been investigated for alleged ritualistic abuse of children in the last few years. Similar cases can be found in preschools and neighborhoods in every state of this country.

The stories these children tell are so inconceivably horrifying that few individuals in the court system believe them. But then again, it was only a few short years ago that we had a problem in believing that incest was rampant. How much harder it is for most of us to accept the fact that there are groups of parents and teachers, doctors, lawyers, ministers, or other "pillars of the community" who are involved in devil worship and ritual abuse of children. Law-enforcement officers and detectives have told me that in many parts of this country their officers no longer even bother to record the ritualistic aspects of a crime. They know that the chances of gaining a court conviction in any case that even breathes the word "satanic" are virtually nil. As stated in an official report presented in September 1986 by John K. Van de Kamp, Attorney General of the State of California, in reference to a major child-abuse case in Bakersfield, California, "It can be firmly stated that the satanic allegations eroded the children's credibility . . . and ultimately their ability to testify about what happened to them."

If there is one thing that cult satanists do well, it's cover their tracks in such a way as to thoroughly discredit witnesses who might seek to come against them. That task is especially easy for them when dealing with young children, which is one reason why children make such ideal victims. The child may muster the courage to testify that he saw a little animal tortured, killed, and buried . . . yet when and if the site is dug up, no conclusive animal remains are found. He may speak of having "naked pictures" taken . . . but none ever surface in the usual circles. He may talk of having been taken on an airplane somewhere where someone did bad things to him . . . but in the time span during which the child was away from his home, it was impossible to have taken a flight to the stated location. So the child is discredited, fostering the belief that it is old-fashioned and ridiculous to believe that anyone would tell stories like these.

Yet in the past few years adult survivors, defectors from satanist camps, and investigators have begun to shed some light on the satanists' tactics. Animals are indeed killed and buried, but are later dug up and disposed of elsewhere. The children are frequently given a stupefying drug before the rituals so that their senses and perceptions are easily manipulated in the dim candlelight of the ritual scene. The pornographic photographs taken of the children don't show up because they're carefully kept in vaults of private collectors. And the "airplane trips" were guided imagery/visualization voyages taken while the children were on the drugs slipped to them in their lemonade. Or perhaps the plane ride was quite real, but they were flown only a short distance to the abuse site and not to some distant place as the child was told.

It is indeed conceivable that some given child could be mistaken or even lying about having been abused or forced to participate in a ritual experience. It is also possible for a therapist to ask a child enough leading questions to glean the desired declaration of abuse. *But what is absolutely impossible and illogical for us to believe is that every single child telling these stories is lying or has been programmed by parents or therapists. There are simply too many such children all over the country, spontaneously and independently telling the same horrific stories, virtually point for point.* The same holds true for the adult survivors who are now beginning to speak up. Too many of them are telling the same story.

It is painful to hear these stories. It tears at the very depth of one's mind and soul to learn of the unspeakably deliberate evil that man is capable of committing. It is especially hard for Christians to handle. Many of us would rather, as I have frequently been told, "simply talk about Jesus." I understand that; so would I. And yet the victims are here—thousands of them, those who are desperately seeking for a way out of the clutching blackness of demonic cults. To whom shall they go? To whom shall we send them for help, if we who call ourselves by the name of Christ refuse to believe, let alone understand? To help them we must know something of what they have lived through. We must understand something of the basics of satanism and ritualistic abuse. We must understand something of the basic working of brainwashing and mind control. We must, above all, know how to fight spiritual warfare *in a balanced and scriptural fashion*, patiently allowing the Lord to bring healing to these shattered lives in His time. If you do not understand these basics, you will never reach the hearts and souls of victims. I believe that Lauren's story will go a long way in helping you understand.

If you still believe that you can comfortably live in today's world as a Christian and not deal with the reality of satanism, think again. Satanism is on the rise. It is not a passing fad that will fade if we all just ignore it or throw a few positive confessions at it. Not every satanist group is involved in animal or human sacrifices, but a growing number of them certainly are. According to the hundreds of news clippings from papers across the country, according to dozens of police reports which I have read, according to detectives and law enforcement officials with whom I have met or spoken, according to therapists and frightened parents, according to the victims and according to many satanists themselves, *satanism is here*. It will not go away simply because you refuse to believe it.

This story isn't just for detectives and law enforcement to learn from, although they will. It isn't just for pastors, therapists, and mental-health professionals, although the information contained in the end of this book will provide insights vital to their ministry to victims. This book is also for teenagers, because they are prime targets for the satanist who lures them with promises of power and glory. It is for every Christian who believes that "for this purpose the Son of God was manifested, that He might destroy the works of the devil." It is for every believer who understands that God has not given us a spirit of fear, but of power, love, and a sound mind. It is for every Christian who knows Jesus Christ *has already won the victory!*

Ultimately this book is not about pornography or Satan. It is about the overwhelming power and victory of the Lord Jesus Christ. It is about the hope and light and healing and freedom that He can bring into the most hopeless and shattered of lives. Lauren has written this book with her tears. She has written it to tell the world that because Jesus Christ is Lord, she has been set free! You can be too!

CONTENTS

BEHIND THE STORY

Shedding tears that flowed like a torrential rain, I could no longer see to drive. I pulled my car over to the curb and let God have it.

"I can't rewrite the first chapter one more time!" I sobbed. "The little girl in that chapter is hurting too badly, and I don't know how to comfort her. I can see her cowering in a corner of the basement behind a stack of boxes. Her little body is naked and trembling. I can hear her whimpering."

Stopping only long enough to gasp for another breath, I cried out again in anguish, "God, I'm hurting bad enough! It just isn't fair that I have to go back and hurt for that little girl too! I don't want to feel her pain. I can't write any more about her. I just can't. So don't ask me to!"

If cars were passing by, I didn't notice them. If people were watching me, I didn't see them. I was in my own world, agonizing over a decision. Though I already knew the answer, I didn't want to accept it.

Earlier in the day I had received a phone call from a dear friend and author who was evaluating the manuscript of *Satan's Underground*. Her first comment was, "You must let us learn more about the little girl in Chapter 1. Your readers will want to get a better feel for her and what she went through." I knew she was right, but I didn't like it.

I didn't want to deal with the little six-year-old girl who was cowering in the basement on the cold cement floor. I didn't want to feel her hellish nightmare. Only I knew her pain. Only I understood her terror. For the little girl was me, and she would never again know the joy of innocent childhood.

As I rested my head on the steering wheel, the basement scene grew clearer in my mind. Old memories of images, sounds, and smells jumped to life. They were so vivid that I began to feel nauseous. "I've got to start the car and drive home before I throw up," I thought.

Although the drive back home took only five minutes, it seemed like several hours. I tried not to think about that little girl, but it was no use. I had begun to relive the events of that horrible afternoon, and there was no stopping the memories.

Somehow the Lord got me home safely. I stumbled through the front door and slammed it behind me. I turned on the television and held the volume button in until the sound was blaring. Perhaps the noise would blot out the remembrance of that afternoon many long years ago.

It didn't help. I fell into the sofa and buried my head in the pillows. "Go away!" I yelled at the little girl. "I can't help you. I can't take care of you. Just go away!" But she was all I could see in the darkness of those pillows. Her frightened whimperings grew louder and louder.

It was time, I knew, to write about that afternoon, the first of many such afternoons and evenings. I pulled myself off the sofa, turned the TV off, and switched the air conditioner on. Reluctantly I settled into the chair in front of my desk.

My eye settled on a letter from Joyce Landorf Heatherley. She had written it to me after my appearance on her radio program nearly two years earlier. How many times I had read it and found encouragement to continue with my project! Once again I picked it up and read her words:

My Dearest Lauren,

Moments before I walked into the radio studio and met you face-to-face, I was pretty well convinced that no one on earth could ever begin to understand the degree or the depth of my own physical and emotional pain.

I was very mistaken.

It took only one brief look into your pain-filled eyes to tell me that the unthinkable and the unbelievable events of my life were nothing compared to the wounds of your own body, mind, and soul.

You must tell your story! Tell all of it, my friend. Spare no one any agony. This will hurt terribly, almost more than the initial wounding itself, because whenever we write of "life as it really is" there is much pain. But out of your hellacious story countless thousands of women (and men) will have their first taste of the sweetness of God's loving, tender measures of healing and wholeness. Furthermore, it will bring meaning to your own suffering and healing to your own memories.

You've suffered enough, dear heart, but how wonderful that you *have* survived and lived long enough to tell about it.

God will use your recounting to His glory and to our healing. It will not be easy or simple, but like Queen Esther, you are writing this book for such a time as this . . . and your words are desperately needed.

God will use my recounting—to His glory. I pulled out the blue writing paper and picked up the well-used pen I thought would never have to be used on this manuscript again.

And so I'm writing to you about myself as a little girl, a child who was manhandled and brutally abused sexually in a makeshift bedroom in the basement. That girl grew up in a world of abuse and pornography and was eventually forced to become involved in satanism.

It would only be human to write this book as a means of getting back at those who so cruelly abused me and held me captive. But if I am to know any of God's peace, I must rest in His promise, "Vengeance is Mine; I will repay" (Romans 12:19). To nurture hatred for others would only cause me to heap coals of fire upon my own self. Instead, I have chosen to write this book in forgiveness, giving up selfish sins of bitterness, anger, and self-pity.

If I am to believe, as I do, that God allowed me to go through this hell that I might bring hope to others, then I can only say, "Thank You, Father, for the privilege of entrusting me with Your plan for my life."

I must warn you—this is not an easy book to read. Its pages are full of pain, suffering, abuse, and yes, even the horrors of hell itself! Considering how much of this hell to reveal has posed an overwhelming dilemma to me. To dilute the truth would betray my conscience and nullify my purpose in writing the book. To tell it like it is, holding nothing back, would risk shocking readers to the point where many would be hesitant to continue reading.

In turning to those whose advice I greatly respect, their answers were identical and unwavering.

I was admonished by my dear sister in Christ, Johanna Michaelsen, to "have the boldness and courage to speak what I must speak and to write what I must write."

Stormie Omartian, author of the autobiography *Stormie*, wrote a letter to me with the following exhortation: "We have to know the extent of the horrors in order to be awakened to what's happening. This kind of satanic ritual abuse is all around us and it must be exposed. You must write the book and not leave out anything that will serve to make the point."

Others have written or called with these words of advice: "If you don't tell it like it is, there is no point in writing the book."

And so I have striven to be diligent and true to the Lord's leading, to the voice of my own conscience, and to the wisdom of others whose advice I highly respect. In return I ask that you, for the sake of countless others who continue to live in the grasp of Satan's underground, be willing to suffer an anguish of heart as you learn about the realities of Satan and his diabolical schemes. If this book raises more questions for you than it answers, it will have served one of its purposes—to stimulate awareness that these horrors are occurring in our neighborhoods.

We should be horrified. We should be asking why and how such evil can thrive in our midst. We should be praying for and reaching out to victims, showing them the love of God. The worst thing we can do is to ignore what is happening or deny that it exists.

This book is not only for you who need to be informed of the realities of pornography and satanism. In love and compassion I encourage you precious victims whose lives have been torn apart by Satan's schemes to read on. For this is not just an exposé about evil; it is also a demonstration of how evil can be used for good when God steps into the picture. It is a book that points to our only hope—Jesus Christ of Nazareth.

There is a sure escape from bondage and captivity, from the helplessness and hopelessness of the evil one. It does not matter what you have been or are now involved in, voluntarily or involuntarily. Whether it's abortion, sexual abuse and perversion, pornography, occultism, satanism, rituals, or even sacrifices and crucifixions—*there is a way out for you!* I stand as living proof of that fact. The one who has told you there is no hope is not the Lord!

You will note as you read that no specific locations are mentioned. In part this is for my own protection, but it also serves to remind you that what I've endured is not limited to one city or region. I have also changed names and descriptions of many key figures in order to protect the victims. However, the story is very real. This is not fiction. The horrors I suffered are being endured by thousands of other innocent victims throughout the country and the world right now.

As you begin your journey into a world that God never intended to exist, I ask you to keep in mind some words that a therapist and dear friend shared with me after reading a few chapters of the manuscript: "Sometimes this is hard to hear, but it is even harder for those who tell."

Lauren Stratford

❖ 1 ❖
A Little Girl's Terror

A man in his forties had been hired by my mother to do cheap labor around the house. He was filthy and smelly. His hair was greasy and matted. His pants and shirt were torn and dirty. And he looked mean. I kept out of his way.

Every once in awhile from a window inside the house, I saw the man sneak behind a bush and take a swig or two from a small tin-looking bottle he kept tucked inside his shirt. Then he would turn away for a minute to relieve himself before returning to work. I was horrified! I had never seen a man go to the bathroom before.

One afternoon my mother asked me to go down to the basement and get the laundry basket. I hated going to the basement at night. There was something about it that made me feel creepy. But this was a bright and sunny day, and I had no reason to feel afraid.

I started down the steps at a pace much too fast for safety. I knew my mother wasn't watching, and I was in a hurry to complete this chore. I hated laundry day. In no time I was at the bottom of the steps.

As I hurried around the corner, I sensed something blocking my path. Startled, I came to a screeching halt and raised my head. There he was, that dirty man! I froze as my eyes met his. There was the terrible look of meanness that had frightened me before.

Too scared to speak, I waited for him to move out of my way. But he didn't move. As I took a step backward, he grabbed me by the arms. In that instant, what began as a bright and sunny afternoon turned into a dark nightmare of horror.

Years later I could only recall that dreadful scene in fragmented images, like a collage of black-and-white pictures in a war documentary, or stop-action photography showing the horrors of famine in Ethiopia.

Picked up. Thrown onto the bed. He's on top of me. Crushing weight. Gasping for air. Trying to push him off. My arms pinned.

Finally get enough air. I scream. "Mother!" He doesn't stop.

Hot! I'm so hot. Sweaty face on my mouth. Smells awful. He's pulling at my clothes. Laughing.

Where's my mother? Why doesn't she come?

Ripping sound. Pants off. Have to get my pants on! Can't breathe. Hand on my bottom. Have to get pants on! Where's my mother?

Pain! My legs. My bottom. My bottom's going to break! Can't yell. Pain! Can't breathe. Pain! Grunting sounds. I'm pulling his hair.

He gets up. His pants are off. Ugly! Pull myself to corner of bed. Away from him. He pulls pants up. Laughing. He's gone. He's gone.

Start to shake. Cold. So cold. Feel wet. Look down. Blood on legs. On blanket. Have to get off bed. Get away. Can't find pants. I hurt.

Mother will be mad. Was I bad? Want to hide. Find boxes. Hide behind the boxes.

So cold! So scared! So dirty! Want to hide forever. Mustn't tell . . .

I don't know how that little girl escaped from the basement. But I remember the questions that screamed to be answered. Why? Why did he do it? Where was my mother? Why didn't she come when I yelled? Why didn't she protect me? Was it because I was no good? Was I being punished because my real parents gave me away? Did they know I was bad?

There were no answers. There was no understanding. I didn't know that I had lost my virginity—I didn't know what a virgin was. I didn't know that I had been raped—I didn't know what rape was. I didn't know that I had been abused sexually—I didn't know what sex was.

But I knew one thing for sure: The nightmare was over, and it would never happen again. Never!

Sadly, not long after the first time there was a second time. Then a third, and a fourth, and a fifth. They soon became too many to count. The days, the weeks, the months—they all blurred together into one agonizing, terrifying eternity.

There were more men, but they all looked the same—dirty. They all smelled the same—awful. Of course, I always yelled for my mother, but she never came to my rescue. One day as I screamed for her, the man began to laugh. "Honey, don't you know your mama ain't comin' for you?" he sneered. "Don't you know she's the one who gave you to me?"

"Shut up! Shut up!" I yelled. I didn't want to hear any more. It couldn't be true! It just couldn't! My mother wouldn't let this happen to me!

But after too many times of yelling for her, and her never coming to help me, somewhere way down deep I had this aching, sick feeling that maybe he was right. Maybe she had known what was going on all this time after all, and she just didn't care enough to come and rescue me.

I was devastated. The pain of her rejection, the pain of a mother not caring enough to heed the cries of her child, hurt so bad that I wanted to die. Maybe I was bad. But was I so bad that my own mother would permit something this awful to happen to me? Was I so bad that she would refuse to come running when her own child was screaming for help?

My heart, my soul, the most private part of my being was crushed. It wasn't just a twinge of pain. It was an all-consuming ache that began at my toes and worked its way up to the topmost hair on my head. It throbbed with a pulsating beat that never stopped. With each new throb I felt as though my heart would burst wide open.

And so I learned that these men who worked around the house were paid for their services with the use of my body. Gone was a little child's innocence. Gone was a little child's trust. Gone was a little child's smile. Gone were a little child's dreams. Gone was the little child, period. She was captive in a world that no child should ever have to endure.

Hiding under the covers after a sexually abusive episode, I would often scrunch myself up into a tight little ball, trying to feel something that resembled security. I had learned early that I dared not let my mother catch me crying. Sometimes I felt as if my tears made her feel guilty for her actions. At other times she acted as if they made her angry. But always she let me know that I was not to cry by slapping me across the mouth and yelling, "Shut up, you crybaby!"

No matter how hard I tried not to cry, the tears were sure to come when I was finally left alone in my room. The little girl tried valiantly to keep a stiff upper lip, but the pain of the moment was too great to endure silently, and under the covers of my bed I whimpered. Scrunched into that little ball, with my arms wrapped tightly around me, I would rock back and forth until I finally fell asleep.

Never-Ending Pain

The way I was raised was so ugly and traumatic that for many years of my adult life, though the memories haunted me day and night, I refused to accept them as reality, let alone reveal them to anyone else.

I feel that I was birthed into evil. I was not born out of love; I was conceived illegitimately and given away at birth. I was never allowed to forget it. NEVER! I was a bastard, a no-good, an unwanted, a bad-blood. During the formative years of my childhood my mother forced me to stand in front of a mirror and repeat those words over and over. I learned them well . . . and I believed them!

I've heard adoptive parents explain to their adopted children that they were *special* because they were *chosen*. How beautiful those words sounded! But how they made me hurt, because I knew a thousand times over that those words would never be true of me. "Why aren't I special?" I cried. "Why aren't I loved? Why did they take me if I'm so awful?"

On the surface, according to the outside world, I could not have had a more perfect home. My adoptive parents were both professionals. We lived in an upper-class neighborhood. I was always dressed well. The house was beautifully decorated, and the kitchen looked like it was right out of *Good Housekeeping* magazine. By all outward appearances I had every advantage that a kid would want. Why, I was even taken to church!

"Why in the world did they bother to take me to church?" one might well ask. I've wondered that myself. Taking me to church, however, is the one thing for which I can be thankful, for at a very early age I asked Jesus to become a father to me. That decision was the one and only thing that kept me alive through all the years of abuse.

Who would ever suspect a churchgoing family of such terrible physical and emotional abuse? In retrospect, I think at times my mother was sincere in her churchgoing. Perhaps she could have received help for her emotional problems if she had only reached out for it. But to my knowledge she never shared any of her intimate thoughts with anyone. She remained a silent captive to her inner being.

The "perfect" family began to dissolve when I was about four years of age. The fighting between my mother and father had become so intense that he, fearing for his life, packed his bags and left. I surely couldn't blame him for leaving. He had silently endured just about every form of physical and verbal abuse that one human being can give to another.

I was certainly no authority on marriage at the ages of three and four, and I had no idea what went on in their private lives as husband and wife. I could only see that my mother seemed to hate my father; that she yelled at him constantly, but that he never yelled back; that she kicked him and hit him and threw things at him and stabbed him, yet he never defended himself or fought back; and that several times he had to be taken to the hospital after her beatings, yet he never pressed charges against her.

One of my most vivid childhood memories is of an afternoon when I was standing on our front porch looking in the window at my father sleeping on the sofa in the den. I saw my mother come into the room, pick up a bar stool, and to my utter horror raise it over my father and bring it crashing down on his chest. I felt as if I were watching a bad movie, and it would go away if I blinked my eyes. But the scene was for real; it didn't go away.

The next day my father was gone. In one sense I was almost relieved, for I hoped things would settle down. Little did I know then that the horror was only beginning.

Hell Isn't Just a Word

The insane screaming of a person gone mad is one of my earliest memories—silence shattered by ear-piercing, animal-like screams. I never knew why my mother screamed. She wasn't saying anything, just shrieking at the top of her lungs, over and over and over again. She didn't seem to be in pain. Nothing bad had happened as far as I could tell. Without any warning she would just open her mouth, take a big gulp of air, and let out the most frightening noise imaginable.

Sometimes my mother's screaming was accompanied by a rampage of destruction. Whatever was accessible—dinner plates, drinking glasses, cans of food, clothes in a closet or in a drawer, books—went flying through the air and crashing into the nearest wall. At the first sign of her fury I would dash to the closest safety zone, whether it was in a closet, behind some chairs, underneath a table, or underneath the bed. If there wasn't time to reach a safety zone, I would crouch in the nearest corner and cover my head with my arms.

My mother never seemed to be aiming at anything in particular. It was as though there were demons of anger and frustration inside her that would suddenly break loose, and in an effort to rid herself of them she could only scream bloody murder and send things crashing to the floor. With every scream my body would quake. With every crashing sound I would hold myself tighter. I was too frightened to cry, and besides, there was no use in yelling for help. No one was ever around to rescue me.

Only once did I get caught in the line of fire. One morning I heard the crashing sounds of breaking glasses and plates, then my mother shouting, "Get in here, you good-for-nothing _____!" For a split second I hesitated to enter the combat zone, but I quickly changed my mind when I thought of the possible ways I might be punished if I didn't obey. Those possibilities heavily outweighed whatever would happen in the kitchen.

As I fearfully stepped into the kitchen, I saw my mother standing on top of the counter. Already her model kitchen was a picture of devastation. Half the contents of the cupboards were lying broken and scattered on the floor. One swoop of her arm emptied another entire shelf, and all the serving dishes were demolished. She was about to start on the cans of food when she paused long enough to acknowledge my presence and yell, "Look at this mess. You can't even keep one room in this house clean!"

Then one by one she grabbed cans of soup and vegetables that had been neatly stacked on the shelf and threw them down amid the broken plates and glasses. "Well, what are you waiting for?" she growled. "Don't just stand there like an idiot. Get in here and clean up this mess."

I knelt down on my hands and knees, trying to stay on the outer fringes of the combat zone. The faster I picked up the cans, the faster she threw them down. Fortunately, she didn't seem to be aiming at me as she continued her rampage. Two or three cans did hit me, but none of them struck my head and I endured only a few bruises.

Next came the boxes of breakfast cereal. These she couldn't just toss onto the floor. She had to open each one, turn it upside down, and fling the contents through the air like she was tossing confetti on a parade. When she was done with the cereal, she jumped down from the counter top and began to paw through the mess on the floor. Finding a plastic bowl that hadn't broken, she scooped up a handful of cereal from the floor and dumped it into the bowl. To my horror, I saw small pieces of broken glass mixed in with the cereal. After pouring milk over the mixture, she emptied the remainder of the milk bottle over the cereal on the floor. "Here's your breakfast," she snapped as she handed me the bowl. "Eat!"

My hand was shaking so badly that as I took the bowl, some of the milk slopped over the side. I didn't know what to think. Was she trying to kill me? Or was she even aware of what she was doing? I didn't dare ask. Reluctantly, I sat down at the kitchen table and put a spoonful of cereal in my mouth. When I felt a piece of glass, I carefully pushed it to one side with my tongue and swallowed the cereal without chewing it.

Satisfied that I was eating, my mother stomped out of the kitchen. Over her shoulder she hollered, "Don't ever let me catch you leaving the kitchen in such a mess again!" As soon as she was out of sight, I dumped the remainder of my bowl of cereal and glass onto the floor. Then, with tears streaming down my face, I got the broom and began cleaning up the mess. Always it was *my* mess, no matter what my mother did.

Every episode of rage grew a little worse. Every day my mother seemed a little more impatient, a little more frustrated, and her anger seemed to grow with each outburst. In the beginning, after quieting down, she would sometimes ask me to forgive her. During those infrequent moments she honestly seemed to feel sorry for the way she had acted. Though I never felt any forgiveness in my heart, I always told her that I forgave her. There was no way I was going to say "No!"

However, as the same scene was repeated over and over, and the episodes became more frequent, she quit asking for forgiveness. I don't really think it was because she wasn't sorry for her outbursts of violence, but I think she felt so overwhelmed with frustration in dealing with the demons of her mind that she finally gave up.

Will You Be My Daddy?

The word "fun" was not in my vocabulary as a little girl. I had no playtime, no friends, and no toys. The word "love" was only a word I heard others use. There was no warmth and no kindness. There were no hugs or kisses. There was no touching that said, "I love you. I care." There were only touches that said, "I hate you. Go away."

The only place where I sensed any love was in Sunday school. There I heard wonderful stories of Jesus, and how He loved little children. There was a picture on the classroom wall showing Him holding a child on His lap while other children sat on the ground and gazed at Him.

I used to stare at that picture, longing to be the child that Jesus was holding. How I wanted to be held and cuddled. How I craved the chance to sit on someone's lap. Tears often filled my eyes as I looked at the children in that picture. They weren't sad or frightened. They were happy, and loved! I would drop my head and walk away knowing that this could never be me. I was too bad. I was too dirty. I was unlovable.

But the next week, I would look at the picture again, and wonder if maybe Jesus could love me. My teacher said we could talk to Him—she called it prayer. She said Jesus loved everyone, that He came to earth to show His love by dying for us. All we had to do was reach out and accept His love. One Sunday morning, when I was the first person in the Sunday school room, I walked up to the picture and touched it. I touched Jesus' hair and hands and face. I touched the children. I don't know why. Perhaps I just wanted to identify with them. And perhaps, somewhere in my subconscious, I hoped that I could somehow feel like those children felt.

Tears again filled my eyes and ran down my chubby little cheeks as I whispered a prayer to Jesus. I was only five or six at the time, so I don't remember everything I told Him, but I do remember asking Him one very special favor. As I touched His beautiful white robe, I whispered, "Will You be my new Daddy, Jesus? . . . And can I sit on Your lap too?"

I could hardly sit still in Sunday school class that morning. I stared at the picture, waiting for Jesus to answer me. I didn't know how Jesus talked to people; my teacher had only taught us how to talk to Him. But as the hour passed and I didn't hear anything from Him, my spirits began to sink.

On my way home I couldn't wait to tell my mother about how I spoke to Jesus. My hopes rose again as I thought that maybe she could tell me how Jesus talked to people. I don't know why, with all the "uglies" in my life, I would cling to that hope. But I did. Running through the front door I called out breathlessly, "Mother, Mother! I talked to Jesus! I asked Him if He would be my daddy!"

I stopped only long enough to take another gulp of air before I asked her how and when Jesus would answer me. But before I could utter another word she shouted, "Jesus don't want no dirty, filthy kid! What makes you think He'd want you?"

"But, Mother," I stammered, thinking she just didn't understand what I was talking about, "I saw a picture of Jesus holding little children and they were just like me!"

"Not like you!" my mother sneered, carefully stressing the word "you." "Not - like - you!"

I was crushed. That one tiny spark of hope was gone. My little spirit wilted. Walking away from her, I repeated the words "Not like me. Not like me. Not like me."

Every Sunday after that, I would sit in Sunday school and sadly look at the picture, saying to myself, "Not like me. Not like me." Even now, as an adult, when I see a picture of Jesus with little children, I still hear my mother saying, "Not like you," and the little girl in me feels the same sadness and hurt all over again.

Bits and Pieces of Terror

From that point on there is very little worth remembering about my youth. All I want to do is blot out the horrible hurts and pains. A few bits and pieces that surface in my memory reveal what my life was like.

• Leaving the house one evening wearing only my pajamas and slippers. I was going to find the police. But within one block some neighbors saw me and walked me back home.

• Losing a mitten on the way home from preschool. My mother was very, very mad. "You're the most irresponsible child in the neighborhood!" she barked. "Get out of here, and go look for your mitten. Don't bother to come back until you've found it!" I made two trips back and forth to the preschool until I found it. I remember it was getting dark, and I was very scared.

• Being awakened in the middle of the night to clean the house. The house was always clean, but never clean enough to please my mother. I could never understand why it had to be cleaned again in the middle of the night.

• My mother pulling the car over to the curb and yelling at me, "Get out! Get out!" We were in a city far away from home. It was hot, and I had asked for a drink. She didn't answer, so I asked her again. I asked one time too many. She blew up, shouting, "You get out of the car and sit on the curb. I'll come back for you after you've learned your lesson!" I was terrified being all alone in a strange city and not knowing when she would come back or if she would ever come back.

• Hiding my pajama bottoms in the closet because I was afraid for my mother to see them. I had messed them when I had the intestinal flu. When my mother found them, she rubbed the dirty part in my face. Oh, how I hated her for that!

There is no end to these nightmarish memories. Countless days were filled with experiences of terror for that little girl. The pain and hurt have stuck to my insides like glue through all these years. Hardly a night went by that I didn't silently soak my pillow with tears. I don't think a day passed that I didn't want to run away. But where is a little girl in preschool or kindergarten going to run?

When the sexual abuse began, not only did my little body go through a shock, but my mind went on overload. At least I knew what was happening when I had to walk a mile each way to and from preschool to find my mitten. I knew what was happening when I had to get up at three o'clock in the morning to dust the furniture. But dirty, filthy, smelly men picking me up and throwing me onto the bed, smothering and crushing me with the weight of their bodies and doing awful things to me that made me hurt really bad? *That I could not understand!* I could only realize that whatever those men were doing made me feel ashamed and dirty and no-good.

What could I do? Who could I tell? Where could I go? I was scared to death of my mother. And if I really did deserve this because I was such a bad little girl like my mother always told me I was, then was it true that no one could help me?

So the little girl remained silent, silent in a world of fear, terror, pain, and abuse. I was only six years old, but already I wanted to die!

Fortunately, I didn't know that much worse was yet to come.

❖ 2 ❖
Behind Closed Doors

I listened with aching heart as my classmates eagerly shared about the fun times they'd had with their families over the weekend. I tried to imagine what it would be like to go on a picnic. My classmates talked about their parents and brothers and sisters, and sometimes even their grandparents—all gathering together to barbecue hamburgers or hot dogs. They would tell about family baseball games or fishing in a pond or sitting around a campfire roasting marshmallows. Others would tell about trips to the beach where they and their friends would build sand castles or bury each other in the sand or wade in the ocean, letting the waves tickle their toes.

As they told their stories, I tried to imagine what it was like. I roasted marshmallows with them. I helped them build sand castles. I tried to feel the cold water touching my toes. But I couldn't imagine what it was *really* like. I couldn't *feel* the fun of it. I couldn't catch the same air of excitement that I heard in their voices.

I wanted so badly to do all of these things that kids do. Sometimes I would put my fingers in my ears so I wouldn't have to hear the kids telling about their families and fun times. "Oh, God, why couldn't that be me?" I would think. "Why can't I do those things? Why can't I play and laugh and eat around a great big picnic table with a whole bunch of family?"

With every kid who stood up to tell about his weekend on Monday mornings in my second-grade class, I grew more and more bitter. Picnics and trips and parties and movies were so far removed from my way of life that I felt as if I were living on a different planet. And in a way I was, for my weekends were about as opposite from theirs as the weather at the North Pole is from that at the equator.

The worst part was when the teacher called my name, asking me to share. All I could do was silently shake my head. I dared not share any information about my weekend. The first report card that my teacher filled out spelled disaster for me. In the space provided for comments she wrote, "Lauren refuses to participate in our Monday sharing time. She will not share any of the activities that happen on the weekends. Will you please encourage her to share her home activities with her classmates?"

Oh, how I paid for her comment! "What are you trying to do, make me look bad, you good-for-nothing _____?" Mother shouted. "Can't you ever do anything right?"

I knew the danger in that tone of voice. Slowly backing away from her, I raised my arms to shield my face.

"Get your hands away from your face," she ordered as she started toward me. "You always were a coward!"

Wham! I felt the sting of her hand across my cheek. The force of the slap turned my head to the right.

"Don't you turn away from me. You always look your mother in the face," she snapped. Anticipating her next move, it was only out of fear that I reluctantly turned my head back to face her. Splat. Her spit hit me between the eyes.

"I hate you. I hate you. I hate . . ." Before I could get the next "you" out, I felt a horrible sting of pain, first on my left cheek, then almost simultaneously, on my right cheek.

Falling to the floor, I put my arms over my head, knowing that I was really going to get it now. It was not uncommon for her to kick me mercilessly. This time, to my surprise, Mother walked out of the room.

The next day the real cover-up began in earnest. My mother taught me fake stories to share in class about fun things I did on the weekends. If I had bruises on exposed parts of my body, I simply wore blouses with long sleeves or pants that covered my legs. When I received injuries from being slapped or kicked that couldn't be covered up—if they weren't too suspicious—a note would be written with an "explanation" of how I had been hurt. Some of the notes even asked the school nurse to treat the injury.

I lived two lives in two totally separate worlds. School became my refuge. It was the only place where I was free from my mother. It was the only place I felt safe. I always volunteered to stay after school to help the teacher. Even though I knew that I would catch hell for coming home late if my mother found out, the extra 15 or 30 minutes of peace and safety were worth it.

The Walk Home

The walk home from school became a kind of morbid ritual. I knew every house, every fire hydrant, every curve in the road, and every bump and crack in the sidewalk. Each one I passed meant I was that much closer to my house of horrors.

Most kids walked home with their friends. I walked home alone. Most kids whistled or hummed a favorite tune or giggled about nonsensical matters. I was silent. Most kids were going home to play. I was going home to work and to endure whatever abuse I would encounter that evening. Most kids' hearts beat with excitement. My heart pounded with fear.

When I saw the house built of red bricks, my walk became virtually a snail's crawl. That was the last house before mine. When I reached the corner of the red brick house, I would stop dead still. It seemed as if the whole world would stop with me as I dared to peek around the corner to see if my mother's car was in the garage. "Jesus," I would beg in desperation, "please don't let her be home! Please, Jesus!"

If the garage was empty, the heavy pounding in my chest calmed to a flutter of relief. "Thank You, Jesus. Thank You!" I would whisper. A faint smile would spread across my face, for I knew I had at least a few more minutes of peace before my mother came home.

When I saw my mother's car as I dared to peek around the corner of that last house, my face would begin to flush. I felt hot, and I could almost hear my heart beat in panic. I knew there would be no respite before I had to face her, before I would find out what kind of mood she was in.

I had learned early that much of my abuse depended on her mood. If she wasn't at home when I came from school, I raced around to have the house in perfect order. Maybe she would be pleased with me. I planned the evening's meal. Maybe it would delay the inevitable—WAR!

My efforts rarely helped. No matter how perfect things were, if my mother decided that we were going to have a war, we had a war. This meant anything from wild, fiendish screaming to tearing an entire room apart. I used to pray that we wouldn't have a war that day. Incredibly, at times my mother would call me into her bedroom in the morning and solemnly announce, "I dreamed there's going to be a war today. Let's pray there won't be." Every day that she announced the possibility of a war, I agonizingly went through the entire school day with just that one thought on my mind.

I used to think up excuses for my mother's seemingly uncontrollable mood swings on the grounds that she was mentally ill. But as her mood swings grew worse and the abuse became an almost daily routine, I gave up all hopes of her getting well. And in time I decided that she actually wanted to be mean and abusive.

If that was the case, where could a young girl go for help? In my mind, the only place to go was the police. Weren't they there to protect us? One afternoon I got up the courage to call the police. "You've got to help me!" I said.

"What's wrong?" said the kind voice at the other end.

"I can't tell you. You just have to help me."

"All right. Somebody will be out. What's your address?"

As soon as I'd hung up, my mother yelled at me to get down to the basement. I always knew what that meant. I hoped that the police would find me there with my latest abuser. But it was an hour before the squad car arrived, and by then it was over.

When the abuser left, I stayed in the basement, trying to console myself. I was disheveled and bleeding. There was a knock at the door. My mother looked out the window and saw a policewoman. She frantically yelled at me to come upstairs. When she saw the bloodstains on my dress, she ordered me to sit up straight on the sofa so the stains wouldn't show.

When I was settled, she opened the door. The officer identified herself and said there had been a call from a child for help at this address.

"Please come in," my mother said, turning on her charm

and projecting an image of the perfect mother. The police-woman saw me immediately. My mother introduced me: "This is my daughter Lauren."

"I would like to talk with her for a minute," the officer said. She didn't ask my mother to leave the room. "Lauren, are you the one who made the call to us?"

I knew better than to respond, so I said nothing.

She turned to my mother and asked, "Is there any trouble in this house?"

My mother, with a sweet smile, answered, "Just the normal mother-daughter disagreement. You know how it is. We got a little upset, that's all. I don't think there's anything to worry about. I can take care of it."

The policewoman turned back to me and asked, "Is that right, Lauren? Will everything be all right now?"

I had no choice but to answer a weak, "Yes, Ma'am."

She smiled and said, "I think all that's needed is for you to mind your mother and do what she tells you to do. Then everything will be all right."

"Would you like some tea?" asked my mother.

"No, thanks. I've got another call," said the officer. As she walked out the door, I felt a hopeless cloud settle over me. As soon as she was gone, I painfully stood up and saw that the sofa cushion was stained with blood. "Get in the bathroom and clean yourself up," my mother ordered. As I started down the hall she yelled after me, "You'll pay for this!"

So the wars continued on and on and on. Her violent fits of rage grew worse, and I was the only one around to bear the brunt of it. I was her punching bag. It seemed inevitable that the punching bag would explode.

It happened when I was in the fourth grade. One day, after several successive days of being horribly abused, I blurted out in my overwhelming anger, "If you don't start treating me like a human being, I'm going to run away, and you'll never see me again!"

For a moment both of us were stunned. I think my mother was just as shocked as I was that I had the nerve to threaten her. Her silence, however, lasted only for a few moments.

The Nightmare Worsens

I paid an awful price for those words. "You think I've treated you inhumanely before? You ain't seen nothin' yet!" my mother yelled. I had never seen her so angry. She was so mad that her face turned bright red and the veins in her neck stuck out. "You just wait and see. You don't talk to your mother that way and get away with it!"

My mother was right. I didn't know just how low the meaning of the word "inhumane" could get until a few days later when a man came to our house after school. I didn't know who he was, and my mother wasn't particularly friendly with him. Their conversation was brief, and, though I couldn't hear what they were saying, their voices sounded businesslike. Then my mother told me that I was to go with him. I didn't want to go, but after threatening to run away just a few days before, I didn't dare disobey her now. I was afraid she would kill me if I made her that mad again. So I got into the man's car.

I huddled against the door, as far away from the driver as possible, and watched as we drove out of town into a wooded area. We finally stopped at an isolated turnout and walked further into the woods. We arrived at a clearing where another man was tending a sheep, a goat, and a dog that looked as big as I was.

"We're going to take some pictures," the driver said. "There are people who like pictures of happy, smiling children. Others like pictures of their family pets. I take pictures of children and pets together in nice natural settings."

All of this sounded fine; certainly it was better than what happened in the basement. Then he said matter-of-factly, "The pictures will be better if you snuggle up to the animals without any clothes on. So take your clothes off. All of them!"

I stood there, frozen in silence. I was numb. I didn't understand what was going on. It wasn't like the times in the basement, but this didn't feel right either.

As the photographer set up his camera, the other man began to move toward me. "Hurry up—we don't have all day," he yelled. "The sun will be going down. Don't you know how to take your clothes off?" Then he laughed at my fear and reached out to touch my blouse. I backed up and slowly began to unbutton it by myself.

"All of them. Hurry up!" he barked again.

Soon the camera was clicking. After a couple of shots I learned that I was expected to do more than just pose in front of a pet animal. Much more. It was getting to be more like my experiences in the basement, and soon it was worse. The animal's sexual part was forced into my mouth. I had to put my fingers in places I didn't want to. I didn't want to touch or feel or smell or taste. I only wanted to shrivel up and disappear in the woods. Again and again I gagged. I kept wiping my mouth with my forearm. That only made the men laugh as the camera kept clicking.

Finally it was over. "You'll get used to it, Honey," the man with the animals jeered. "Maybe you'll even start liking it after awhile."

While the photographer was packing the camera equipment, he suddenly turned his head back toward me as I was trying to put my clothes on and added, "After all, the animals sure like you." Then he made a wolf whistle and the two men threw their heads back and roared with laughter.

I dressed in a daze and stumbled back to the car. On the ride back to my house, I sat in a corner of the backseat as far away from the men as I could get. Tears silently made a path down my dirty face. I started to wipe them away with my hands, but they were dirtier than my face. I smelled like the animals. I was dirty like the animals. And that taste in my mouth—I just had to get rid of it!

The moment the car stopped in the driveway, I jumped out, ran into the house, and headed for the bathroom. I scrubbed and scrubbed. I washed out my mouth with soap. I even brushed my tongue with toothpaste and then with soap. But it was no use—I still smelled like the animals, and the taste would not go away. I looked at my face in the mirror and began to sob convulsively. "I'm just like the animals. I'll never get to sit on Jesus' lap. Never!"

There was no more dignity to take away. There was no more hope to shatter. There was no more innocence to destroy. Whatever they did from now on, they weren't doing it to a child. The "child" in me had ceased to exist. I had become nothing but an object. The tragedy was not that I was an object in their eyes; the tragedy was that I had become an object in my own eyes.

Several months later I found a magazine hidden under my mother's bed. The cover consisted of two children with no clothes on. I glanced through the pages and what I saw was horrible. As I started to close the magazine I caught a glimpse of a photo out of the corner of my eye. My heart skipped a beat and I froze. There I was! It was me, with the animals. And under it, in big bold letters, was the title of the story that followed—BARNYARD BABE!

"Maybe it's just someone who looks like me," I thought. But I knew better. My body began to shake with uncontrollable sobs. The pieces had now come together. That's why all the photos were being taken of me with the animals. My mother was selling my body! *My mother was selling ME!* Everything that was most important to a child—love, trust, a sense of value and worth, warmth, security—all had been betrayed for money!

The magazine slipped out of my hands as I bent over in agonizing emotional pain. It would be futile to attempt to put the feelings of my heart and soul onto paper. Hopelessness, helplessness, loneliness, shock, grief, pain, devastation—none of those feelings even come close to describing my emotions. At ten years of age I felt that I could no longer live two lives in two worlds. No longer could I pretend in the outside world. No longer could I endure the abuse behind closed doors. Yet what choice did I have?

The "businessmen" who had taken me to the wooded area started coming into the house. In the basement they took the same kinds of pictures that they took of me with the animals. Only now the pictures were of me and the dirty bums while they were in the act of abusing me. A few times they even brought one or two other children with them, both boys and girls, and took pictures of all of us together in perverted sexual poses. When the other kids would cry for their mommy or daddy, I would tell them, "It's no use. They're not going to come for you."

How humiliating it was to stand without clothes in front of a strange man with a camera. The bright lights made me feel even more naked. I was touched all over to get me in the "right" poses. Standing in front of the camera, I became a nonperson. I felt like a nothing, a nobody. I hated my body. I hated myself. At that moment the only thing I wanted was to die.

I was getting older and I was beginning to understand what was going on. I still felt the heartache and the fear, but I was also beginning to feel bitterness, anger, and intense hatred. For two years the fear and the anger and the hatred grew— grew until I felt like it was going to devour me.

No Hope

So it was that in seventh grade, out of total desperation, I dared to go to the school counselor. I was embarrassed to go. I didn't want any of my classmates to know about it. I didn't want the kids to think I had done something wrong and was going to the counselor for correction. That was what normally happened. So I quietly asked my health teacher for a pass to go to the restroom and went to the counseling office instead.

Once there, I haltingly told her in what I thought were such simple and clear words, "I cannot live at home any longer. If I do, I will die." I breathed a sigh of relief. I had done it! It was over! I had told. Now I would get help.

Seemingly unmoved, the counselor pulled out three pieces of legal-size paper. With a blank face and a monotone voice, she instructed, "You need to write down why your home is unfit to live in. Write one reason on each page. I will take these to the authorities and they will conduct an investigation."

"While I'm still living in the house?" I asked in alarm.

To my horror she answered, "Of course."

I was certain about two things. First, an investigation would turn up nothing, for the perfect house outside would suddenly become the perfect house inside. My mother had a way of turning her moods on and off at a moment's notice, just like a light switch. All hell could be breaking loose in the middle of one of her wars. She could be screaming and throwing around everything that wasn't nailed to the floor. Yet if the phone rang or someone knocked on the front door, she could change the blackest mood to one of downright congeniality. No one would ever suspect the insane madness of the preceding moments.

Second, I also knew that in asking for an investigation of what went on behind those closed doors, I was only inviting additional abuse. That could possibly end in my being killed during a fit of uncontrollable rage, or in my committing suicide, or in my simply going insane from an inability to handle the added abuse.

How utterly helpless I felt sitting in the counselor's office, silent and motionless. Obviously, she wasn't interested in getting involved in what she considered a family dispute. Her primary job was to handle discipline or academic problems. In those days counselors stayed out of family matters. Impatiently she asked, "Well, what do you want to do?"

I thought to myself, "It's all so cut-and-dried to you—so black and white. If you only knew . . ." My thoughts drifted back to my home, back to my hell on earth. How desperately I wanted to share this with her! But I was afraid—afraid I wouldn't be believed, afraid I would be blamed, afraid of verbally expressing the horrors that were locked inside that house. And so that all-consuming fear kept me silent.

The counselor didn't try to interpret my silence. As she began to put the papers back inside the drawer, I knew that she had given up on me. Shaking her head in apparent disgust, she stood up and let me know that it was time for me to go back to class.

There was only one other place where I could think to go for help—the Sunday school teacher at my church. Would she understand? Surely, of all the people, she would be the most sympathetic. Still, it took several weeks for me to muster up the nerve to ask her for help.

I approached her after class one Sunday and simply said, "I can't stand it at home anymore. Will you please help me?"

Here she was, Bible in hand, ready to dash into the sanctuary for Sunday service. She looked at me, unable to ignore the terrified look on my face. She couldn't pass this off lightly, yet I could tell she also wasn't sure if she wanted to get involved. "Honey, I think this is something we should take to the pastor," she said. "I'll make an appointment for you."

A few days later I was escorted into the pastor's ostentatious office. I had never met this man; I had only seen him behind the pulpit. To me he was an unreachable, untouchable man—almost like God. He sat behind his huge desk and motioned for me to sit opposite him in a heavy leather chair. I felt so insignificant in his presence. He no doubt had so many other important things to do.

There was no small talk. "What can we do for you?" he said, not unkindly but rather businesslike.

"Would you *please* help me," I pleaded.

"Of course. How can I help you?"

What would I tell him? The pastor did look more sympathetic than the school counselor, but what would he think if I told him the whole truth? "Like I told my Sunday school teacher, I don't think I can live at home any longer. My mother is very mean. I can't take it any longer. Can I live somewhere else?"

"Honey, I don't think there's anything we can do about that. We have to let the police handle it. But we sure can take it to the Lord and pray about it."

With that he bowed his head and prayed. I can't remember the words he said, but I remember thinking that his talk with God was awfully short for a matter of life and death. As soon as he had uttered "Amen," he patted me on the back and ushered me to the door. "God will take care of this," he said with a sugar-coated smile. "Everything will be fine. You wait and see." I left with the feeling that he felt I was making a big thing out of something very small.

A few Sundays later my mother was terribly mean. By the time we got to church that night I was an emotional mess. I cried throughout the whole service. When the pastor gave an altar call, I ran down to the prayer room. I knelt and sobbed until the tears formed a puddle in the metal folding chair. I begged God, "Please don't make me go home tonight."

I stayed there until the room was empty. Surprisingly, my mother hadn't come for me yet. Usually she didn't let me out of her sight. This was my chance. I remembered that the youth pastor seemed especially kind, and he and his wife had a tiny two-room apartment right next to the sanctuary. I went over and knocked on their door. The youth pastor opened the door and invited me in. "Come in. I noticed you crying downstairs. What's the problem?"

I slumped into his sofa and started sobbing again. "I'm afraid of my mother. I just can't go home with her tonight. Can I please stay with you?"

The couple were very kind, and they obviously felt for me. They spent a few minutes discussing the options. Finally he said, "I don't know what we can do. We don't have room for you to stay here. We really would like to do something."

His wife softly said, "I wonder if there's anyone else who could take her in?"

Just then there was a knock on the door. It was my mother. "I've been looking all over for you," she said when the door was opened. "This was the last place I knew to look. It's time to go home."

I looked at the youth pastor and his wife and saw the concern in their faces. They wanted to do something. It was also obvious that they felt helpless. They looked at each other, saying nothing, and I knew there was nothing they could do. Slowly I got up and followed my mother out the door.

It was obvious I had been crying. My eyes were red and my nose was runny. As soon as we got in the car my mother said, "By the look on your face, I know you must have told them something. You have been very disobedient. I'm going to take you to the pastor right now and he's going to straighten you out."

"Good!" I said. "Let's go right now."

There was silence. She started the car and headed toward home. Apparently I had called her bluff. She wasn't about to risk my saying anything to the pastor.

At that point I gave up all hope of ever finding help. I had gone to the police, the school counselor, my Sunday school teacher, and two pastors. Who else could I turn to? My neighbors? My mother loved to tell them what an unruly child I was. One of them even told me that I should be kinder to her.

After all, she was a single parent, trying to do the best she could. So who could I tell? Who would believe me? I despaired of ever being rescued, of ever finding peace, joy, and love.

The next three or four years were a blur of endless abuse and pain. The outward facade continued. I played the school routine quite convincingly. I performed in a robotlike fashion, seldom smiling and almost never laughing. Nary a teacher ever questioned me or sent me to the school counselor for evaluation. In gym class I used every possible excuse to not take a shower, because I was afraid to take my clothes off. I didn't want anyone to notice the bruises. I also felt horribly ashamed of my naked body. To me it was shameful, dirty, and bad.

No doubt there were many signs that indicated I was an abused child. Yet no one picked up on them. Or if they did, they never talked to me about it.

Teenage girls are usually consumed with panic decisions like "What dress should I wear to school today?" or "Will my boyfriend like my hair this way?" or "I've got to put more makeup on to hide these gross pimples." However, my priorities were not those of a typical teenager. I was not allowed to have any friends. My mother dominated my life. When I wasn't in school or church, she kept me under her control at home. I was never allowed to go to someone else's house or participate in any extracurricular activities.

A day didn't go by that I didn't want to run away. Daily my mother's violent mood swings became worse. The abuse increased. It is amazing that either of us managed to put on a convincing front to others, for inside the home was total chaos and depravity. I began to fear that one day she would literally turn into some sort of wild animal.

A Mother's Betrayal

When I entered high school, I began to view my home life from a different perspective. The excuses I had so desperately clung to as a child had fallen apart. I saw that my mother was not just a helpless victim in the scheme of things. She was not so mentally unstable that she could not control her actions. She could be a raving maniac at home and yet go to church and be the meek and misunderstood single parent who only wanted the best for her child. She could rave at me in the car, driving like a maniac, and when the police stopped her, she could softly explain how she was deserted by her husband and left to raise a child all by herself, and talk her way out of a ticket. She could present a well-dressed, clean, and controlled appearance in the neighborhood and at work. No one saw her the way I saw her. That was hard enough to accept. Yet when I realized that not only was she allowing the abuse, but even seemed to *direct* it at times, my bitterness, anger, and hatred multiplied tenfold.

I vented my anger in a prayer that I began to pray daily, and sometimes even hourly: "God, just let her die." I had little hope of escaping. I had even less hope of anyone believing me. And I had no hope that the abuse would end. My only hope was that she would die.

The others who abused me—the bums, the pedophiles, the pornographers—weren't supposed to love me. I didn't expect anything but abuse from them. But my mother? Who does a child look to for love? Her mother. Who does a child look to for protection? Her mother. Who does a child trust? Her mother. Whose betrayal of these life-giving fundamentals hurts the most? Her mother's!

Oh, how I longed for my mother to love me. How I longed to climb up onto her lap and feel her arms holding me safe and secure. How I longed for her to protect me from all those bad people. I couldn't understand what I had done to deserve the punishments I constantly received from her. It gradually dawned on me that I would never have the mother I longed for. However, the acceptance of that fact didn't diminish my longing.

I thought only occasionally about my father. I was very young when he left home, and I had very few memories of him, positive or negative. The one question I found myself asking over and over was, "Why didn't he take me with him?" Had he too betrayed me?

In my attempt to make the pain of his leaving more bearable, I could find only one acceptable justification for his abandonment of me. I told myself that he had no way of knowing what was really going on at home. The possibility that he had left me behind even though he knew how I was being abused was too painful to consider.

Once, as I approached my teen years, a friend who had recently visited my father gave me a snapshot of him. I hid it under my pillow, but my mother found it just a couple of days later. In a rage she ripped it into tiny pieces. Over time I forgot what my father looked like, and he became a nonexistent person in my life.

There was no reprieve from the abuse while I was in high school. Every morning I walked to school with one thing on my mind—the dreaded walk home. I walked home with one thing on my mind—the abuse that surely would be mine that evening. I went to bed that night with one thing on my mind—the terror-filled nightmares from which I awakened screaming and fearful of going back to sleep. I got up in the morning with one thing on my mind—the fear of hearing my mother greet me with the words, "We're going to have a war today."

Warning Sign

I had heard about it in school, a condition called hysterical paralysis. I was convinced I had it one morning when I woke up and found myself unable to move or speak. I could hear my mother moving around, and I knew that in a few minutes she would fly into a rage if I didn't begin dressing for school. But no amount of willpower could budge my body. At the age of 15, after years of hell on earth, I wondered if this was the end.

As my body lay frozen in fear, morbid thoughts raced through my mind. "What if I stay this way? I can't defend myself. I'll be paralyzed for life. Is this the way I'm going to die?"

One part of me wanted to die, for that seemed the only hope that I would find relief from the pain. Yet another part of me silently cried out to God, "Please help me. Please get me out of here. Please God, please."

How many times before had I cried out to God for help? There were too many to count. So that morning in bed I didn't pray my prayer with much hope of it being heard, much less answered. But within only a few minutes the impossible happened: I felt my body relax; strength returned to my muscles. I opened my eyes and pushed past the fear as I tried to bend my fingers. They moved! Then I checked my hands, my feet, my legs . . . I could move everything! "You did hear me, Jesus! Thank You!" I prayed with relief.

There was no doubt in my mind that I would soon be dead if I didn't get away from my mother. I had always been scared to think of what would happen if I tried to leave, but at that moment I had no fear. It was as if the experience in bed gave me the added degree of courage that I needed to leave. I determined that this would be the day!

Running Away

We were pressed for time as usual that morning, and I was unavoidably detained in the bathroom. Mother was waiting impatiently in the car. She honked the horn several times. I tried to rush, but there was nothing I could do to hurry nature along.

Mother, not one to wait for anything or anyone, stormed back into the house and into the bathroom, yelling about my irresponsibility and disobedience. As she continued shouting her accusations, she grabbed a rubber bulb syringe from the bathroom cabinet and turned on the tap water in the washbasin. When the water was steaming hot, she filled the syringe.

"Take your pants off and get down on the floor!" she barked as she slammed the bathroom door behind her. "I'll teach you not to keep your mother waiting, you good-for-nothing _____."

There was no escape; mother was blocking the door. Terrified, I lay down on the floor. She spread-eagled my legs with her feet and rammed the syringe of steaming hot water into my behind. Instantly I felt it burning as if my insides were on fire.

Mother stomped out of the bathroom, oblivious to my screams as she yelled, "That'll fix you so you won't sit on the toilet forever anymore! Now get up and get in the car!"

The ride to school was agony. How could my mother be so mean? What was it in her past that had made her so inhumane? Had she been abused as a child? I knew nothing about her past, and now it didn't matter. In the heavy silence, I cemented my decision to run away that day. Never, I vowed, would I be hurt again.

With every ounce of effort, I managed to lift myself out of the car in front of school. A couple of classmates saw me and immediately recognized that something was very wrong. "What's happened to you? You look terrible!" one of them said. Their expressions of concern gave me the courage to confide in them.

"Look, you guys," I explained in desperation, "If I go back home tonight, I think I'll be dead before tomorrow. My mother will kill me if I don't leave."

Other classmates joined in a circle around me. To my relief and surprise, one of them asked, "How can we help?" "Yeah!" said another student, "we've got to do something."

This was my chance. I had to get out of the city. I had to go as far away as possible. With a courage that surprised me, I blurted, "Will you guys chip in so I can buy a bus ticket?"

Instantly, hands went into pockets. Wallets and purses were opened. Students went to other students. One classmate emptied her lunchbag and used it to collect the money. A few minutes later she handed the sack of dimes, quarters, and dollar bills to me. As I reached out to accept it, I realized that this would probably be the last time I would ever see them.

"You know you'll never get your money back, don't you?" I said. "I'll never be able to come back to this school." As I was talking I could feel the tears running down my cheeks, and some of the students were wiping tears away from their eyes. I could hardly believe what I was seeing. I had never realized that any of my classmates even knew I existed, much less cared about me. For the first time I recognized that I had had friends all along and didn't even know it.

"Bye, you guys. I'll never forget what you've done," I said, trying to thank them but finding no words adequate.

As I turned to walk to the bus station, one of the students came trailing behind me. "I'm going to the bus station with you," he explained. "I'll watch out for the truant officer and the police. I don't want anyone stopping you from getting out of here."

Though I was scared as I walked to the bus station, I had not one doubt or hesitation. I knew that I had made the right decision, and no one could have convinced me differently. I purchased a ticket to a large city about 200 miles away and boarded the bus with high hopes. I would never spend another night at my mother's house, and I would never again be abused.

❖ 3 ❖

Deeper Evils

Pain shot up my body as the bus bounced over an uneven road by a construction site. I tried to ignore it, but every time I shifted in the seat or the bus hit a bump, I was reminded of the horror of that morning. "Concentrate, Lauren!" I ordered my mind. I had to think of a plan. Where would I go? What would I do once I arrived at my destination? I had no contacts and only a couple of dollars left in the lunchbag.

I had accomplished the escape. I was out of my home, no longer suffering from my mother's physical and mental beatings, no longer having to endure those men in the basement. Now I would try again to find someone who would help me and protect me. There wasn't much I could do about the men in the basement. In those days I had never heard of the term "sexual abuse." It wasn't talked about on television or in newspapers, and certainly not in the classroom. In seventh grade, the highlight of our sex education was a lively discussion of what date we should allow kissing. The majority said you should wait until the third date. So my experiences in the basement had to remain a secret.

However, certainly someone ought to be able to do something about my mother. I didn't know what went on in other homes; my mother didn't allow me to go to other houses. But without her around, maybe I would have the nerve to say more about what went on in my home. Maybe now I could find out if my situation was unusual.

By the end of the four-hour bus ride I had reached a conclusion. I would go to the police. I was going to a large city that had a large police force. But more important, my mother wasn't there to defend herself. Back in my hometown I got the impression that the policemen were her friends. At least they tended to believe her story rather than mine. I had to believe they were on her side.

My remaining money was just enough to pay a taxi to drive me to police headquarters. My limited courage evaporated as

I walked into the imposing building. Everyone seemed busy. There was all kinds of activity. Who would have time to listen to me? They would consider me a nuisance. However, a policewoman did consent to hear me out. She took me into her office and asked what I needed.

"I think my mother is becoming a wild woman," I said in practically a whisper. "I'm afraid she is going crazy and will do something horrible to me. If I go back home . . ." I couldn't finish the sentence.

"What do you think she could do to you?" the woman asked in a very businesslike manner.

"If I spend one more night at that house, I might not live to tell about it. She could kill me." There, I'd done it. Certainly that was enough information for the police to take action.

"What's she doing to you?"

"This morning I woke up and I was so afraid I couldn't move. Nearly every day she has these screaming fits. She beats me or kicks me. A few days ago she started locking herself in the bedroom for hours at a time. I never know what she's going to be like when she comes out. She's almost like a wild woman. She does terrible things to me. They're getting worse and worse. I don't know what's happening to her. I'm afraid she's going crazy."

In those days they didn't have children's protective services. Children were rarely taken out of the home. But I thought surely there had to be a way to protect me if my life was in danger.

"How old are you?" the officer asked.

"Fifteen," I answered.

"When will you be 16?"

"In five more months."

"I suggest you go back home and live there until your sixteenth birthday. After that you can legally choose who you want to live with. Just be a good girl and do whatever your mother tells you to do. You'll see how time flies. Are you willing to do that? There's nothing we can do for you here."

For a moment I stared at her. How could she say that? Obviously she didn't understand. Had she even heard what I'd just said? If I went back home, I might not be *alive* by my sixteenth birthday.

But what else could I say? Meekly I mumbled, "Yes, I'll go back home." In dejection I walked out of her office with no money and nowhere to go.

I wound up sleeping underneath the bushes in the city park. It was the rainy season, and I was wet, cold, and hungry. In desperation I begged for money. Many passersby kept on walking. Some made snide remarks. But a few paused long enough for me to explain to them that I had run away from home, but that now I was lonely and broke. Some of them offered comments like "Repent and be saved!" or "You're nothing but a trashy streetwalker!" Once in awhile someone would reach into his pocket or purse and hand me a couple of quarters or a dollar bill. I would thank him and promise that the money would only be spent on a bus ticket home.

Thinking back on the two days and nights I spent in the park, I realize that it was a miracle I wasn't picked up by the police. As soon as I had enough money, I bought a bus ticket back to my hometown. I was still determined not to go back to my mother. That left me only one other alternative. In complete desperation, I walked over to the Juvenile Hall, turned myself in, and asked them to help me.

Of course they let me in. I was a runaway, a delinquent! Promptly they locked me in a small room that looked like a jail cell—bars on the window, a narrow cot, and a toilet. There was no light switch on the wall and no doorknob on the inside of the door. A three-inch-by-six-inch slot in the door gave full view of the room, including the toilet.

As the reality of my situation gripped me, I clutched the bars in the window with both hands and screamed at the top of my voice. "Somebody help me! Please help me!" I yelled and sobbed until, spent with exhaustion, I dropped in defeat to the cold, hard floor. *They* had won. *I* had lost.

As I sat motionless on the floor, I heard the sound of keys in the door. Looking up, I saw a guard standing over me. As he saw me cowering in the corner he said softly, "You haven't done anything wrong. You're not supposed to be locked up in this room." He helped me to my feet and added, "Don't worry. You'll have a chance to tell your story in Juvenile Court in a couple of days. Until then, we'll protect you. No one can hurt you here."

That was on Friday. For two precious days there was no abuse, pain, or torment. I was determined that in court I would tell everything.

The Awful Choice

On Sunday afternoon I was told I had a visitor. It was my father. I hadn't seen him in 11 years, when he had moved to another state to get as far away from my mother as possible. It didn't take me long to figure out why he had come back for me. Obviously my mother had been told that I was to appear in court the following Monday. No way was she about to let me tell my story to people who just might believe me. So she had called my father; the only person to whom the juvenile authorities would release me in lieu of my testifying in court.

Quickly I had to recover from my shock and evaluate my options. I didn't have to go with my father; I could stay and testify. I felt torn between the two possibilities. If I agreed to go with this stranger, my father, at least I wouldn't have to go back to that house and live with that woman! If I chose instead to stay and tell my story, I had no assurance that I would be believed. I might still be sent back home. All of a sudden, horror struck me like a ton of bricks. "Oh, dear God," I prayed, "after all I've gone through, they wouldn't dare to send me back home—would they?" That possibility was unbearable. There was no way I would survive at home after telling my story.

And so, with an odd mixture of emotions, I reluctantly decided to go with my father. I wasn't at all certain that I was making the right choice, and I was filled with a nameless fear that I couldn't shake. But I figured that anyone and anywhere had to be better than what I had run away from.

On the long plane trip across the country, I sat next to this stranger, my father, daring to whisper under my breath, "Maybe I've found someone who will love me. Maybe I'm safe. Dear God, please make it so." Still, I couldn't rid myself of those lingering fears while I dared to entertain a few dreams of a happy future.

My father was a gentle, soft-spoken man. Much of the time he was away from home because of his work. When he was home, he was usually tired and spent much of his time in his room resting. He never yelled or did wild, unpredictable things. He was also very lonely and seemed to welcome my presence. I did all the things the woman of the house was supposed to do—housework, washing, ironing, and cooking. I didn't mind, because he was fairly easy to please—in direct contrast to my mother, who was absolutely impossible to please.

At first I heaved a sigh of relief, thinking, "I can get used to this real easy." But at the same time that nameless fear gnawed away in my mind. Though I was not in the midst of continual "wars" with my mother, I felt that an unexplainable and impending doom was soon to surface. That doom turned out to be my mother.

I never have been able to figure out the hold that my mother had on my father. Was she blackmailing him for something he had done in the past? Had she set him up, and had he innocently fallen in the trap? Did he have such a blind love for her that he would do anything, absolutely anything, she wanted him to do? Or did he simply not have the guts to stand up to her even when he knew she was in the wrong?

Whatever the reasons, it soon became evident that my father was under a great deal of pressure. My mother phoned him every day, sometimes several times. From what I could tell, he seemed to be weakening under my mother's incessant verbal attacks. He never told me what the conversations were about, but after he would hang up the phone he would look totally distraught. Sometimes he would go into his bedroom and slam the door behind him—for him a rare show of emotion. From the references to me, I could tell that I was the center of their discussions, but for what purpose I could not tell.

The Phone Call

It came to a head one evening as I overheard him on the phone.

"I don't want this to go on!" my father said emphatically. "She's been through enough. You've already made her into a robot. What more do you want from her?"

I could hardly believe what I was hearing. "Is my father really sticking up for me?" I thought to myself. It was too good to be true! Of course, I could hear nothing of what my mother said, and I heard only part of my father's responses. But the more I heard, the more the fear and uneasiness increased. Somehow she was wearing him down. She was determined to run my life. She would not surrender whatever financial returns I had provided her.

"All right, I'll let her go with them when they come for her," my father finally said, "but I don't want to be connected to it out here. I don't want to be that involved now that she's here." Repeatedly running his hand through his hair in exasperation, he stated emphatically, "I don't agree with it. It's against everything I believe. Besides, I can't afford for anyone to find out. It would ruin me. Just keep me out of it."

There was a long pause of several minutes. Whatever my mother said, it worked. "You know I've wanted this to end," my father finally responded, his voice ringing with a futile sound of resignation. "I've never agreed with the way you've handled her. But I do agree, she's never been anything but trouble. You've always been the boss . . . of everything. I'm too old to fight you. Whatever you say, whatever you say . . ."

I had been leaning against a wall as I listened to their conversation. As I fought to make some sense of what I'd heard, I slowly sank to the floor. Tears streamed down my cheeks. The dream I had dared to entertain was shattered. I had run away in hope that the bad would be ended and a new life could begin. I had done all I knew to do, but it wasn't enough. A cloak of despair fell over me as the dream that had kept my desperate hopes alive was gone. I realized then that my parents were separated in distance only. The "business"— ME—would continue. My father was too intimidated to stop it. My mother would continue to inflict pain, hurt, and ugliness.

I began to rock back and forth, wrapping my arms around my body in a futile effort to comfort myself. "No more hope," I cried. "No more way out. No more dream." Then I looked up toward heaven through eyes that were wet and blurred and cried, "Why God, why? Where are You? Don't You care?"

God's answer was a deafening silence. Not only had my dream of finding a way out been shattered, not only had my dream of being loved been crushed, but now I felt that even God, whom I had clung to through all those agonizing years, had turned His back on me. If God didn't want me, who did? That was the worst hurt of all.

The Same World—Only Worse

Either my father would be gone, or he would stay in his den when they came to pick me up. "They" were the men who worked for the pornographer, a man named Tony. I had learned since childhood that they were to be obeyed. And even though I was now in my late teens, my fear of them was just as devastating and unshakable. And so it was on occasional weekends that I was taken to the pornographer's studio.

The first time they injected me with some kind of drug that left me in a relaxed, dazed state. After that first session I knew what to expect before every picture session—an injection that put me into a stupor, leaving me in a state where I didn't care what happened. It wasn't long before Tony gave me pills to take on a regular basis, even at home. He said that they were to counteract the effect of the injections, so I wouldn't become addicted. I was only too willing to take them, for I certainly didn't want to become a drug addict. Only later did I begin to realize that Tony had tricked me. By then it was too late; I was hooked.

Most of the work for the porn magazines, films, and (in recent years) videos was done at this studio. From the outside the building looked impressive. I was always blindfolded for the last 15 minutes of the ride, so I never knew exactly where it was located. However, it appeared to be in a very ritzy business district, surrounded by other "high-class" offices and stores. The entryway and front office were elegantly decorated. No opulent extravagance was spared in giving this business the look of professionalism.

However, the front office was only a facade. Behind that was where the real world began for me and for countless nameless and faceless others who had come looking for fame and fortune. Little did they know that when they signed on the dotted line they were signing themselves into the same world as mine—HELL!

If you ask the man on the street what pornography is, he'll more than likely mention *Playboy* magazine. He has in mind a beautiful woman who has spent a few hours in the lap of luxury while doing a centerfold. For that one or two days of "work" she may have received a fur coat and several thousand dollars. That is just window-dressing, the tip of the iceberg.

The real world of pornography is a vast multibillion-dollar industry that is destroying thousands of lives. The *Playboy* centerfold is tame compared to the filthy perversion that I was forced to endure. I was not there to make a sexy centerfold. I didn't receive any fur coats, fake or otherwise. I didn't ride in a limousine. I didn't receive $30,000 for a day's work. I wasn't paraded on the arm of a handsome, sexy guy. I was used in the most depraved and lewd ways that man could devise. Nothing was too immoral, too shameless, too perverse. The most obscene picture imaginable will touch just a part of the lewdness in which I was forced to be photographed.

Two Worlds Collide

Once again I was two people. One was the girl who went to college and was seemingly the average girl who lived next door. The other lived in a world that most people don't even want to imagine might exist. I had learned well how to live in two worlds as a child. But now, for the first time in my life, the emotional scars were beginning to seep through the veneer I had learned so well to hide behind. Whereas school had long been my "safe place," college life was another story.

In college the emotional traumas of my other world began to seriously affect my ability to concentrate. The drugs I was on and the horror of the occasional weekends in the pornography studio made it hard to pretend that I was a normal person. I kept to myself, unable to make close friends. I never allowed any boys to get close enough to even ask me for a date. My grades began to drift downward from mostly A's to mostly B's and even a few C's. I can see now that I was making an attempt to cry out for help. Unfortunately, the cries were too subtle for others to hear.

I cried out by refusing to study for classes I thought were stupid. In World Geography, I didn't care what the rainfalls in South American jungles were, or what kinds of currents controlled the oceans of the world. So I quit attending the class. Since it was too late to legally drop the course, I received a failing grade. In Comparative Governments, I didn't care how the French government differed from the government of the Soviet Union. So I didn't show up for the tests. Even in the classes I thought were worthwhile or interesting, I couldn't concentrate. But in college, no one cared if I struggled. No one cared if I dropped out. No one ever inquired to try and learn if there was something wrong. In fact, I could vanish from campus for one or more terms and return again without anyone except a clerk in the registration office noticing.

Church was the other place where I cried out for help. But again, the cries weren't specific enough for others to identify the world behind my pain. I'm certainly not faulting the church people. Who could possibly have guessed what my tears were really about unless I had spelled them out in specific detail? That I was never able to do. That I never *dared* to do. I remembered my Sunday school teacher and the pastor, and I could not bear the possibility of being misunderstood again.

However, the church remained a retreat where I could cry my heart out to God. Many a Sunday, when I wasn't taken to the studio, I would go forward to the altar and plead with God for His forgiveness. I felt so guilty and so dirty that I couldn't accept the possibility that God might love me. The sermons meant nothing to me. I never remembered any of the messages. They never touched the hell I was living. All I could grasp was the concept of God as Father. And often was the time when I cried out to Him to put His arms around me and hold me. It was the simplest of faiths, but it kept me going.

A few faithful worshipers would see me crying and pray with me as a soul who obviously was hurting very badly. As the burden of being forced to live two lives in two worlds became harder and harder, I did find some strength in the prayers of those precious God-sent prayer warriors. But it was impossible for me to open those closed doors I had lived behind for so long. I simply could not find the keys that would unlock those secrets. Today, my friends whom I've now told about my life understand that, but some still ask, "Why didn't you try to run again now that you were of age?"

The answer to that question is easy for me to understand, yet difficult to explain. From as early an age as I can remember, I was made to believe that I was nothing, that I was not worthy of being loved. My mother, and later Tony, the pornographic photographer, and others so degraded and terrified me that they were able to control me.

Then there were the pornographic pictures of me with animals, with other women, and with children. Most victims of sexual abuse, and especially prolonged abuse, end up feeling that they are guilty. I certainly felt that way. It didn't matter that as a child I was forced into these activities. It didn't matter that very mean people had controlled every day of my life. It didn't matter that I was often beaten into submission. In my own mind I was guilty.

In addition, there was the control through drugs. The injections made me lethargic and submissive. In between I was given pills, and it wasn't long before I was hooked on them. The drugs made it easier to endure the physical and mental pain. I didn't even care as much about resisting. I became like a robot, and that was exactly what they wanted.

I was shocked out of my lethargy one day when I saw a fellow victim die of a drug overdose during one of our sessions. Immediately I informed Tony that I was getting out and I refused to take the pills. The following day I broke into a cold sweat and I felt like bugs were crawling all over me. I stood in a cold shower for an hour, but the feeling wouldn't go away. Then I began to hallucinate. I saw gigantic bugs crawling on the walls. Before the day was over, I was begging Tony for more drugs.

"You pull that stunt one more time and you'll end up dead, pretty baby," Tony threatened. Then, as he handed me the pills, he added with a wry smile, "You can't get along without us."

I knew he was right. They had me. I had tried to get help before, but it hadn't worked. I had run away before, but that hadn't worked either. And now? With the countless lewd photographs they threatened to send to anyone I knew, with my watching another victim like myself die from a drug overdose, with the fear that they would track me down and kill me if I ran—I saw no way out!

So, feeling now more than ever that this was my fate, I resigned myself to the abuses in passive submission. Whatever the pornographers wanted, I did. Whatever physical abuse, I silently accepted it. Whatever sexual abuse, I endured it without a word of protest. The tears flowed. My heart cried. My soul wept. And yet, miraculously, I still loved my heavenly Father, for He was my only hope. Now I can see that He was protecting me, keeping me until the day when I would see His sun shining into the darkness. Apart from His presence, I have no doubt what my fate would have been, for I saw it enacted in the life of a teenage girl who died in my arms.

Rhonda

The pornography business is like a revolving door. Devious men entice people in, use them until their minds and spirits are broken, and then throw them away. In and out they come and go—a never-ending circle of horror. I had long ago gotten over caring and hurting for the others. I had lived in a hell for every one of my 19 years. I was hurting as badly as they were. And after all, some of them had come through those doors of their own free will.

But for some reason Rhonda touched my heart. She was typical of the runaway teenager. She had hopped a bus that she believed would take her to a new life, freedom, and maybe even fame. She was just innocent enough to think that fame went to the beautiful, and Rhonda was certainly beautiful. With a slender figure, long blonde hair, large dark eyes, and an irresistible smile, she had all the qualifications for stardom—or so she thought.

She knew one thing for certain—nothing could be worse than the alcoholic parents she had left behind. Rhonda was wrong, dead wrong. She found herself in the big city, living on "the strip." Turning tricks was the only way she could survive. ("Tricks" are men who pick up a prostitute.) It didn't take long for disenchantment to catch up with Rhonda. She wanted to go home. But she was afraid of her parents, and she didn't want to end up in Juvenile Hall.

It was a Saturday night, and Rhonda was coming up dry in finding a trick. She was penniless, cold, sick, hungry, and frightened. It was at this point that Rhonda had to make a decision. A man named Tony had told her about a place that would take her in, feed her, provide her a bed, and give her money. All she had to do was pose in the nude for a photographer.

Rhonda wasn't streetwise enough to recognize that Tony's line—"I work for a photography studio that's looking for girls like you who need a break in life to try out as models"—was just that, a line. She didn't know that Tony was really working for a pornographer, not a reputable photographer, and that his real job was to find pretty but desperate girls—preferably runaways who wouldn't be missed—who were just gullible enough to fall for his line. She didn't know that Tony's show of concern and offer to "show you the ropes until you get your feet on the ground" would last only as long as it took him to convince her to walk through the doors of his studio.

And so it was, in the cold and rain of that Saturday night, that Rhonda made the worst decision of her life. Tomorrow she would go to work at this place. On Sunday afternoon, after making herself look as presentable as she could, Rhonda walked through those revolving doors.

I watched Rhonda as I had watched dozens of Rhondas. The so-called "photographer" cleaned her up, fed her, and made her feel important. Rhonda was on her way up. But Rhonda wasn't told what she would have to do on her way up. They didn't tell her that once she walked through those revolving doors she was their property—they owned her. They didn't tell her that she would be kept on drugs to keep her in line. They didn't tell her that this was hard-core pornography. They didn't tell her that she would have to perform acts of sexual perversion—with men, with women, with children. They didn't tell her that some of these films would include sexual "games" of bondage where she would be tied to the bed and whipped. No, they just didn't bother to tell her.

Just six weeks later Rhonda was on her way out of those revolving doors, but not the way she had planned. She had served her purpose well. Rhonda had been used. Rhonda had been abused. Rhonda had seen things a 15-year-old should never see. Rhonda had seen things no one should see. Rhonda had been forced to take part in activities that stripped her of every ounce of self-respect, self-worth, and most importantly, her will to live. Raped in body and mind, Rhonda wasn't needed any longer.

How vividly I remember holding that young girl in my arms. Once beautiful, she was now emaciated, her body wasted from the abuse and drugs. Her face was gaunt and pale. That once-irresistible smile was now twisted into a taut grimace of pain. Those large dark eyes had lost their sparkle. Her hair was no longer shiny, but matted and dull.

I listened to her halting, almost incoherent speech as she tried to share the pain of her life with me: "Mommy. I want my mommy. . . . Ran away. Daddy beat me when he was drunk. Thought he didn't love me. Better I leave home. . . . Tony said he'd take care of me . . . love me. He lied. . . . I'm dirty. I'm so dirty. Take me home, Lauren. Please . . . (there was a long pause as she struggled to get her last words out) . . . take me home."

This was no woman of the world who had collapsed in my arms. This was a disillusioned young girl who had fallen into the hands of one of the most evil, depraved, and perverse professions in this country—the porn business.

As I gently held Rhonda in my arms, slowly rocking her back and forth, I whispered, "Jesus loves you." Then I felt her body go limp. This precious young life, who should have been enjoying carefree days of fun and laughter in a loving home, died in my arms from a drug overdose.

As I laid her head on my lap, I was overcome with grief. "It should have been me," I sobbed. "It should have been me."

The Porn Business

Pornography is not just a picture on a piece of paper. Pornography is not just "a work of art." Pornography has a living definition. I know. I'm one of them.

And my experience is not unique—not by a long shot. Though accurate figures are impossible to obtain because of the secretive nature of the industry, it has been estimated that up to 600,000 children in the United States are used annually by the "kiddie porn" industry.[1] That figure makes sense when one considers that many victims are runaways with little or no money. According to a report sponsored by the Department of Justice, it is "estimated that between 700,000 and 1 million children run away from home each year. Adult exploiters can pick them up at bus stations, fast-food stands, and street corners and offer them money, gifts or drugs for sexual favors."[2] The report also recognizes that there are children (like I was) whose parents have sold them for use in child pornography.

Pornography is about living human beings. It's about people, especially those who are the most vulnerable in our society—babies, children, teenagers, homeless young adults.

There are two victims of pornography: the victim whose body is used to produce the pornographic picture and the victim who reads and feeds into the pornographic breeding ground. Both types of victims are physically and/or psychologically abused. There is no question that pornography is a major contributor to child abuse. It helps explain why so many middle- and upper-class "respectable" citizens are involved. One study sought to identify who reads magazines such as *Playboy*, *Penthouse*, and *Hustler*. It discovered that 10 percent of all men who serve on school boards read *Playboy*. Likewise, 13 percent of business club members, 8 percent of local government officials, and 6 percent of church board members read the magazine.[3]

Charles H. Keating, founder of Citizens for Decency Through Law, said in testimony before a U.S. Senate hearing that one research study revealed that 77 percent of child molesters of boys and 78 percent of child molesters of girls admitted imitating the sexual behavior they had seen modeled in pornography.[4] And they didn't get the ideas only from what is called hard-core porn. Dr. Judith Reisman, through an 800,000-dollar grant from the Department of Justice, studied the images of children, crime, and violence in *Playboy*, *Penthouse*, and *Hustler*. She identified more than 6000 photographs, illustrations, and cartoons depicting children in 683 issues of these three publications. *Hustler* depicted children most often, an average of 14.1 times per issue, followed by *Playboy* (8.2 times per issue), and *Penthouse* (6.4 times per issue).[5]

Pornography is big business. According to estimates presented to the Attorney General's Commission on Pornography, it's an eight-billion-dollar-per-year industry in the United States.[6]

But statistics don't begin to reflect the Rhondas—the starry-eyed, gullible teenagers who fall for the empty promises of the dream-come-true. It doesn't reflect the young woman who has been bound, chained, whipped, and degraded to the lowest low. It doesn't show the babies and young children who are abused and battered in perverted sexual acts with adults, or the ones who are used in snuff films—where they are tortured and then killed during the filming of pornographic videos.

As the demand for this garbage increases, pornographers stoop to new lows. There is no bottom line. There is no standard of morality or decency beyond which they cannot pass. The pornographers have thrown decency and morality to the wind.

Victims of the porn business experience a slow death. Through the years I was robbed of everything that counts the most to a human being. I was robbed of my identity—not just my name, but my identity as a human being: first as a little girl in my basement or in a dirty garage and then as a teenager and young adult in a pornographer's studio, where I (and others, like Rhonda) ceased to exist as human beings.

And who is behind this evil business? Who could possibly exploit so many fellow human beings solely for the purpose of making money? I was about to find out, for without realizing it I was part of a pornographic empire. I was going to meet the man responsible for ruining my life and the lives of countless other victims.

❖ 4 ❖
The House of Victor

It was a typical day at the studio. I was waiting for instructions when suddenly a man approached me and said, "Let's go; we're taking a ride." Before I could respond, he had grabbed my arm and ushered me out the service door into the alley, where a van was waiting. The motor was idling and a driver was sitting behind the wheel. The man half-pushed me into the van, got in after me, and slammed the door shut.

Quickly the man tied a blindfold around my eyes. I was used to being blindfolded, so that didn't surprise me. However, I had never been taken anywhere else from the studio. I had heard of other victims being taken away for good—those who were causing trouble or rebelling. We never learned what happened to them; they just disappeared. The mere suggestion of foul play was enough to keep the rest of us in line.

Soon I felt myself rocking from side to side, and had to grab the armrest to keep from sliding across the seat. I could tell from the sounds that we had left the city, and now we were going up a hill on a road that had a lot of curves. No one said a word, and I had learned long ago not to ask questions. So I sat in my own silent prison of terror. What if they were taking me into some isolated hills to do away with me? I didn't think I had caused any trouble, but I couldn't be sure. Maybe they were finished with me and wanted to make sure I would never talk. I didn't want to think these thoughts, but the further we went, the more such a possibility loomed in my mind.

Suddenly the van slowed to make a sharp turn. I heard a crunching sound under the tires as we proceeded slowly over a gravel road. My fear mushroomed. This could only mean that my suspicions were correct. But then the van suddenly stopped, and that didn't make sense. They hadn't bothered to take me very far off the main road.

The blindfold was removed from my eyes. To my utter relief, I wasn't in some remote wilderness, parked behind a huge rock. I was on a beautiful estate. The grounds were perfectly manicured. There were flowers and tall trees, and several sprinklers watered the vast lawn. Then I saw the massive house that looked more like a mansion, the kind I had seen only on television.

The driver got out and opened the side door. The other man grabbed me by the arm and barked, "Get out." I was marched between these two men to the huge double front doors of the mansion. There a servant greeted us and ushered me into a room that looked like a library. Behind an elegantly carved desk a man looked up from his paperwork. He had jet-black hair that was combed straight back and piercing, olive-colored eyes. His muscular chest and finely tuned body bulged under an expensive silk suit. His fingers, wrists, and neck were draped with heavy gold jewelry.

Suddenly I realized that I had seen this man many times at the pornography studio. Was this the person the other girls had talked about? I had heard them whisper about a house on a ranch—The House of Victor.

With a smile the man rose and greeted me. "Hello, I'm Victor."

A million questions raced through my mind. Why am I here? Why am I meeting the boss? Why is he being so kind? What does he want with me?

"Please, sit down," he beckoned as he walked around his desk to position the chair.

My mind said "Run" but my body sank into the sumptuous chair.

"I'm sure you're wondering why I had you brought here," he began. "As you probably know, I am the proprietor of the photography studio. I also provide a first-class service for high society here at my estate. . . ." His explanation droned on for several minutes. Finally he came to the point. "I've been keeping my eyes on you at the studio, and I like what I see."

My mind instantly thought, "That's the most absurd compliment ever paid to me." But I held my tongue.

"You have a certain something that the other girls don't have. I'd like to bring you up here to my home, and if you pass the test I have for you, I'm going to make you my special woman!"

"As if I had any say in the matter," I thought. As Victor began reciting some of the benefits of being his woman—nice clothes, furs, the good life—all I could think about was Rhonda and the other girls at the studio. He had to know what was happening to them. He was responsible for their abuse, their drug addiction, their ruined lives which supported his lucrative business. I hated this man, and I most certainly did not want to be his special woman.

But what choice did I have? If he was truly that evil, as I was sure he was, then there could be no escaping him. I thought about the other girls who had rebelled, and how some of them had simply disappeared. To resist him could cost me my life. So it might just be better for me to go along with him, if not in spirit, at least in body. Perhaps that might keep me from suffering the sick kinds of sexual abuse I had heard that other victims endured at "The Ranch."

". . . you're going to go through a testing period where I'll have you service some of my clients," Victor said. "If you service them well and there are no complaints, then I'll bring you into the main house to do my bidding.

"You've already passed several tests without knowing it," he remarked rather proudly. His tone of voice was both approving and sarcastic. "You do what you're told. You keep your mouth shut. You even show compassion to some of the other girls who are having problems. That's a new twist in my line of work, and I kind of like it. I think you just might be the one to make me feel better when I'm down."

I was so angry that I felt like putting my hands on his 200-dollar silk shirt, pulling him out of his genuine-leather overstuffed chair, and yelling at him, "Yeah, if you'd been used like I'd been since day one; if you'd tried to run away only to be trapped and brought back to worse conditions; if someone else had forced you to get hooked on drugs; if your very life was in danger if you so much as looked cross-eyed at those perverted men—you'd mind your p's and q's too, just to save yourself from a little of the hell you put your girls through!"

But of course I didn't say a word. I just sat there and silently seethed. I must have hidden my thoughts well, for Victor didn't seem to notice. "Come!" he said, "Let me give you a tour of the house."

The home was elegant, yet tasteful. Artworks that must have cost a fortune adorned the walls. There was a hand-carved staircase, crystal chandeliers, and the finest furniture in every room. But all I could think about as I walked through this mansion was the blood, sweat, and tears that had been spilled to pay for this man's lavish lifestyle.

Finally the tour was over. As Victor showed me to the door, his parting words were, "By the way, you won't be going to the studio any longer. You'll be coming here. And you'll be mine . . . soon."

Victor's Connections

During the next few weeks as I waited for his call, all I could think about was my introduction to Victor, his house, and his incredible conversation with me. I went through the motions of college classes, church, and tending to my father's home, but my mind was on Victor. "Why me?" I kept asking myself. I was so confused, so tired, so beaten down, and so strung out on drugs that it was almost impossible to think logically. Victor had made it sound like I had a choice. But what kind of a choice was it? A choice to try and run, only to be found and suffer ungodly consequences? A choice to rebel during Victor's testing of me and remain as one of the girls who were sexually abused and tortured by his clients?

And so I prayed even harder for God's love. "Lord, if You don't hug me, I'll go out and hug a telephone pole." I had an undying craving for love, and He was the only person where I found it. He was the one sane place in an insane world. I couldn't understand why He allowed me to suffer, but I couldn't afford to leave Him. He was all I had.

One thing was certain: I would not get any love from Victor. Though I doubted that he had any real affection for me, even if he did, I would never love him. I despised him. He was lord over his underground kingdom, and I was his slave. I had learned that he was into providing sexual services of every conceivable kind. He was into all forms of pornography, including kiddie porn, homosexual porn, and snuff films that show the abuse, torture, and ultimate murder of humans, usually children.

Gradually an appalling realization came to me. Without realizing it I had probably been connected to Victor since early childhood. All the pieces fit. He was the mastermind of a national pornography ring. He had legmen working for him throughout the country. These men worked as contacts or middlemen with parents who were willing to allow their children to be used in pornography as a way of making easy money. My mother was obviously one of those parents.

No doubt about it, children made big money for the pornography business—and Victor kept meticulous track of his investments. Just because a child moved from one parent to another, or from one city to another, didn't mean that the child couldn't continue being used. Just because I was brought to live with my father in another state didn't stop my mother from using me in the pornography business. In fact, whereas before Victor only had long-distance control of me through my mother, now that I was living in his own backyard he had literal control of me.

When I talk about the money involved in pornography, I don't mean to imply that the children ever received money for their services. They didn't. They only made money for their parents. The children were the product used and sold for profit. I was never offered—and I never would have accepted—one cent from my mother or from the pornographers, either as a child or as an adult victim.

The House of Torture

When Victor's men finally came for me, I was exhausted from the sleepless nights. When the blindfold was removed, we were in front of his house, just as he had promised. That weekend was spent servicing his clients in a smaller house on Victor's property. Originally it probably was a servant's cottage, but now it was used as a place where evils of the worst kind took place. I quickly labeled it "The House of Torture."

It had several small rooms, each equipped for a different purpose. There was a room for bondage sex acts that was equipped with restraining devices and leather straps for whipping the victim. Another room had hooks and a rope. The client could hang his victim upside down while performing acts of sexual perversion.

There was a third room that was equipped with whatever the client had ordered. Even the most creative mind cannot conceive of the weird sexual desires that these perverted men had, or of the equipment they would request in order to perform their sick desires.

I spent the entire weekend in The House of Torture. Two days and two nights with Victor's so-called "high-society types" were more than enough to make me want to either end my life or tell Victor that I would be his woman. Yet I hated that man so intensely that I held out for several more weekends, for there was nothing I wanted less in life than to be known as Victor's woman.

Who were these clients of Victor's? You might be picturing the traditional "dirty old man" as the typical client who would engage in such perversion. Not so! They were doctors, lawyers, and men in the highest management levels of major corporations. They were judges, politicians, and entertainers. They were even law-enforcement personnel and clergymen.

These men, and even a few women, were more than willing to bare their souls to the girls who serviced them. After a round of drinks and a line of coke (cocaine), or whatever their choice of drug, they told about anything and everything. I found out about their jobs and their job problems. I learned about their wives and their marital troubles. They told me stories about illegal messes they had gotten themselves into. Some even talked about illegalities they were into with Victor.

Evil is not restricted to the uneducated. Wickedness is not limited to the indigent. The dirty old man does not hold a monopoly on sexual perversion. Victor's clientele were men with money, prestige, position, and power. They knew how to use it, and they knew how to hide behind it.

Victor began each evening by entertaining his clients with striptease acts and porn films while they imbibed in extreme amounts of alcohol and satisfied their drug habits. By the time the entertainment started winding down, they were wound up—ready for anything and everything. They were wired!

This is when the clients ceased to be the men they were in the outside world. When a politician takes his clothes off, he ceases to be a politician. When a clergyman takes his clothes off, he ceases to be a clergyman. When the mask is off, the real man is revealed. One policeman had a thing about wearing only his gun as he abused me. I can still recall the sound the gun made as it slapped against his thigh. A certain clergyman liked to keep his backward-turned collar on. I can now look back and see how downright silly they looked, but at the time these men filled my mind with terror and my body with pain.

High on drugs and drunk on alcohol, the perverted sexual cravings ran rampant. For most of these men, it probably started many years before with a magazine like *Playboy* and an X-rated movie, but soon their sexual fantasies were not satisfied at this level. It took hard-core porn to satisfy. Natural sex was left behind along with the softer-porn magazines. Once the line of "normal" is crossed, the flames are fanned into an ever-increasing abnormal, uncontrollable craving for perversions that end in abuse, torture, animalistic behavior, multipartner sex, and sex with children. The cravings become more and more deviant, finally culminating with sexual acts that are almost unthinkable to the mind that hasn't been polluted with hard-core pornography.

On a typical night of activity at The Ranch, I would be used and abused sexually by anywhere from one to ten men. Sometimes it was one at a time and sometimes two or three together. Sometimes children, usually 10 to 14 years old, were included in the orgy. Many of Victor's clients were so perverted in their sexual desires and in the kinky sex acts they demanded from the girls that some of them became nothing less than pure torture.

Those long, never-ending nights blurred together. The brutality, the depravity, the lewdness, and the degradation of mind, soul, and body mingled together into one long, fiendish nightmare. Much as I was repulsed and nauseated at the thought of "graduating" to Victor's house, I began to feel that this was the only way I could survive.

After one particularly brutal night with several clients whose sexual demands left my body bruised and battered, I began to cry. Staci, one of Victor's other girls who had spent the night with clients in the room next to me, rushed in and quickly put a hand over my mouth. "Shhh," she whispered. "You mustn't let them hear you crying. You know the boss will find out, and he'll put you with one of his meanest clients just to punish you. You know he doesn't like his girls to be crybabies."

Staci's voice was kind and understanding, but I didn't care. I pushed her hand away and blurted, "I can't take it any longer. I've done all I can to please these creeps, but they still do every dirty trick in the book with me."

As she wiped the tears from my face, Staci began to explain, "Honey, that's why they're here. The men who come to the ranch know they can get away with anything and everything. These are the kind of clients Victor wants. He gets paid big bucks for offering this kind of service."

I was startled as Staci took my head in her hands and looked into my eyes. "Honey, you'd better take Victor's offer and run with it," she said. "I would if I had the chance."

I couldn't believe I'd heard her right. She couldn't be advising me to be the woman of the man we all hated.

As I began to shake my head, she held it still and whispered, "Don't you see, you can't last much longer? At least try it. What do you have to lose? If you run, he'll go after you and find you. You know he will. And if you spend many more weekends in this hellhole, you won't make it."

Weakly I nodded my head. I knew she was right.

"Just remember one thing," she added in a stern voice. She was so serious that I didn't think I wanted to hear what she was about to say. But I listened anyway. "Remember, Victor is a dangerous and unpredictable man. *Don't you ever forget it!* I've been here a lot longer than you, and I saw what happened to his last woman who got out of line."

Staci didn't offer an explanation, so I asked, "What could be worse than what I've already gone through?"

"You don't want to know," she answered. The look in her eyes convinced me that I really didn't want to know. "Just think about what I've said. Will you?" As she got off the bed and walked out the door, I knew that I indeed had a lot of thinking to do. Time was running out. I surely had gone through enough testing, and Victor would soon approach me about being his woman.

Who Are the Victims

Those of us who were taken to The Ranch as "regulars" to be used and abused by Victor's clients were not women or children who enjoyed this type of activity. A few, like myself, had been victims all their lives. They had had no choice from the beginning. Some were much worse off than I. At least I was allowed to attend school and church. Some victims were not recorded births, and they experienced nothing that could be called normal in their entire childhood. Perversion and abuse was their world 24 hours a day. They were not given the option of living two lives.

Those who were used at The Ranch or elsewhere, and knew of no other life, either managed to commit suicide or eventually, almost mercifully, died somewhere along the way from the extreme abuse. Some were dumped on the streets as excess baggage. They never made it off those streets. Their bodies were used, their minds were burned, their will to make it had long ago been methodically destroyed. They died on the streets.

Others who ended up at The Ranch were like Rhonda—unsuspecting and gullible, looking for an exciting way of life and willing to surrender a few morals to find it. Unfortunately, they ended up on a dead-end street with a one-way ticket to nowhere.

The worst tragedies of all were the young runaways who were brought to The Ranch. Their parents may have been heartbroken at their disappearance and were searching for them. More likely, the parents couldn't have cared less. Many of the children weren't even reported as missing. It really didn't matter why the children left. Whether a rebellious runaway or an unwanted child, they usually ended up in the same place—on the streets of Dallas, Seattle, Los Angeles, or New York: big cities, exciting cities, glamorous cities, cities that offered everything but what they needed most—love, food, and shelter.

Needing the basic essentials for self-preservation, the runaways are easy prey for the scums, the slimes, the scavengers, and the hawks who lure them into their trust by promising anything and everything. These were the tragic victims who ended up in the clutches of men like Victor.

Once the victims were in their grasp, these men had many methods of control. For example, Victor knew which of his clients indulged in particularly sadistic sexual acts. His girls also knew. If one of the girls wasn't playing the game to his liking, he only had to threaten to assign her to one of these men. Usually the threat was enough. It was bad enough to draw one of these men for a single night. To get him for a successive number of times was pure hell.

But the worst and most inhumane scare tactic was when Victor threatened, or actually assigned, a girl to the studio to be photographed with little children in sexual poses, or to the ranch with a client whose sexual preference included using little girls and/or boys and one of the women in sex acts. Nothing repulsed us more, or made us feel more dirty and guilty, than being forced to do these things with or to children.

The threats were endless: the threat of cutting off a girl's drug supply if she was hooked, or the threat of giving her a forced overdose; the threat of sending pornographic photos of her to her parents (that is, if she had parents who cared); the threat of physical torture. The few who continually defied Victor just disappeared. Whenever I inquired about someone, the answer was always the same: "You'd do well to keep your nose out of other people's business!"

Stolen Minutes

Some of us who were repeatedly brought to The Ranch got to know each other over a period of time. The stories we told may have been different, but the pain and devastation we shared was very much the same. We were frightened. We felt hopeless and alone. We had been forced to participate in the most shameful, vulgar acts imaginable.

The stolen minutes we found to share our hellish nightmare with each other became priceless. We felt like soldiers in a hopeless war. We weren't fighting to win. We were only fighting to hang on until maybe, just maybe, we would find a way out—a way to be free of the total degradation that kept us beaten down in spirit; a way to be free of the threats we knew would be carried out if we talked; and a way to be free from our own personal hell that each of us was living within our own mind.

If ever there was a group of human spirits that molded together instantaneously, it was the few of us who got together occasionally. Our talks got right down to where "the rubber meets the road." There wasn't time for niceties. Every second counted. Every word counted. Every expressed feeling was loaded with emotion. We weren't afraid to hug, to hold, to weep, or to admit fear, helplessness, hopelessness, or even the ever-present thought of suicide.

There was Cicely, or at least that was the name she changed it to when she came to the big city straight out of high school. She thought the name would look good on magazine covers. Cicely had left a good home and parents who loved her and had turned down a college scholarship to pursue her childhood dream of becoming a model.

Marsha had no dream. She hadn't turned down anything. The only thing Marsha left behind as a 14-year-old was two alcoholic parents, an older brother who had committed suicide a year before, and a younger brother who was doing time in a juvenile detention center.

Then there was a young teenage girl who wouldn't tell anyone her name. All of us, at one time or another, had tried to communicate with her, for in the midst of our own pains the look of emotional suffering on her face was so pitiful that we each felt drawn to her. Yet she chose to remain silent in her internal world of hurt.

The four of us met together behind that house of torture one cold morning just before dawn. That night had been particularly horrible for each of us. The clients were all of the "sicko" perverted type, and we were all at the end of our rope, physically and mentally.

Cicely had dragged a blanket behind her and we all tried to make it cover our arms and legs. For a minute or so we huddled together in silence, trying just to keep ourselves from falling apart.

The silence was interrupted by the sound of crying. I looked up and saw Marsha bent over, her body heaving from the stifled sobs. Cicely put her arm around Marsha and drew her close. Marsha laid her head on Cicely's shoulder. "I'm scared. I'm so scared," she managed to say between sobs. "I don't have anyplace else to go."

All of us felt the same. There wasn't much to say; there weren't any answers. But there, with that handful of aching, wounded hearts, I mentioned my faith in Jesus Christ. I told them that I never would have survived this long without His love.

When I said, "Jesus is my Father, and I am His child," tears began to well up in the eyes of the teenager whose name we had never known. She had never said a word before during the few times she had joined us in our stolen minutes together. To our surprise, she spoke up as the tears spilled down her cheeks.

"My mama got real sick and died," she began. "My daddy started having sex with me. When he got a girlfriend, they didn't want no one else around. So he packed a shopping bag with my clothes, set it out on the front porch, and told me, 'You're old enough to be on your own. Here's a hundred bucks. Go find yourself a new life.' " All four of us were crying now as she added, "I guess this is my new life."

I still didn't know the girl's name, but I had an understanding of her silence. And I was so thankful that at least I could tell her about the love of Jesus.

Sadly, there were also times when I shared some of my bitterness and anger at Him. Yet the girls seemed to respect my feelings. I think if I had told them that everything was always just great with Jesus, they would have looked at me like I had rocks in my head. "I don't know why life has been this way for me," I confided to Cicely, Marsha, and our unnamed friend. "I wish to God I had a real home, with real parents and real love. But I don't. I only know one thing for sure: Jesus loves me, and in the middle of the night when I'm crying myself to sleep, I know I'm not alone. I'm never alone."

There wasn't one of these girls who hadn't been through every dirty, vulgar, demonic act that Satan could shovel out. They had developed an exterior toughness just to make it through their fate in life. Yet in spite of their toughness and their "I don't care about anything" attitude, that hard exterior always came off when they heard about Jesus. They became like little children who were starved for love. Just the mention of His name brought a glimmer of hope to their pain-filled eyes.

As our stolen minutes were coming to an end, I began to softly sing the simple little song I had learned long ago in Sunday school. Cicely sang with me. Marsha hummed along. Our silent friend listened.

> Jesus loves me, this I know,
> For the Bible tells me so.
> Little ones to Him belong;
> We are weak, but He is strong.
> Yes, Jesus loves me.
> Yes, Jesus loves me.
> Yes, Jesus loves me,
> The Bible tells me so.

Not even Victor could take the love of Jesus away from us!

The Decision

"Lauren, come into the study," I heard the deep, gravelly voice command. I didn't have to turn around to know it was Victor. "I want to talk to you. You'll be pleased," he added, as if to keep me from running out the front door.

I was both terrified and surprised—terrified because I was certain of the reason he was calling me into his study, and surprised because this was the first time any of these creeps had called me by my name. Usually it was "Hey, broad," or "Hey, woman," or "You girl." It sounded nice to finally hear someone use my real name.

As I entered Victor's study, the same room where I had first met him weeks before, I heard Staci's voice whispering, "Remember, Victor is a dangerous and unpredictable man. Don't you ever forget it!" I could still feel the intensity with which she spoke that warning.

Victor directed me to the same chair I had sat in before, only this time he pulled up a similar chair and sat down next to me. "Next comes the big spiel," I thought, "and I don't even know what my answer is going to be. Some choice I have anyway—pervert clients or pervert Victor!"

"Lauren, I'm very pleased with you," Victor said. "My clients have had nothing but praise for you." His voice was so sugary sweet that I felt like throwing up all over his tailor-made suit. "I've put you up with just about every type of client I have," he continued. "They say you took it like a trouper. You know that pleases me, don't you?"

My thoughts went back to the room where I'd been tied to the bed with leather straps, and I thought to myself, "You _____, what else could I do but lie there and take it?" I began to grip my chair. My knuckles turned white. My teeth were clenched together so tightly that my gums ached.

My tension was obvious to Victor, who said, "Relax, my dear. You have nothing to fear. I know it hasn't been very pleasant lately, but things are going to be different now. Very different."

As he said the words "Very different," I looked into Victor's face for the first time. He had a crooked half-smile that made me feel anything but reassured. However, I apparently had no choice; the decision had been made for me.

"I've been grooming you for a very long time, my dear. You're ready to be mine!" he stated. Victor then reached over and pushed a button on the side of his desk. I heard a buzzer ring, and in a few moments a man entered the study and handed Victor a small box. As he opened it he said, "I know you will be pleased to be my woman, and that you will be proud to wear my mark." Out of the box he produced a shiny, single-edged razor. My eyes could not have gotten any wider.

The man who had brought the box to Victor positioned himself behind me and held my head in his hands. I tried to wiggle out of his grip, but his hands were large and his arms strong. My head remained still in this vise. Victor knelt in front of me, the razor blade in his right hand. As his hand drew near to my face, I closed my eyes so tight that it scrunched up my entire face.

"Relax, Lauren, I'm not going to hurt you," he said in a vain attempt to talk gently. "You must relax so your forehead will be smooth."

There was silence. I sat motionless, not even daring to breathe. Suddenly my body jerked as Victor's voice solemnly announced, "With this mark I take thee as my woman." I felt a stinging pain on my forehead, then felt what must have been a kiss over the wound. A couple of seconds later a warm trickle of blood crawled down my forehead and over my tightly closed eyes. Someone, either Victor or the other man, wiped the blood from my face.

Ever so slowly I opened my eyes. Victor was still kneeling in front of me, wearing that same devilish smirk. "You will forever bear the mark of Victor," he said. "You will forever belong to me."

"No!" I protested inwardly. "I belong to God, not you."

Life didn't change much as Victor's woman. The weekends and summer evenings that I was taken to the ranch always began with two men coming to get me in a van. There was the usual blindfold and the silent ride. The only thing that was different was that I no longer spent my time with clients. I now spent my time with Victor, and with every passing encounter, the warning Staci had given me rang truer.

Victor was dangerous and unpredictable. I soon learned that his sexual preferences weren't much different from those of his clients. Just because his bed had a canopy over it and the sheets were made of satin didn't cover up the horrors of sexual abuse. Just because I was abused by the same man every time instead of a variety of men didn't make the physical or emotional pain any less. I was no less abused, and I was no less a victim. I really wasn't Victor's special woman. I was Victor's special fool.

In the beginning I was used only as Victor's sexual toy. Then he began to show me off to the more important clients whom he entertained in his elegant living room. He used me as an object to paw over, which made them all the more anxious to get their own girls in the other house. I was forced to do all sorts of things in front of these men that I can't bring myself to describe.

There was another change. I received more phone calls at my home, either from Victor or from one of his men. No doubt he thought that leaving him or running to the authorities was on my mind. He was right. There was no way that I could pretend to enjoy the life I was forced to have with him. "You talk and you're dead," the voice would say. "You run and we'll hunt you down. You disobey and you'll curse the day you were born." The warnings were never-ending, and I knew they weren't just empty threats. No one crossed Victor and got away with it.

Besides, much as I wanted to run, where could I go? To the police? They would want particulars, like Victor's address, and names of his clients, and I couldn't provide them. I was always blindfolded before being driven to Victor's house. I wasn't even sure Victor was his real name. And his clients surely didn't advertise who they were and where they lived. The police would want me to detail my complaint, and I felt sure that my abuses were so bizarre that I would not be believed. And then I thought of the policemen who visited The Ranch. Was Victor paying them off? Would they sabotage my efforts? If I failed, it could mean my life. And if I decided to just leave town instead, where would I go? Victor had his people all over the country. I had no doubt that he could hunt me down. I was trapped, and Victor knew it.

The more time I spent with Victor, the more careless he got about what he said to me. He drank a lot, and when he was drunk he talked about things that should never have reached my ears. I learned some of Victor's businesses. He operated a drug ring. He bought and sold black-market babies. His pornography empire was more extensive than I had imagined. But Victor wasn't worried. He knew that I knew that he could put my life on ice at the snap of his fingers.

Descending into Hell

Victor's lust for evil was insatiable. He had partaken of just about every sin this world has to offer, yet it wasn't enough to satisfy him. I could see it coming. Victor was getting bored!

One night after what seemed to have been a very lucrative evening of "business," he began to bemoan how jaded his interests had become. As he paced the floor, he kept saying over and over and louder and louder, "Lauren, there has to be more. I know it's out there somewhere. I can feel it. But I can't find it."

A few weekends later I detected a sudden change in him. With an air of excitement and anticipation he exclaimed, "Woman, I've found it! I've found it! I've finally found it!"

When I dared to question just what he had found, he gestured toward me with his right hand. To my horror he was holding up his index finger and little finger. Suddenly my heart was in my mouth. My flesh began to creep. I felt chilled to the bone.

I had noticed several of Victor's clients using that same sign. Just a few days before I had mustered up the nerve to ask one of the men at Victor's "entertainment" parties what the symbol meant. The man explained that it represented the horns of a goat's head. "It's the sign of Satan!" he declared proudly.

Now Victor was holding up the same sign. I tried to scream, but the words came out in only a whisper. "Victor, no. No, no, no!"

He looked at me with a glint of evil in his eyes and tauntingly whispered, "Yes, yes, oh yes!" Then he threw his head back and began to laugh a laugh not only of pleasure, but of frenzied glee. Victor had always been evil. Victor had always been wicked. But that night I felt an evil presence in him darker than any evil I had ever felt before. It was hellish. It was fiendish. For the first time in my life, I felt as if I were looking into the face of Satan himself. Never had I seen such a look of demonic hell. Never had I heard such a laugh of depraved insanity.

Victor would never be bored again, for Satan knows no limits in his diabolical schemes. Victor had dared to step into the realm of Satan himself. The only fact that terrified me more was the knowledge that I would be forced into that world with him. There was no comfort in knowing that my life would be spared until he was through with me. I would have welcomed death, for I knew that despite the insanely wicked life I had already endured, the horrors were sure to get worse as Victor progressed deeper into satanism.

✦ 5 ✦

Basement of Death

Victor's men always came to pick me up late in the evening, probably because there was little chance of them being seen. One Friday night I heard their knock but refused to answer the door. I just couldn't stand the prospect of being with Victor that night. His wicked grin and the evil expression in his eyes sent chills up my spine. I had become obsessed with thoughts of escaping his ever-increasing insanity.

It seemed ridiculous to keep living this nightmare. One way or another I had to get out. I knew I couldn't escape in any conventional sense, so I had thought about suicide. One night I emptied the medicine cabinet of all the pills, hoping that they would end my life. But all they produced was a long and fitful night's sleep. The next morning I awoke with a gnawing realization that my halfhearted suicide attempt only proved that I didn't really want to die. I wanted freedom from Victor's bondage, and the opportunity to experience the fullness of God's love.

What if I simply didn't answer Victor's summons? What would happen? I wouldn't run; I wouldn't tell anyone. I just wouldn't go when his men came. What would be his reaction? Would he leave me alone? Since I didn't see any other obvious options, I decided to find out.

As usual, my father was gone this evening. His business commitments gave him a convenient excuse; he probably suspected that Victor's men were coming for me. At the sound of their knocking, I hid in my room, hoping they would just go away. Maybe they would think I was sick. Instead, I heard the sound of a key being inserted into the front door, and then the doorknob turning. How had they gotten a key? I hadn't considered that possibility. Quickly they entered the house and found me. One of the men grabbed me and I felt a sharp sting in my arm. Within seconds I was out cold.

I awoke to the slaps of Victor's hand across my face. I had never seen him so angry; it reminded me of the rage I'd seen on my mother's face so many times before. I was still groggy, but not enough to keep me from understanding the grave meaning of the next few minutes.

Victor grabbed my arm and pulled me off his bed. Without giving me a chance to get my footing, he dragged me across the room to one of his huge walk-in closets. He flung open the door, then jerked me upright. "Do you see these clothes?" he shouted. "Do you know who these clothes belonged to?"

Just one glance revealed fur coats, sexy negligees, expensive shoes—the kind of wardrobe most women only dream of having. Victor yanked one of the negligees off its hanger and held it in front of me. It was torn and stained by what appeared to be blood. "This was my last woman. She tried to turn me down too!" he roared as he ripped the negligee in half and threw the pieces to the floor.

Instantly I recalled Staci's words when I had asked her what had happened to Victor's last woman: "You don't want to know." I began to shake as I wondered if I was about to find out. Victor shoved me out of the closet and I fell to the floor. Shaking his finger at me, he warned, "Don't you ever forget what you just saw, woman!" I never forgot.

In the following months as Victor progressed deeper into satanism, his interest in pornography took a back seat. Learning the powers of Satan became his new "profession," as he called it. Each time I was taken to his home, Victor told me a new story about what he had seen in a ritual. At first the rituals seemed fairly innocent, and I wasn't too frightened. There was fire changing colors and ghostly apparitions coming out of the smoke. Bodies were levitated. Objects were moved by the power of the mind. Once he even described how the powers of Satan (which he always insisted were good powers) had healed a woman who was dying. The high priest had used magic to make the cancerous tumor come out of her body. "She coughed it up," said Victor. "I saw it with my own eyes!"

Initially I thought that all my fears might have been for nothing. But gradually the stories became more sordid. When he told me about a ritual in which a young pregnant woman had sold herself to Satan, I knew there was nothing "good" about satanism. "If only you'd been there, Lauren," he said with great animation. His wild excitement in simply recalling what he saw made him act as if he were high on drugs. "The woman was so brave. She just held her arm out and let the high priest cut her wrist. She let the blood drain into a chalice, and then do you know what she did? She sold her soul to Satan. She used her own blood to sign her name on the pact! You had to be there. You just can't get the same feeling by my telling you about it. You have to be there to see it and feel it for yourself!"

Victor's words were spilling at high speed. When he stopped long enough to grab a breath, I blurted, "Stop it! I don't want to hear anymore about it. Please, don't tell me any more."

"Oh, but you've got to listen, Lauren, because I'm going to do the same thing, and you're going to be with me."

I felt as if I would choke on his words. Before I had time to even begin to deal with his declaration, he raced on. "This is going to blow you away, woman. Listen to this! The high priest prayed this really weird prayer. He asked the demons to come forth. I couldn't see them, but I guess they did because he started to talk to them. He asked them to give this woman's baby a name because Satan was going to be its father."

Victor paced the floor as he spoke, walking faster and faster. The way his eyes darted around the room, it was as though he could see the ritual taking place right in front of him. Then suddenly he stopped dead in his tracks and lowered his voice, as though he didn't want anyone else to hear him. "Lauren, when the high priest asked the demons what the baby was to be named, I heard the most eerie-sounding voices I've ever heard. I thought, 'Someday I'm going to have the power to make demons talk to me.' Then the high priest spoke a name to the woman, but I couldn't understand what it was."

He started pacing again as he said, "Do you know what the woman did next? She sold her baby's soul to Satan too, by signing its name beneath hers on the pact. Doesn't that just blow you away—selling your soul to Satan? Do you know how much power I could have if I did that!" With that exclamation he raised his clenched fists into the air as though he were celebrating a great victory.

I knew then that there was no turning back for Victor. He was headed straight into the hands of Satan, and he intended to take me along with him. This would be different from the studio and the house of torture. Here the rules weren't clearly defined. I didn't know what to expect.

High Priest of Satan

Victor was faithful to his promise that I would go with him to a satanic ritual. What I didn't expect was that it would be in his own house. "Guess what?" he said one evening with a wicked smile. "I am now a high priest. A high priest of Satan!" He motioned for me to follow him and we descended through a cellar-type door in his floor to the basement. I had not even been aware that there was a basement; a rug had covered the entrance.

The basement was cold, damp, and dark, with a musty smell. A heavy, eerie feeling pervaded the atmosphere and seemed to settle on me as I entered, making it hard to breathe. "You can feel him!" declared Victor in a hushed voice. "That's Satan!"

Satan may appear as an angel of light at times, but in Victor's basement there was only darkness. The walls were draped in black fabric, and the only light was from candles and the glow of a black kettle on the floor. I stared at a large slab of smooth rock that was partially covered with a purple-colored velvet material. "That's the altar," Victor explained. Then he pointed to a silver bowl. "That's the chalice that we drink from—our communion cup." Then he pointed to a cross. "It's placed upside down to mock the crucifixion of Jesus Christ."

A glance around the room revealed other objects. There was a goat's head positioned at the front of the altar. I saw an upside-down star within a circle drawn on top of the altar. And to the side was the black kettle. "That's the cauldron,"

Victor whispered. "Demons are summoned from the fires of hell that are burning in it." I shuddered, for its glow seemed like a silent omen, foreshadowing the very activities of hell.

As my eyes adjusted to the darkness, I saw the glint of the blade of a very large sword that was lying on the end of the altar. A terrifying thought—what do they do with the sword?—raced through my mind. I quickly shifted my eyes, afraid that Victor would notice and explain what it was for. Right now I didn't want to know. In fact, I didn't think I ever wanted to know.

As I tried to calm my racing heart, a door suddenly opened on the opposite side of the basement, and black-robed men, humming in unison, slowly moved in single file to the altar. Victor tugged at my arm, but I didn't budge. I wasn't about to go anywhere, unless it was back up the stairs.

The humming stopped abruptly and was replaced by chanting, "All hail to the father, Satan. All hail to the father, Satan. All hail . . ." While the chanting proceeded, one of the men who was cloaked in a black cape over his robe walked over to the sword and picked it up. "He's a high priest like I am," Victor whispered. As the high priest pointed the sword to the north, south, east, and west, I shuddered as I began to wonder why Victor had brought me down here to witness a ritual.

My wondering soon became terror. Spirits were conjured up to curse certain people whom the members wanted harmed. Other spirits were called on to give the coven members more power. Several of the members allowed their wrists to be cut, and the blood was drained into the silver bowl. Then they urinated into it. Finally, wine was mixed in and they each drank from the bowl.

Now these robed men began to get unruly. Gone was the initial sense of hushed decorum. I wasn't sure if they were drunk or high on drugs, or if they actually were receiving some kind of supernatural power from the demon spirits they had summoned. They began to indulge in what looked to me like a sexual orgy. I was surprised to see two or three women. I wasn't sure whether they were coven members, or if they had been brought in just for the orgy. Whatever the case, I had seen enough, but as I turned to try and go back up the stairs, I felt Victor's grip tighten around my arm.

"You can't leave!" he hissed. "I'm giving you to Satan tonight."

With every ounce of my energy I jerked to try and get free of his grip. But Victor was too strong. He pulled me up to the altar, and two coven members lifted me onto the slab of stone. My clothes were removed and I was positioned and held down so that my private parts were on top of the circle and upside down star.

I screamed and begged the men to let me go. But the more I screamed, the more excited they seemed. "Louder. Louder. Satan is pleased," they chanted. Then the abuse began. One after another, members of the coven brutally abused me sexually on the altar. After each one was through, he drank from the bowl of blood, urine, and wine and announced, "Satan is pleased." With each vulgar act, my will to resist lessened. I felt myself weakening physically, as though I would pass out. As each man climbed on me, I felt as if Satan himself were assaulting me.

Finally, after the last man had taken his turn, the high priest picked up the bowl, took a drink from it, then flung the remainder of it over my body. With that he threw his head back and laughingly mocked, "Satan has had you!"

The entire coven picked up the chant. "Satan has had you. Satan has had you. Satan has had you." My spirit was crushed. I was too weak to move, too bruised and ashamed. Finally I was lifted off the altar and returned to the arms of Victor. As he carried me up the stairs, he proudly declared, "Now we both belong to Satan."

But that was not true. Silently my heart spoke for me: "I will never belong to Satan. Never!"

Coven Members

Those who put on the black robes, who stood in a circle, who lit candles and uttered unending chants until they saw the very face of Satan—they were not surprised at the fiendishly diabolical acts that were sure to follow. For it was those very acts that would please their father, Satan, and bring more power to them.

These participants were not players in a game. They were not there to have fun. One does not play with Satan. Neither does one have fun with Satan. One follows Satan. One serves Satan. In obedience to him, one does Satan's bidding.

The evil practices of the satanic rituals I was forced to attend and participate in were not performed in symbolism. They were actually carried out. Those who practiced them were serious about their deeds of evil. Their allegiance to Satan was absolute. They were there to follow Satan explicitly, uncompromisingly, without question, even when he demanded sacrifices of parts of their own bodies. They willingly allowed the tip of a finger down to the first knuckle to be cut off as a sacrificial offering. There was great motivation to do this, for these members believed that through this show of loyalty they would please Satan and experience more power, fulfillment, satisfaction, and success in their own lives.

Evil begets evil. Perversion begets perversion. Acts of sadism, sexual abuse, torture, mutilation, and evils that go far beyond that generate a craving for participation in deeper and deeper evils. Satan does not take pleasure in good. The name of his game is evil, and as the members of many of the more self-styled satanic covens find out, one must always top last week's acts of evil. To gain more power and continue to please their hellish father, one must eventually go beyond even what the human mind can conceive. Only the Father of Evil could conceive such diabolical acts of perversion and wickedness, and only the Father of Evil could seduce a human being to carry out such acts. I heard demonic spirits order deeds of such a heinous nature that even the bravest would cringe.

Usually I heard only the voices, but on a few occasions I saw the demons materialize. Sometimes they took on the most hideous and grotesque forms imaginable. Usually, however, they appeared as ghostly apparitions with a vaporlike quality that I couldn't quite decipher. At one ritual, several demonic spirits appeared as hairy little creatures with sharp, pointed teeth and eyes that I felt were looking straight through me. Another time an evil spirit appeared as a slinky, slimy creature that looked like it was about to wrap itself around me and cling to me.

Regardless of whether they chose to materialize or not, when the demons spoke, Satan worshipers listened and obeyed. I heard demons order curses of the vilest nature— cancerous growths, even acts of suicide—put on unsuspecting victims. They ordered acts of sexual perversion that went far beyond the descriptions of lewd, perverse, and vile. They ordered the literal sacrifice of animals and even humans— both willing and unwilling victims.

You may wonder how any human being could actually carry out the orders of such evils and feel that he has done what is right and good. I wrestled with that question myself, for I did feel that some of the members sincerely believed that what they were doing was right.

One day, years later, while reading my Bible at home, I found a verse that answered that question for me. Speaking of Satan, John 8:44b says that "there is no truth in him . . . he is a liar and the father of lies" (NIV). From what I had seen and learned about satanism, that verse was true. I began to realize that Satan has never told the truth, but is such a master of deception that the coven members who opened their hearts and minds to Satan's schemes were blinded to the truth. Good became evil and evil became good. Once they gave themselves over to that false truth, all barriers to evil were destroyed. The door to the most diabolical evil was opened wide.

Victims of Rituals

Nudity and sexual lewdness and perversion are commonplace at most rituals. It does not matter if the female is willing or unwilling. In fact, it is believed to bring more pleasure to Satan if she is unwilling.

The female "sacrifice" is put on the altar, which is commonly draped with a red velvet cloth (red being the satanic color for anything of a sexual nature). She is raped, oftentimes brutally, by any of the male members who wish to have her. They often are so drugged by heroin, coke, or some other drug, or so bombed out on alcohol, that the rape becomes pure sexual torture. To satisfy their own perverse cravings and do what they think will bestow upon them stronger satanic powers, the male members perform crude sexual acts, often of a bestial-like nature. Sometimes the female is seriously injured physically. To keep her from even thinking about telling the police or anyone else, the high priest calls upon demonic spirits to do something of such a diabolical nature that she will be frightened into silence. She is told that these evil spirits will get her if she steps out of line. And well might she take that threat to heart, for it is not just an empty threat. Those spirits are real!

One time Victor told me about a young housewife and mother who had become bored at home. She accepted an invitation from a couple of her closest friends to attend a meeting. It turned out to be a meeting of witches. At first she was leery, but something kept drawing her back until months later she joined a satanic coven.

In her eagerness to be accepted, and through much coaxing by the other members and a word of admonition from the high priest, she offered herself as the sexual offering at the end of one of the rituals. As is often the case, the woman was put through more than what she could excuse as part of a religious ceremony.

That night when she went home, she suffered some physical complications. She phoned one of the two friends who had invited her to the initial meeting and told her she was going to the hospital to be examined. She asked the friend if she would come over and babysit her children, since her husband was away on a business trip.

The friend told her she would come over, but reminded her of her vow to secrecy and warned her that she might regret it if she told anyone what had happened. The young housewife told her friend that she didn't care—that she couldn't live this kind of life any longer. She would rather die than go through anything like that again.

So the friend came over. The victim started her car and drove toward the hospital. But she never made it. She died instantly in a grisly car accident. One of the police officers on the scene told the victim's husband that he had never seen a freak accident quite like that before. He couldn't explain how or why it had happened. In fact, from all he could determine, it shouldn't have happened at all.

When Victor reached this point in the story, he put his hand up to the side of his mouth and secretly said, "What the policeman didn't know was that the lady's friend had called the high priest before she went over to babysit and told him that they were about to be ratted on." Victor went on to relate how the high priest had summoned an evil spirit to place a curse on her that would cause her to die in whatever manner it chose before she reached the hospital.

To my disgust, Victor stuck out his chest and proudly announced, "You know what? It worked! The screws [cops] won't ever know what happened."

That kind of incident was not as unusual as one would like to think, and they were all too eagerly recounted to any victim who gave even the slightest indication that she might cause trouble. Understandably, the stories were most effective.

A New Business

The sexual perversion during satanic rituals interested Victor not only as a high priest, but also as a pornographer. He was an astute businessman, and it didn't take him long after he was installed as a high priest to recognize that there could be a very lucrative marriage between his rituals and hardcore porn. There was sure to be a market for such heretofore-unknown types of films and videos. There could hardly be too much blood and gore. There could hardly be too loud a scream of pain and agony. There could hardly be too much mutilation. There could hardly be too much partaking of the flesh of sacrificed body parts or too much drinking of blood that was drained into a crucible.

These films, videos, and photographs were not sold to the stereotyped "dirty old man" in seedy porno shops. Victor marketed them to doctors, lawyers, corporate businessmen, and high-level political figures. Only they could afford the thousand dollars per photo or the five to twenty thousand dollars per film or video. The more barbaric, cold-blooded, and unrestrained the acts of Satan were, the more Victor could get for the film. In fact, the more diabolical they were, the greater the demand.

Because I was Victor's "woman," I was privy to information that most of the other victims never learned. Occasionally I'm sure I heard discussions that were not intended for my ears; in fact, I wished I had not heard them. But Victor was very proud of his little empire. He was fond of bragging about how he had started with nothing. If you didn't know better, you could easily get misty-eyed listening to stories of his boyhood poverty. Then with a sweeping gesture of his arm, after making you feel so sorry for him, he would boast, "And now all of this is mine. All mine!"

One evening he had had too much to drink. As he was boasting about his accomplishments to me, the phone rang. When he answered it, he forgot that I was there. It was obvious to me that he was talking to someone he knew quite well. They were discussing the buying and selling of some of his photos and films.

"Look, Bud," Victor said impatiently, "You're offering peanuts for a product that's worth more than gold. Do you know what the market is? These are one-of-a-kind. You won't find them anywhere else. So stop playing dumb with me!"

For the next few minutes, sums in the thousands of dollars were bandied about. "All right, fifteen thousand for that one," Victor agreed. "You drive a hard bargain."

Once during the discussion, I jerked in my chair in response to what he was saying. Victor looked up and suddenly realized I was still in the room. "Get out of here and shut the door behind you," he barked.

My Own Hell

Not all of the rituals took place in Victor's basement. Some occurred on the far side of his estate, or deep in the hills. Occasionally we ventured into a church or cemetery. But no matter where they occurred, it was my own personal hell! I was not Victor's woman for the purpose of becoming a satanist. I was never trained to be a satanist. I only attended the ceremonies because Victor took me with him. However, I was seldom just a passive observer. Victor believed that Satan would give him the power he so desperately craved if he offered his woman as a sexual sacrifice. So I was seldom taken to a ritual where I was not abused.

My one small defense was to carry a little New Testament with the Psalms hidden in a pocket. Whenever I had a chance, I would sneak it out and read a verse or two. Usually I found myself reading from the Psalms. It comforted me to read about David's despair and how God kept loving him and giving him the strength to go on.

Once when I was offered as a sexual sacrifice the New Testament fell out of my pocket. Victor saw it and was livid. He picked it up and tore it into tiny pieces, then threw the pieces on the ground and urinated on them. When he was done, he commanded me to never touch another Bible. "I'll not have my woman being a Jesus lover!" he yelled. "And neither will Satan!"

To my shame, I remained silent. I wanted to yell back at him that there was nothing he could do to make me stop loving Jesus. But I was too scared. However, Victor was now convinced that offering me to be used by the satanists would be doubly pleasing to Satan because of my faith in Jesus.

I don't know how many nights I was laid on that cold, hard slab of rock—naked, shivering from the cold of night, while listening to unending chants that beckoned Satan. Every time, the same horrifying fear would grip my heart as the demons were conjured up to give their orders as to how my body would be used. The steel of a purified knife glistened in the candlelight, and I wondered if it would be used on my body. Already there were scars on my body, for it was commonplace to drain blood into the chalice from a cut they made on me. Sometimes, when a knife was poised above my heart, I wished to God that the high priest would plunge it swiftly into my body, putting an end to my hell. My life was a slow, torturous death that never ended.

Suffer the Little Children

Another element of some of the rituals was the sacrifice of animals, and even infants—sometimes taken directly from the young pregnant mother. I hesitate to write of these sacrifices, but I must.

I witnessed the ultimate sacrifice of a baby—skinned while still alive. I heard its screams which must have reached to the heavens. But even God seemed to turn a deaf ear. I often wondered why He allowed the hideous torture of a helpless, innocent little child. Didn't He have the power to protect the little ones? Didn't the sound of the screams that only an infant can make bother Him? Was He a God of love or was He a cold, uncaring God? Bitterness and anger toward this "God of love" began to grow in my heart. How could this Person show no pity on an innocent baby? That question would ring in my mind until I would find myself looking up to the heavens, screaming at Him in anger and resentment.

Victor told me that the purest sacrifice, the sacrifice that pleases Satan the most, is none other than an infant or young child. Why? Because children represent purity and innocence; they belong to God. Animals are offered to Satan. Adults, willingly or unwillingly, are offered to Satan. But Satan revels in the most macabre, inhuman, and bestial evil he can conceive in the diabolical machinations of his mind. There is no evil more perverse than the murder of a little one whose life has been robbed from God and sacrificed to Satan.

Where do they get the children? That is a valid question. I'm sure that it is very difficult for people to believe that children can be used for sacrifices in this country. If I had not witnessed this atrocity, I would ask the same question. Believe me, I would like to deny it, or at least doubt it. But I can't. I learned the answer the hard way.

Tom was a Master Counselor in satanism, and Victor frequently brainstormed ideas for rituals with him. One night I heard Victor blurt out, "I've got a good one, Tom. Listen to this. This is too much, man. I mean, this will blow your brains out!" Victor tried to describe his idea, but he was so consumed with the brilliance of his newly devised horror that he couldn't speak. It was as if his brain was working faster than his mouth.

I had seen Victor like this before. His voice always rose to a higher pitch and ran on fast-forward when he was trying to explain a new idea for a future ritual. I always felt I was hearing Satan speak when Victor was this way. I anticipated that each new revelation would be a little more demonic, a little more sadistic, a little more perverse than the last one. I was usually right. This one was no exception.

"Tom, I want Satan to give me more power than any other high priest," exclaimed Victor. "My Master Teacher has always expected great things from me. I don't want to disappoint him. I've been racking my brain thinking about what I can do that will make me more powerful than anyone else. I think I've found it!"

"I'm afraid to ask," Tom said dryly. "Don't lay too much on me if I have any part in your new plan." Though a close friend of Victor's, Tom had always been a little leery of these brainstorms.

"It goes like this." Victor's speech slowed and he was now talking in dead earnest. "We'll get a teenage boy and girl off the street and bring them up here. Then we'll get a baby from a gal we've been keeping our eyes on. Or maybe we'll even use the mother. Yeah! That would be even better."

"Wait a minute," Tom interrupted. "Where are we getting this baby from?"

"Oh, you know, Tom. That babe we've been hiding out. That one who thinks we're going to find a good home for her baby. She's going to have the kid any day now."

"Oh, yeah, I know the one. I can't believe how dumb these girls are. Who does she think we are, anyway—the fairy princess?" Tom was laughing so hard he could hardly speak.

As the laughter died down, Victor continued. "We'll marry the two kids off to each other during the ritual. Then we'll present this little kid to them. We'll make them a family— Mom and Dad and the new baby—the whole family scene."

Victor was getting excited again. Speaking faster and faster, he began to describe his plan for presenting this entire "family" to Satan. The two teenagers would be forced to sanctify their marriage union by having sexual relations with each other on the altar. Then the teenagers and the baby would be sexually abused by the coven members.

The grand finale would be the sacrifice of the baby. When I heard that, once again, as I had done so many times before, I raised my head to the heavens and silently cried out, "My God, what more can Satan do?" Once again, the heavens remained silent.

What particularly shocked me was the way Tom and Victor, and occasionally some coven members, discussed where and how they would get the babies. I learned from Tom that there were fraudulent people who represented themselves as case-workers of adoption agencies or heads of placement homes. They carried so-called "legitimate" identification papers, but they were either satanists or were acting as go-betweens. Their purpose was to get the unsuspecting and well-inten-tioned unwed mother to sign her baby away to a porno-graphic ring or to people connected with satanic cults.

One afternoon Victor and Tom were laughing about what they called "want-ad babies." "Did you see the ad I placed in the paper the other day?" Tom asked. "I said that Janie and I were prospective parents who were searching for an unwed pregnant young woman who would give her baby up to us for adoption after it was born. Man, you wouldn't believe how many gals answered the ad! We've got a supply of babies all set up whenever we need them. We could have enough babies to last us a whole year!"

I cringed. I'd never heard of babies referred to as a *supply* before. This was too much. I got sick and threw up. Victor and Tom laughed and called me a wimp.

On another occasion some coven members sat around and talked about their breeders. The word "breeder" was new to me. One of the members explained that breeders were women who were born, marked, and raised for the sole purpose of having babies that would be used by satanists— either to be raised in satanism or used in ritualistic sacrifices. Since there was never any public record of their births, they were never missed when they were abused or killed.

I thought I had heard it all until a high priestess approached Victor after a ritual as he and I were about to leave. She informed him that she had completed the assignment. "I convinced Judy (a new female coven member who was eight months pregnant) to assume the highest honor. She agreed to give her baby by C-section while lying on a purified altar."

I gasped. Victor turned and chuckled. He was always amused when I reacted in shock. Then he asked the priestess, "Did you make arrangements for a doctor?"

"Yes, I've engaged the services of a licensed doctor," she answered. "I understand that he is one of ours."

I'm sure this seems too horrendous for many of you to comprehend. It was for me. But I heard it and saw it. It's true. I know these practices are shocking and repulsive. That is the intent of those who do such evils—to make the horrors so shocking, so heinous, so fiendish, and so barbaric that they will not be believable. If you do not believe, you have played into their hands, and they have accomplished their purpose.

I thought that the rituals I had witnessed in Victor's basement were as evil as evil could get. I could not imagine anything worse. I did not want to imagine anything worse. Little did I know that the next ritual I would be forced to attend would take me into the pit of hell itself!

❖ 6 ❖

Brainwashed and Broken

A few weekends later, Victor was talking as usual about the glories of satanism. "It's the greatest thing that's ever happened to me!" he said as he paced across the room. "It's given me everything I ever wanted. This is power, Lauren—real power."

I was about to tune him out when suddenly he announced, "I've been thinking! It's about time for you to take an active part in the rituals." Up till now I had been forced to attend rituals and service the coven's perverted lusts. But I had never had to chant or in any way demonstrate allegiance to Satan.

"Never!" I protested. "And you can't make me. You may have a certain power over me, but Satan will never have power over me! And if you try, you will live to regret it!"

Victor swung his head around, glared into my eyes, and shouted, "You *will* do it. You will!" With that he stormed out of the room, slamming the door behind him. I knew I had made a big mistake. No one challenged Victor. He would feel compelled to break my defiance. He would make sure he had absolute control over me.

It took a few weeks for Victor to finalize his plans, but there was no doubt about his intentions. I knew he was highly agitated about my love for God. He didn't treat me as he had apparently treated his previous women. There were no gifts, no nice clothes, no special recognition. He became obsessed in his desire for me to give my allegiance to Satan. And he knew I would never willingly give that.

It was only many years later that I understood why this man I loathed held so much control over me. It was as though I was a prisoner of war. Most of us have an image of a POW being tortured and broken by the enemy. We've heard of sleep deprivation, isolation, untold hours of questioning, needles under the fingernails, the use of drugs, and various forms of bondage being used to brainwash soldiers. It can bring the strongest man to his knees begging for mercy, totally pliable in the hands of his captors.

That kind of thing happens in Asia or eastern European countries, not the United States. Or does it? Are people brainwashed in the land of the free? We might not call it that, but the results are the same. There are people who have been so controlled, sometimes from their preschool years, that we could rightly consider them brainwashed. I realize now that I was one such victim.

Dr. Judith Reisman is a noted expert in mass-media effects and was a principal investigator for the Department of Justice. She has done exhaustive study in the area of child sexual abuse. When I asked her why I couldn't run from my captors, she explained, "Thousands of children and young adults are in a similar situation to yours, and it has nothing to do with the will of the individual to escape. If they have been appropriately brainwashed, they become paralyzed in their effort to remove themselves physically from the situation. We know that paralysis has to do with threats of specific kinds of violence when one tries to escape. But setting that aside, the behavioral finding here is that brainwashing creates a psychological paralysis in the victim. There is no way to deny that because it holds across all races and religions. Your situation is not unique to either time, gender, or place."

Of course, as a four-year-old, I wouldn't understand the process of mind control. But I can understand now what was happening. It began with my mother having me stand in front of a mirror and say over and over, "I'm no good. No one wants me. I'm bad blood." It was reinforced when my mother told me that the children Jesus loved were "not like you." "Not like me"—I repeated that lie over and over again. I didn't know it was a lie. I believed it.

The humiliating experiences with the dirty men, and posing nude and in vulgar positions in front of the camera, reinforced my belief that I was worthless. Much as I desired happiness, I believed I didn't deserve it. I didn't know why I was so bad, but my mother constantly reminded me that I was. As I got older and began to realize that maybe my mother was bad, and I found the courage to try to find help, I was crushed by the repeated futility of my attempts.

On top of that was the total control my mother exerted over me. Until I ran away from home, I was never allowed to have a friend. I was never allowed to go to another girl's house. I was seldom allowed to play. I never enjoyed any birthday parties or Christmas gifts. Whatever she told me to do, I had to obey instantly or face terrible consequences. When I moved across the country with my father, that control shifted to Victor.

Victor's methods were more brutal, but just as effective. There were the drugs that sedated me so I would be cooperative during the pornographic sessions. The drugs clouded my mind, and bound me to Victor as the supplier. There were the numerous threats, with enough examples to demonstrate that they were never uttered idly. If I didn't cooperate, they could inflict the most heinous punishment. If I talked, they could arrange an accident and end my life.

There is no question that Victor and his men had almost total control of my life. But it wasn't absolute. Despite their thorough programming, they could not make me worship Satan. This was where I drew the line. My allegiance was to Jesus Christ, not Satan. Victor knew that. And he was determined to break that last hold on my life.

One day I was again picked up at home and driven to the ranch. Victor met me at the front door, grabbed my arm, and rushed me down into his basement. By now I had made many trips to that basement, but I never got used to it. It was dark and musty and I always sensed that same eerie feeling of evil hanging in the air.

The silence of that darkness was broken by a voice. I knew it had to be Victor's, yet it sounded as if Satan himself were speaking to me. "The father has chosen you to present your purest offering to him. Not only will you present that offering, but you will lay that offering on the altar and sacrifice it to the father, who will be pleased to accept it."

Horror seized my mind. Terror froze my heart. The purest sacrifice, the most pleasing sacrifice—the one sacrifice I could never make unless my mind and will were completely broken—was the sacrifice of a child to Satan!

Victor could call it an offering. Satan could call it a sacrifice or gift. They could put any label they wanted on it. But to me,

IT WAS MURDER! I would not do it. They could not make me do it.

Or could they? I heard footsteps go up the stairs and I knew that Victor had left me alone to ponder the most diabolical act I would ever be asked to perform. In the darkness of the basement, I fell to my knees. Tears streamed down my face. My fists pounded the cement floor in outrage.

A Voice in the Dark

By now I was so confused that I didn't know whom to pray to, whom to beg for mercy. How many times I had prayed to God, and He still had not rescued me. Maybe if I pleaded to Satan he would let me off. I had seen miracles, real miracles, performed in his name. Maybe he did hear. Maybe he would answer. Obviously he had power—awesome power.

I had certainly seen satanists perform powerful deeds of evil. I wasn't interested in that. But I had also seen Satan's power used for good. I thought about the time when one of the witches in the coven was having financial problems. Her husband had left her, unable to deal with her "religious" lifestyle, leaving her with three children, no job, and no food in the house. She had prayed to Satan during a ritual and asked him to provide her needs. I knew she had sold her soul to Satan, and I was curious to see if Satan would take care of his own.

The woman returned home that night and found her kitchen cupboards and refrigerator fully stocked. Cans, bottles, boxes, and fresh food weren't just left on her porch; they were all put away in the right places. I was shocked, for this was the first time I had seen anything that showed Satan actually cared for his children.

Then I thought of the time a high priest from another coven interrupted one of the rituals. He was carrying his little boy who had just been severely bitten in several places by a dog. The wounds were gaping, and pieces of flesh were hanging loose.

The father placed his son on the altar, and coven members stood around him in a tight circle. Placing their left hands on the boy's body and extending their right arms toward the goat's head, they began to hum in unison as the officiating priest prayed over the boy.

Suddenly I saw beautiful lights of soft, pastel colors hover over the child. A few minutes later, the humming stopped abruptly. The worshipers began chanting, "All praise to the father, Satan," and dancing around the altar. The boy's father gave an invocation of thanks to Satan, the healer, then picked his son up in his arms. My mouth dropped open. The wounds were closed! Not only were they closed, but there were no scars. Apart from the torn clothes, you could not tell where the ghastly wounds had been moments before.

Now, in the basement, these memories triggered other instances of Satan's "good." It was as if Satan were whispering, "Try me. See what I can do for you."

Never had I considered praying to the father of all evil. Yet now, faced with Victor's ultimatum, and remembering all of my past prayers to God and wondering if He had heard or cared, I thought, "It certainly can't hurt to try."

I tried to form the words "All praise be unto my father, Satan," as I had heard others pray. I lifted my head to get a sense of where he was. As I felt Satan's presence begin to surround me, another voice invaded from somewhere beyond that presence: "My child, I am with you. I have never left you, nor have I forsaken you. Your darkest hour is upon you, but I will be with you in it, and I will bring you out."

I had heard Satan's spirits speak before. *This was not his voice. These were not his words.*

Kneeling in a puddle of tears, I felt a hand gently rest on my shoulder. A warmth began to surround my body. There was no question that God had spoken to me! Whether I had heard His voice out loud or in my mind, it didn't matter. God had heard my prayers! Even though He had allowed me to experience physical and mental torment beyond belief, He had not deserted me. His encouragement gave me the determination and strength I needed to stand against these sinister men and their wicked schemes.

The joy of that moment with my God abruptly ended when Victor jerked open the basement door and yelled, "You will make a sacrifice to Satan. You will. You will. You will!"

Brainwashing Begins

The next few weeks were uncommonly quiet. I tried to exist in my "other life" routine, but it was virtually impossible. I was so terrified at what I feared lay ahead that I could think of nothing else. I ate little. I slept only when my eyes simply could not stay open any longer. I paced the floor. I kept hearing Victor's shout: "You will make a sacrifice to Satan. You will. You will. You will!" Those "you wills" resounded over and over in my head. No matter what I did to distract my attention, they would not go away. Even the warmth of God's word to me became a distant memory.

Life seemed totally hopeless. I couldn't think of anything to do except to somehow endure until I couldn't endure any longer. Then what? Would I simply go crazy? Maybe I would sit down wherever I was—in the middle of the street, on the sidewalk, on the floor at church, in the aisle of the grocery store. Then someone would have to take notice. They would have to take me away, somewhere. They would have to take care of me. Somehow that resolution gave me a strange peace.

It was four weeks, and Victor's men had not come for me. I began to think, to hope that perhaps Victor didn't have what it took to carry out his threat. I should have known better! One Saturday the familiar van arrived. I was driven up to The Ranch and placed in the hands of John—the man whose job it was to break me.

I did not think that I would ever meet a man more evil than Victor. I was wrong. John had some creative ways of forcing Victor's will on me. He began his work by stripping me and placing me in a large box. There I sat in a cramped position, naked and in total darkness. Then I felt something slithering over my body. And another. There were snakes in the box with me! I froze, afraid to move or even breathe.

After what seemed to me like an eternity, the box was opened. As soon as John released me from the box, he asked, "Will you willingly make a sacrifice to Satan?"

Instantly I thought of the words, "Your darkest hour is upon you, but I will be with you in it and I will bring you out." With that reassurance I felt the courage to say, "No! I will not make a sacrifice to Satan!"

The process of breaking my will was established. Over and over John asked the question, "Will you willingly make a sacrifice to Satan." Each time, as I remembered God's promise, my answer was the same. "No! I will not make a sacrifice to Satan!" We were involved in a titanic clash. I couldn't help wondering why Victor would go to such efforts. Why did he want me to make a sacrifice to Satan? Up until now his delight was in the torturing and the taking of human life. Now, for some reason I couldn't comprehend, it was of crucial importance that I be the one who committed the act. And he knew that it would take nothing but the total breaking of my will to make me commit such evil.

I have no idea how long the struggle went on. In Victor's windowless basement, time had no meaning. It could have been a day, a week, a month . . . I just couldn't tell. I do know that as each hour passed, each minute became more agonizing. I was forced to endure sleep and food deprivation. Certainly I was familiar with torture, but not this type. There were no rituals. There was no sexual abuse, sexual perversion, or pornography. This was the kind of breaking process I had heard that prisoners of war went through in concentration camps.

Loss of the basic essentials of life does terrible things to the mind. Slowly my will to say "No" weakened. I began to feel as if I really were a prisoner of war in a foreign country. I had no idea how to fight this war.

Along with the food and sleep deprivation, I was forced to sit on a chair for hours on end. Anytime my head nodded, and I began to fall off the chair, John would switch on a spotlight and bark, "Sit up straight!" Then he would repeat the question "Will you willingly make a sacrifice to Satan?"

One time I began to mumble, "Your darkest hour is upon you, but I will . . ." Wham! The chair was jerked out from under me, sending me sprawling onto the cold, hard floor. Then I heard the door slam. And silence.

I crawled over to a corner, hunched up against the wall, and waited for the next routine. Somehow, mercifully, I fell asleep.

The Final Scheme

"You will give in. You will give in. You will. You will!" I was jolted into consciousness. On came the bright light. John's face was only a few inches from mine. Lines of demonic pleasure were etched into his face. His smile was one of devilish glee. I felt as if I were face-to-face with Satan's chief henchman. I shuddered, for I sensed that a diabolical scheme of fiendishly wicked extremes had been devised—one, I feared, that would force my surrender.

"For every week you refuse to make a sacrifice to Satan, a baby will be sacrificed in your name."

John's words were so heinous that I could not react. My body had frozen; my mind was paralyzed.

John uttered the words again, this time yelling at the top of his voice. I could feel his breath against my face as he screamed, "Did you hear what I said? I said that for every _____ week you refuse to make a sacrifice to Satan, we will sacrifice a _____ baby for you in *your* name! Do you hear me?"

I was numb. I couldn't even nod in acknowledgment to his question.

Do I say "No?" If I do, a baby is sacrificed. Do I say "Yes?" If I do, a baby is sacrificed. "Yes." "No." "Yes!" "No!" I could not win.

The next Saturday night I was abruptly awakened by the horrible screams of a baby being sacrificed. The sounds were coming from a tape recorder that John had put beside me. As I shot up from the floor he spoke only two words: "Number one." The next week I heard, "Number two."

The method had its calculated effect—horror mixed with guilt. Still, my mind mercifully rationalized that they were only pretending that a baby had been sacrificed. After all, the baby's screams were only from a tape. Maybe it was just a wicked trick. In a desperate attempt to free myself from this impossible decision, I declared over and over again, "Yes, a wicked trick. That's what they're doing. They are trying to fool me."

And so I continued to hold out. I was strong again. Nothing was going to make me sacrifice a baby to Satan.

Hell in a Barrel

It was a Saturday night. Sometime around midnight, I was rudely awakened. Before me was a large barrel, like an oil drum. I was lifted up and dropped into the barrel, and a lid was closed over my head. The darkness was total. And the silence.

A few minutes later, the lid was opened and something was dropped on top of me. As it slid down my skin, another something was dropped on me . . . and another . . . maybe three or four. The last object was positioned directly in front of me, on top of my stomach. Then the lid was slammed shut. Again, there was only darkness . . . and silence.

There was a smell. A horrible smell. What could it be? With so little room in my small prison, I slowly maneuvered my arms and hands above my knees so I could grasp the last object that was put in.

There is no right way to tell you this. There are no right words to choose. However, this experience is so crucial to your understanding of my decision—the impossible choice between the yes and no—that I must include it.

Slowly, fearfully, I touched the object that was pressing against my stomach. It took only a few seconds to realize it was a small body. A baby's body. It was lifeless, but not stiff. It had probably been sacrificed that evening, just a short time before.

Something within me wanted to cradle the baby in my arms. But fear gripped me. I knew what they did to babies in their sacrificial rituals. Mutilation. Skinned alive. I could not bear to explore any further.

I thought I had known fear. I thought I had known rage. I thought I had experienced every emotion possible. But at that moment I felt emotions that I could not put into words. For I realized that the objects Victor and John had dropped into the barrel were bodies of sacrificed babies. Three or four weeks had gone by since I had first said "No." There were three or four objects in that barrel with me.

I tried to scrunch myself into a tiny ball so the bodies wouldn't touch me. It was useless. Even in the darkness with my eyes closed as tightly as possible, vivid images of the bodies of these babies flooded my mind. I could not take it anymore. I began to scream in torment and anguish. No words—just screams.

Suddenly the darkness turned to light. The lid of the barrel was taken off. One by one the bodies were removed. I shut my eyes. I refused to see. Ever so slowly I heard Victor say, "Number one." Then John followed with "Number two." They took turns counting the bodies as they removed them. With each number I felt another sentence of guilt descend on me. I began to scream again in a vain effort to block out their pronouncements of "Guilty!"

At last I was lifted out of the barrel. I crumpled to the floor. All strength had been drained from my body. I did not want to see. I did not want to feel. I did not want to hear.

But hear I did when John assaulted me with that same, never-changing question.

"Now, you _____, will you willingly make a sacrifice to Satan? You will now, won't you?"

I tried to think of the words I had clung to for dear life, the words of God—His promise. But they were gone. All I heard were the sounds of Victor and John's devilish snickering.

They picked me up and set me on a chair. I was face-to-face with them. I could see the look of triumph on their faces—that look of final victory.

This had been no game. They weren't pretending after all. This was for real. And I knew it would go on and on until I surrendered. They had no morals, no values, no conscience. Nothing would stop them unless I gave in to their diabolical, unholy demand. I was damned if I did and damned if I didn't.

They forced me to look at the babies they had dumped on the floor. Then John repeated the question. I grabbed my stomach, bent forward, and threw up. After an anguished groan, I whispered, "Yes."

"Louder," John demanded. "We can't hear you."

I lifted my head, and screamed at the top of my voice, "YES!"

It was over. I was broken. Brainwashed.

❖ 7 ❖

Halloween Night

Victor sent for me on Halloween. That is one of the most important dates on the satanic calendar—THE CELEBRATION OF DEATH! "This is your night!" Victor informed me when I arrived at his home. I did not need to ask what he meant.

A few minutes later, after receiving a heavy injection of sedatives, I climbed into the backseat of Victor's car. As usual, I was blindfolded. This time I didn't mind the blindfold, because I didn't want to know where I was going. I just wanted this to be over as fast as possible.

During the ride, my mind shifted into neutral. In fact, I was almost calm. It was as if this night wasn't really happening. I felt as if I were moving in a dreamlike trance.

As I felt the car slow down and make an abrupt turn, the blindfold was removed. There it was—a church. "No, God. Not in a church! Please, God, not in a church," my heart cried.

Victor turned around in the front seat to look at me. The pain in my heart must have registered on my face. He grinned that devilish grin I had seen so many times before and with a sound of delight he said, "That's right. A church. Just the right place for someone who worships God, don't you think?"

I had been to a few churches before for satanic rituals. A couple were held in the sanctuary itself, but most were conducted in rooms like a church basement. I had often wondered if the pastor knew what was going on. It was difficult for me to believe that a church could be used for that type of activity without anyone connected with the church knowing about it. I did know that coven members were masters at performing their rituals in secrecy.

It was always a time of celebration when a church was found that could be used for a satanic worship. As Victor so wickedly insinuated, a church is the perfect setting for a ritual. Performing an act that worships Satan in a place dedicated to the worship of God is the ultimate mockery of God. And mocking God is the highest pleasure of Satan. That is why the cross is turned upside down. This is why the Lord's Prayer is read backward and the communion drink is a mixture of blood, urine, and wine.

My belief in God had been a great source of displeasure to Victor. I have to think that he knew it was my faith in God that had kept me together through all those years. No doubt, that is one of the reasons why a church was chosen for the ritual in which I was to make a sacrifice. Victor knew that the conscience of my heart would be seared even deeper. Perhaps he also had hopes that the church setting, the ritual, the sacrifice, and the cemetery—all so carefully devised—would make me feel such guilt that I would turn against God, curse Him, and perhaps even give in and join the forces of Satan.

The car rolled to a stop in a dark corner of the parking lot behind the church where it could not be seen from the road. We got out and entered a side door to the church. Though it was very dark, I knew the moment we walked into the room where the ritual would be held. I could feel the overwhelming presence of evil, a feeling I had experienced at every ritual. But this presence was even stronger, more overpowering, much darker. I had never before sensed such a suffocating darkness. It was as if I had to push against it to even move.

As candles were lit, all the trappings of a satanic ritual slowly came into view: the goat's head, the upside-down cross, the velvet cloth on a table, the crucible. Hooded robes were donned by the handful of members in attendance while I was seated in a corner. Victor occasionally glanced at me as he whispered comments to someone I couldn't recognize. It was obvious that I was the center of attraction this night.

I wanted to disappear. I wanted to wake up and find that this was all just a dream. I almost felt that if I held my breath, the whole scene would vanish. I closed my eyes and let my mind drift.

"Lauren!" Victor's voice aroused me from my desperate thoughts. "Come forth. Satan's time is upon you." I had been totally unaware of the proceedings of the ritual up to this point, though it obviously had been going on for some time.

I slowly, agonizingly approached an opening in the circle that the members had made around the altar. My gaze was directed toward an object on the table, impossible to distinguish in the flickering candlelight.

Was this my sacrifice? I gasped and froze in my tracks.

"Come forth!" Victor commanded.

My feet would not move. I felt the arms of the hooded members on either side of me gently push me forward toward the altar. My feet began to move, taking me closer to the the inevitable moment. There it was. The sacrifice. My sacrifice. Hidden under a piece of cloth. What it was? I didn't know. I did not want to know.

"Pick up the knife!" a voice commanded from the head of the altar. "Offer your sacrifice to Satan as you have promised!"

Again, I could not move. It seemed as if my arms weighed a thousand pounds. My mind could not force them to move. I could not even look at the knife lying on the altar. My eyes were riveted on the object, the sacrifice now immediately in front of me.

I heard Victor whisper, "We'll have to put the knife in her hand. She's in too much of a daze to act on her own." He had given me more drugs than usual to keep me from resisting. Perhaps he believed he had given me too much.

He was wrong. It was not due to the drugs that I was incapable of following his commands. I was simply paralyzed with horror.

As I stood there unable to move—unable to even take a breath—I felt someone grab my right hand and pry open the tightly clenched fingers. The knife was placed in the palm of my hand and my fingers closed around it. I wanted to drop the knife. But my fingers were cramped shut.

Suddenly something snapped within me. The numbness left. The fear fled. In their place, I saw the faces of all the people who had ever used me, abused me, and tortured me. I saw that each face was laughing cruelly at me. Then I began to hear the laughter. Louder and louder it swelled, like the roar of an ocean.

I felt as if my body were going to burst with an overpowering and uncontrollable rage. The fury grew as the laughter of my tormenters pounded in my ears. I felt my arms raise themselves, the knife now grasped firmly in both hands. With the knife poised over my head, I let out a frenzied scream, a scream that reached beyond the present and echoed back through all the years of my tortured life. To my mother. To every bum who assaulted me in the basement. To every pornographic photographer who used me for his smut. To every one of Victor's wicked clients. To every single coven member. And to Victor himself. I was screaming at them. They had destroyed my life and now they would destroy my spirit as well. But they were wrong. They could never have my spirit. Never!

Down came the knife with every ounce of my strength. Up, down. Up, down. Up, down. Until the faces no longer laughed at me. They were gone, every one. In my mind, the knife had impaled each one of them.

It was over. They thought they would finish me. But I fooled them. I had finished them. I had won!

The knife slipped out of my hands. I crumpled to the floor in total physical and mental exhaustion.

The Cemetery

How long I was unconscious, I do not know. The next thing I remember was my being led through a wire gate into a cemetery. It was very dark. Stumbling over the rough hillside, two of the members took hold of my arms and led me to the bottom of a ravine. We stopped at the base of a tree.

A deep, oppressive stillness hung in the air. The cries of the little ones were silent that night. The sobs of teenage and adult victims were silent that night. Even the overpowering grief that was exploding within me could not shatter the stillness of that night. I understood why. It was the stillness of death.

The ending of a ritualistic sacrifice was usually an occasion of jubilee, of making merriment and indulgence in every conceivable lust of sexual perversion. But tonight was different. The mood was a total antithesis to the usual reveling. There was no jubilation, no merriment, no sexual orgies.

The small group of coven members who had followed the high priest into the cemetery silently formed a circle around a small plot of ground near the tree. Even as they began their usual humming and chanting, they did so in such hushed voices that I could barely hear them. I couldn't put my finger on the reason why, but something was different.

My body, still supported by two others, stood in the circle. But my mind had mercifully turned itself off. I was in a confused state of mental and emotional shock. Mental comprehension was impossible. I could only obey orders mechanically, not mentally.

Victor, the high priest, raised his arm. The chanting ended in obedience to his signal. Not a sound was to be heard. I began to tremble uncontrollably. Even though I felt very cold, beads of perspiration rolled down my face.

At that moment, light from the candles revealed the outline of a shovel that a coven member was holding in his hands. Victor motioned for two of the men to do something with the shovel. Carefully they placed their lighted candles upright in the dirt where they had been standing. It was crucial to the burial ritual that the circle remain unbroken.

As they dug, the chanting started. "Dust to dust. Earth to earth. Back to Satan whence it came. Dust to dust. Earth to earth. Back to Satan whence it came."

Though the words were chanted in hushed voices, the words seemed to reverberate throughout the ravine and grow, as though they would surround every hillside, mountaintop, valley, and city across the country.

"Dust to dust. Earth to earth. Back to Satan whence it came."

Over and over and over and over. "My God, will it ever end?" As the chant crescendoed, my heart began to pound with the beat of each syllable, until it felt as if it would explode in my chest. Nausea swept over me, and those on either side strengthened their grip, bearing more of my weight.

Just as suddenly as the chant of death began, it ended. Once again a shroud of deadly silence settled on the group of evildoers like a cloak of dense fog. The two coven members had finished digging a shallow hole. They returned to their places in the circle, being careful to pick up their candles without putting out the flame. The flame must not go out just as the circle must not be broken.

Then I saw the object. It was covered with a cloth, lying in the center of a pentagram that had been drawn on the ground with chalk.

I tried to pray. "God, do something. Get me out of here. Let me die, God. I want to die. Get me out of here! God . . ."

My prayer trailed off as I heard a voice coming from afar off. I couldn't hear the words. I didn't want to hear the words. But want to or not, I began to hear the high priest call my name.

"Lauren."

I don't know how many times he called my name. But each time I heard it, the sound came closer.

"Lauren . . . Lauren . . ." His voice commanded my attention. I could ignore it no longer.

The look of evil in Victor's eyes cut through the darkness of the night. I tried desperately to look away, but somehow I was transfixed by his glare. His stare of evil was so intense that I began to feel evil. Victor was in control. I was powerless. I was truly his captive, subject to his every whim, to his every demonic desire.

As Victor raised his right arm, the two gems in his ring focused my attention. Those gems represented the eyes of Satan. Victor wore that ring only during rituals. A special incantation had been chanted over that ring when he became a high priest, supposedly giving the stones supernatural power to summon demons. I had seen the ring many times before, but never had those gems glowed like they did this night, as though the fires of hell were shining from the very center of the ring. I felt as if they were summoning me to step forth into the middle of the circle by the tree. I feared that if I tried to step out from under the support of the two coven members who were holding me, I would collapse. To my amazement, as I took that first step with my eyes still transfixed on Victor's ring, strength flowed into my legs. As I walked toward the tree, the chanting began once again.

"Dust to dust. Earth to earth. Back to Satan whence it came."

Suddenly I thought, "Oh my God, they're going to bury me alive!" I can't say that I became more terrified, for I was already as terrified as I could get. But I felt a sudden panic to run as fast as I could.

"Run, run, run, run." The words raced faster and faster through my mind. I knew, however, that I would not be able to break through the coven's circle.

I stumbled as my foot touched something, freeing my eyes from the spell of Victor's ring. I looked down to see what my foot had touched.

There it was again . . . at my feet.

Instantly my thoughts returned to the church altar. Bits and pieces of the ritual flashed across my mind. The altar . . . the faces of my tormenters . . . the knife . . . rage . . . screaming. . . . Round and round the memories flashed in a frenzied whirl. Waves of nausea swept over me and I felt myself beginning to faint.

Victor's stern voice jolted my thoughts back to the graveyard. "Your sacrifice." He was pointing at the object on the ground in front of me.

"Dust to dust. Earth to earth. Back to Satan whence it came. Return your sacrifice to the father, Satan," Victor commanded.

Obviously, I was expected to pick up the sacrifice. I let out a scream that should have wakened the very dead.

"NO!"

I'm certain that my involuntary scream spared me from having to touch the object. Victor must have realized that I was beyond my limit of endurance and that I was in danger of risking their safety.

Victor bent down and laid the object in the shallow, grave-like hole. Dirt was hurriedly shoveled over it. Then, obviously nervous, he hurriedly ushered the coven members away from the gravesite.

I looked back one time. I couldn't quite comprehend what I had done, if anything. I really didn't want to know. Still, I felt an undefinable need to look back.

At that moment the moon broke through the clouds, casting enough light on the gravesite for me to see the shadow of a satanist who had remained behind. He was doing something to the ground.

I knew that he was doing one of two things that were always done immediately after a sacrificial burial. He was either digging the sacrificed object back up or he was disguising the grave and leaving the sacrifice for a removal soon after. (Satanists rarely leave a sacrifice buried. For one thing, it is too dangerous. But also, the parts of the sacrifice, especially if it is human, are too sacred to abandon. The few parts that are not used for another ritualistic purpose are cremated to destroy all remaining evidence of the sacrifice.)

I had seen enough. I looked away from the gravesite, unable to think any more about what had just taken place. A heavy grief consumed me. I wasn't certain what had taken place. I knew only one thing . . . it was over. It was finally over!

It was the last time I ever participated in a satanic ritual.

Secret Pains

"I'm sorry, he's dead," the fireman said gently.

I guess one is never totally prepared for the death of a family member. Whether you liked or disliked him; whether you were close or distant emotionally; whether you lived with him a year or 50 years—death is never easy to face.

In the few years that I lived with my father, I never really got to know him. He was a very busy man and was seldom home. When he did come home in the evening, he either had to go back out or he was so exhausted that he went straight to bed.

I had not grown up with a man in the house, and the only men with whom I had had any contacts had been abusive. So I kept my distance from my father, and even though I felt he liked my presence in his home, I always felt that he was equally uncomfortable with me.

My mother remained a taboo subject. Neither my father nor I wanted to talk about her. He never confided any of his feelings about her. I only knew that he seemed completely subservient to her.

Only one time did I dare to step into the forbidden zone. I was driving my father's car and I started to tell him my fears, and how I never wanted to see my mother again. He quickly interrupted: "You know, Lauren, you've been more trouble to me than anyone else in my life."

The crush of those words brought a rush of tears, making it difficult to drive. "After all she's done to you?" I thought. "You left me with her because you couldn't take any more from her. Yet you say I've given you more trouble? I've cooked your meals, cleaned your house, washed and ironed your clothes, and mowed your lawn. And you say I've given you trouble? You're the one who adopted me. Why? Why?"

That day I erected a barrier between us that would have prohibited him from getting close to me even if he had wanted to. Life in his home became like living in a peaceful but meaningless vacuum. The fact that my father and I never had a normal father-daughter closeness was irrelevant to me. I now had a certain amount of peace in my life, at least when I was at home. That was all that mattered. Peace was worth more than solid gold. I didn't know enough about normal human relationships to desire any more.

My father provided for all my basic needs—food, clothing, a nice home, spending money. But there was one sentence I longed to hear my father say: "Lauren, I love you." Although I never heard him say it, I made myself believe in my heart that his love for me was there, though unspoken.

After I would be brought home from Victor's, my father never asked me anything, and I never told him anything. I figured that he either knew what was happening or else he didn't want to know. I was scared to death that if I made waves at home my life would become a hell there too. My confused rationale was that I was better off going through hell for a weekend now and then to insure the relatively sane life I found at home. It's easy to look back now and think, "How stupid of me!" But back then, at 20 years of age, it made perfect sense.

The weeks before my father died were spent in relative calm. My mother continually phoned my father to check up on me, leaving me with the feeling that I would never be free from her control. But I didn't see her—blessing number one. And following that final ritual on Halloween night, Victor's men had not come for me—blessing number two.

My father came home from work one day, late as usual. He walked into his bedroom to change clothes. Suddenly I heard a groan. Then silence. I waited a few minutes, but heard no sounds or movement. Something was wrong. Slowly, with great hesitation, I opened his bedroom door and peeked in. My father was slumped over his bed.

I called the fire department, then waited for them in the living room. They arrived quickly and went into the bedroom. A few minutes later they came back out and gave me the news. The fire captain tried to gently ease the words out, but they shot through me like a round of machine-gun bullets. "I'm sorry, he's dead," the fireman said as he hung his head.

It was impossible to believe. My father—dead? He hadn't looked sick when he came home. He hadn't complained of any illness. Yet this stranger was telling me he was dead. I sat in numbed silence in the rocking chair, rocking back and forth, back and forth, hearing the words over and over, "I'm sorry, he's dead."

I felt such opposite emotions. I had clung to that desperate need to believe that someone cared for me. And in a way, I think my father did. Somehow I think that he was just as much a victim as I was.

On the other hand, my father's death enabled me to make a break from the circle of horror. There was no reason for me to stay put. I immediately packed up and moved to another city.

My ties to Victor changed abruptly after that. The only reason he had to make any contact with me was to make sure I kept quiet. His purposes had been served. He and his men had used and abused me. They had made money from me. I had finally succumbed to their demonic acts of brainwashing and had participated in a ritual. And worst of all, they had forced me to experience the most agonizing emotional pain a woman can know in order to service their diabolically evil purposes.

The bottom line was that they had gotten what they wanted. Now they were through with me. So as long as I agreed to keep my mouth shut, they left me alone—except for an occasional threat just to make sure I stayed in line.

A vivid reminder of what they would do to me if I talked was more than enough to keep me quiet. They didn't have to use a gun. They didn't even have to keep me drugged. All it took was a threatening note covered with blood left on the front door, a phone call of fiendish screaming and obscene threats, the blackmailing threat to send pornographic photos of me to my friends, or the most effective silencer of all—the memories and guilt of my participation in a satanic ritual. All of these kept me as their captive, captive in spirit and captive in mind.

Never Alone

There was one other way they kept me in their control—if not physically, then certainly emotionally. That was through the use of an evil spirit that kept me in bondage. This is an area that I hesitate to write about, for it is so difficult to explain. Even I don't fully understand just *how* spirit guides work. I only know that they *do* work.

I had only heard about spirit guides in conversations with coven members before and after rituals. They would talk about how they had asked for and received their own spirit guides from Satan. Surprisingly, they often talked rather fondly about their guides and the occult powers they endowed. However, occasionally they confessed a fear of them. They expressed how their spirit guides were not only guides but controllers. A few even said these guides were *in* them, making sure they remained faithful and obedient to their orders.

One satanist I overheard talking about her spirit guide expressed rather bitterly that she was afraid that if she was ever disobedient to the spirit's commands, Satan might give it orders to kill her. I was glad that I didn't have a spirit guide, and sincerely hoped I never would. I had enough troubles with people controlling me without adding a spirit to the list. Besides, I figured that you had to be a confessed and initiated satanist to have one.

Soon after my father's death, I found myself becoming more and more angry at the people who were harassing me. I surely had no intentions of making my life any more miserable by daring to talk about them. It made me mad that they were still messing with me. I began talking to myself out loud. "Just get out of my life and leave me alone," I would say. "I don't want to have anything to do with you. Why can't you get that through your thick skulls?"

One night after one of their obscene phone calls, I let off steam by verbally assaulting them as I walked around the house. Suddenly I heard a voice. It startled me, for I knew I was alone. Then I heard it again.

"Little one, I've come to help you. I've come to guide you from now on."

There was no doubt about it. It was an unusually kind and gentle voice, spoken in almost a whisper. It seemed to be coming from behind me. Slowly I turned around. There it was, the form of a person. At least, it looked like a person. It wasn't a solid body, but rather an untouchable yet visible form of a body. I don't know how to explain it any other way.

The face was a female likeness, the most compassionate-looking face I had ever seen. There was only the head and the upper part of the body. The head was covered with a black shawl that draped down over the arms and chest. Instantly I was drawn to the eyes. They seemed to beckon me.

I took a step back as I said, "This can't be happening. You aren't real. I must be dreaming."

"No, my little one, you're not dreaming," the voice replied. "I am real. You may touch me if you like."

I stood stiff as a board. No way was I going to reach out my hand. I had witnessed many strange apparitions at satanic rituals, but nothing like this had ever come into my own home. I wasn't about to encourage it or even acknowledge it.

Yet one thing bothered me as I stood looking at this form. I wasn't frightened. Startled, yes; frightened, no. The compassion, almost a look of love, that emanated from its face made me feel as if it could be my friend. The smile was so compelling that I felt almost mesmerized.

Once more it spoke. "You're all alone now. I've been sent to be your spirit friend. You may call me 'Mother,' for that is what I will be to you. You'll never be alone again. I will always be with you."

As it spoke the words "I will always be with you," the form disappeared.

It was true. I had been feeling very alone, without direction. I was always on the run, but never knowing where to go. And even though I had not asked or prayed for a spirit of any kind, much less a spirit guide, nor did I really want to have anything to do with this so-called "friend" or "Mother," as it called itself, yet in my loneliness and desperation I was tempted to call for it to come back. For I did long for everything it had promised—help, guidance, direction, and someone to be a mother to me. The face on the form of this spirit friend looked like the face of the kindest mother I had ever seen.

As I sat on the edge of my bed and thought about what had just happened, I remembered the conversations about spirit guides that I had heard among the coven members. This was just like many of their stories. Sadly, I had allowed Satan to deceive me. I failed to recall the words of the satanist who was afraid that if she ever disobeyed her spirit guide, Satan might order it to kill her.

From that night on I felt that I was being kept in line by "Mother." It only made its presence known when I needed direction or correction. It seldom appeared visually; usually I only heard its voice. But when "Mother" chose to speak, I listened. Even when I did not see or hear it, I never felt that it was far from me. I always sensed its presence.

I finally managed to finish my college credits and graduate. I had no trouble getting good jobs. My college work was broad enough to qualify me for a number of professional positions. However, those positions required counseling troubled individuals, and that caused two problems. First, I found myself becoming increasingly unable to handle pressure and stress of any kind. And my jobs were certainly stressful. Second, in listening to others unload their stories of suffering, I couldn't help but identify with their pain. It became increasingly difficult to stay in a job that reminded me of my own life of abuse.

Mercifully, I managed to deny some of the most evil acts that I had witnessed, shoving them so far back into my mind that I didn't have to deal with the memories. I had to do it for self-preservation. No one could live with a lifetime of untold horror and survive. The only other alternative was insanity.

While many of my memories as a child had been removed from my consciousness, they had not been sent to a never-never land, forever lost in a sea of forgetfulness. Instead, the most painful of memories had become like creatures lurking around a corner in the recesses of my mind, needing only the slightest nudge to pounce back into my consciousness.

When the pressure became too great, I would quit my job and move to another city to escape Victor's harassment. However, within a month or two he inevitably found me. The cycle would begin again. Obscene phone calls, threatening notes, and the stress and pressure of my latest job would build once again. I also began to feel the inevitable accumulation of the years of physical abuse. I became too tired and was fast becoming too ill to keep running. Finally my body gave out and I was hospitalized.

Memories Unleashed

"Relax. Let go. Imagine yourself floating . . . down . . . down . . . down . . . you're light as a feather." The social worker was speaking in a calm, monotone voice. "You're okay, Lauren," she reassured me. "You're doing very well."

For several years I was hospitalized off and on for treatment of a chronic and life-threatening disorder that was possibly triggered by my years of abuse. The accompanying pain was so severe that at times the prescribed pain medications brought precious little relief. As a last resort, my doctor wrote an order asking that the hospital social worker take me through guided imagery sessions as a means of reducing the pain. I was willing to try just about anything, even if it did sound a little "off the wall" to me.

The first session started out very well. Terri, the social worker, explained the basic steps that she would take me through. Contrary to my initial apprehensions about someone messing with my mind again, I felt that this just might work.

"Relax. Let go. You're doing fine," Terri continued. The process of relaxation took 15 to 20 minutes. No part of my body was left unmentioned, from the toes on my feet to the top of my head. This was no joke to me. I was giving it all I had—concentration, breathing, relaxing, letting go. With my body as relaxed as possible, it was time to begin the guided-imagery phase.

I had always liked the peaceful serenity of meadows, so I asked Terri to put me mentally in a meadow. Moss-covered rocks alongside a gurgling brook, lush green foliage, tall evergreen trees giving off the scent of pine with birds chirping on the boughs, perhaps a deer off in the distance slowly wandering down to the water—this was the place in which I had chosen to visualize myself, hopefully free from pain.

Terri began to describe the meadow to me. I was to picture myself experiencing and enjoying all the sights, sounds, and smells as she introduced them. Gently she encouraged, "Lauren, take yourself back to your childhood. Picture yourself as a little girl playing in the meadow, doing the fun things you used to do."

Instantly I jerked, and every muscle in my body tightened. My teeth clenched together involuntarily. Both hands retracted into tight fists. From one second to the next, my body went from total relaxation to total rigidity. Realizing that she must have touched on an uncomfortable subject, Terri quickly backed off and skillfully guided my thoughts to another area.

I was so desperate to find something that would relieve the pain that I forced myself to continue with the session until it was over. But I was unable in the remaining 20 minutes or so to regain a relaxed, tension-free position, mentally or physically.

"I'm going to count backward from ten to one," Terri announced as she slowly began to bring me out of the meadow and back to reality. "When I say 'one,' you're going to open your eyes. I'll be here with you holding your hand. You're safe."

"Ten." The countdown began. "Nine . . . eight . . ." Terri proceeded very slowly, aware that it can be quite a shock when one returns to her present surroundings, especially when it's a hospital room. "Seven . . . six . . . you're doing fine. Five . . . four . . . you're okay. Three . . . two . . . you're going to wake up relaxed and refreshed. I'm here. You're all right. When I say 'one,' open your eyes." There was a long pause. Then decisively she said "One," and snapped her fingers.

My body reacted as if every muscle had been waiting for that final number. Gripping the bed rails, I pulled myself up with a strength that surprised me. "Don't you ever mention my childhood again!" I snapped. "Thinking about my childhood does not relax me!"

My response not only shocked Terri, but me as well. How could she know that a thousand memories long hidden in the darkened recesses of my innermost being had darted across my mind like scenes from a horror movie?

Terri, sensing how frightened and confused I was, wisely chose not to pursue the subject any further at that time. Rather, she let me know that she was there if and when I felt the need to explore the reasons behind my violent reaction to the mention of my childhood.

That was the beginning of my struggle to face those horrors that I had so desperately tried to forget. As Terri regularly visited my bedside to check up on me, I began to reveal bits and pieces of my life as a child. Those bits and pieces were meticulously chosen and carefully worded. I still wasn't even close to letting it all hang out. But it was a start.

Dealing with Secret Pain

People who have made the commitment to deal with the secret pains in their past will identify with me when I say it can be a frightening and painful experience. Many victims of abuse—whether physical, sexual, or emotional—elect to get off their road to recovery soon after they begin. They find it too painful to discuss the past, for it is almost impossible not to relive it. That can almost be as traumatic as the actual abuse.

I was no exception. I often felt as if I were about to "lose it" as I tried to face the onslaught of unwanted, yet unavoidable, memories. At times they attacked me like a swarm of angry bees.

In an effort to counteract those inevitable side effects, Terri suggested that I start a journal. "It will be your companion," she urged, noticing the hesitant expression on my face. "The journal will be a safe place to express your feelings. And if you would like, I'll write in your journal, too, as we ride out this storm together."

Beginning the journal was no easy task. Hearing myself talk about my childhood was hard enough. Seeing the words written down on paper was downright scary! At first they seemed bigger than life, almost jumping off the page to attack me.

Terri had said that writing down my feelings would act as a

catharsis, cleansing the wounds of my emotions. In time, she said, I would come to regard the journal as my friend. I questioned that, but after many tear-filled writing sessions, I began to see that my writing did have a healing effect. In the process I was relieved of a big chunk of guilt—guilt that no victim should have to carry.

Never, until writing this book, have I shared my journal with anyone but Terri. I used to think that I was the only one who felt the way I did. That feeling of aloneness is devastating. I've since found that victims and survivors share the same pains, sorrows, and fears. I've learned that I am not the only one who responded to the past in the way I did.

So I share my journal of secret pains with you. To you who are victims, I pray that you find comfort in identifying with my pain. You are not alone!

* * *

Lauren:

"How can I go on when life has crumbled into a thousand pieces? How can I make it through another battle? Is there no end? Do I have the strength to go on? I'm so alone, so very alone."

Terri:

"Lauren, I am your counselor. I will be here for you until you have come to some resolution with what you are dealing with. I will not desert you."

(Note: I desperately needed this affirmation.)

Lauren:

"Oh God, how it hurts to remember. I'm beginning to remember things I had buried so far down I didn't even realize they were there. It is so frightening. How can I handle it? What did I do to deserve this? I feel so dirty."

Terri:

"Lauren, I don't see you as a 'dirty' person. I feel that you have been the victim and that you had no other choice at the time in any participation. It's easy to look back and say how you should have handled it. But you are looking at it at another age, another time, and another place. Please live."

(Note: I felt that I would rather die than to have to remember and relive any more painful memories.)

Lauren:

"I had vowed I would never, ever tell these things. Is it possible I let someone else know? Why have I let my defenses down? I lasted for so long. The more I talk, the more I remember. The more I remember, the worse I feel. I feel so guilty."

Terri:

"You were a victim of a very bad situation. Stay away from guilt. It serves no good purpose! You did what you had to do. Look at that child outside of yourself and you will feel the pain for that child, not guilt."

Lauren:

"I don't want to be brave anymore. I don't want to be strong anymore. Don't want to think anymore today. How do I turn it off? Oh God, can it be? Was it really this way? I wish I could pound all of you to pieces in my pillow! I hate you!"

(Note: Several weeks go by between these two entries. Notice the change in my attitude.)

Lauren:

"Oh Lord, can the memories destroy me? I must tend to my emotional pain. I have to find out how to live in spite of the past. I just have to!"

Terri:

"Lauren, I know it's been rough for you. I can see it in your face. I can feel it. But I think you're going to make it because you want to. You won! Say, 'I survived it!' Since you survived, you can say, 'Yes, it's been rough!' But you can also say, '*I made it.*' "

* * *

The journal was only the first step on my journey toward healing. Since then I have often thanked God that He doesn't let us see what lies ahead too far down the road. I sometimes wonder if I had known how rough the road, how deep the valleys, how steep the climb—would I have had the will to go on? God, in His wisdom and mercy, led me just one step at a time, and I, in my naivete and impatience, hoped that each step would be the last step to healing and freedom.

Terri offered to continue seeing me on an outpatient basis once I was discharged from the hospital. I did so for a few weeks, but as the memories kept surfacing, I felt a compelling need to back off. I was simply afraid to face even worse memories. Talking about my childhood was bad enough. How would I ever talk about my teenage and young adult years? Fearing Terri's reactions to those years, I chose once again to put up my front.

Most of my friends knew that I had lived a rough life as a child. But only a handful of close friends knew that this included sexual abuse. I felt that few would understand if I told them any more—even the "lesser" evils of sexual abuse, much less the worlds of pornography and satanism.

I have written that those who abuse a person purposely make the abuse so horrendous that it is unbelievable. Believe me, Victor and his people had done their work well! No way in the world was I going to talk. Even though the physical abuse had ended and I had less and less connection with them, I was always aware of their presence. In my mind I felt as if they were always with me—every minute, every hour, every day.

I also knew that "Mother," my spirit guide, was watching me. It had occasionally spoken to me since the time it introduced itself. Unlike that time when it appeared as a kind and gentle mother, now it was frequently a harsh taskmaster, verbally ridiculing, debasing, and chastising me for even thinking of trying to find a way to be free from my past.

Its admonishments became more and more cruel after I began talking to Terri. One afternoon after returning home from a successful session with Terri, "Mother" appeared. There was no gentle smile this time. There was no sound of compassion in its voice. "Little one!" it barked. "You have angered me greatly. You have tested my patience to its limit. As a mother who has to look out for her child, I must warn you that you're walking on dangerous ground by letting others mess with your mind."

Then, in a voice I can't adequately describe except to say that it made me believe every word it said, the spirit threatened: "If you can't stop yourself, I will stop you!" With that it disappeared.

After that appearance, I became more and more frightened. I knew that the spirit meant business. And I knew that as long as Satan had this point of contact, seeking to control me through this spirit, I would forever remain a victim, captive and in bondage.

Flashbacks

The nightmares never ceased. I woke up almost every night in a cold sweat, feeling that I was drenched in the blood of sacrificed children. I would get out of bed and soak in the bathtub, trying to cleanse myself of the blood. But it was to no avail. No amount of external washing could cleanse my body or my mind of the demonic horrors that haunted me.

One afternoon I lay down to take a nap. I was fine before I went to sleep, but during the short nap I had a flashback of one of the ghastly rituals I had witnessed. Abruptly I awoke to hear myself yelling words of unintelligible gibberish. I would try to say a sentence, but all that came out was "aye, aye, aye, aye." Every once in awhile the word-sound changed, but the ability to speak English was gone. A side effect was a continual shaking of my hands. I don't mean just trembling—my hands from my wrists were shaking as hard and as fast as possible.

One of my friends tried to stay with me at home, but I was uncontrollable. Once I even shoved her away with my fists when she came near me. I was aware of everything I was doing, but I couldn't control my actions.

I was hospitalized, and a psychiatrist was called in. His diagnosis was that a pain medication I was taking had triggered a memory in my past so traumatic that I couldn't express it in English. My description of the trauma could only be expressed in unintelligible gibberish. He prescribed a tranquilizer and advised me to begin seeing a psychiatrist on a regular basis. Exploring my past, he concluded, might shed some light on my current emotional problems.

In my own evaluation of the situation, I concluded that "they" had finally achieved what they had been working toward for several years. By my own diagnosis, I was crazy. If I talked now, no one would believe me. My enemies were safe.

Even though the gibberish phase lasted for less than a day, I was hospitalized for several days because of my continued emotional outbursts. In my mind, everyone was a threat to me—the nurses, my friends, even other patients. Two dear friends who had driven for several hours to visit me stood by my bedside with tears in their eyes because I kept yelling at them to not hurt me. I begged the nurse to get them away from me.

To every nurse who came near me, I yelled, "Don't hurt me!" "Don't rape me!"

It took several days for the medications to restore my self-control so that I was well enough to be discharged. As the psychiatrist gave me a prescription for tranquilizers he cautioned, "These flashbacks will probably happen again. If they do, take two of the tranquilizers and try to relax."

I thought to myself, "Happen again? How often? For how long?" I was terrified! For the first time I began to fear the future as much as I had feared the past.

❖ 9 ❖
Turning Point

The flashbacks were a turning point for me. As difficult as they were to endure, they forced me to face my past—all of it, not just my childhood. I needed to find help desperately. My mind and body could take no more. I could no longer keep the life I had lived behind closed doors a secret.

What I really wanted was to be freed from the pain and bondage I was suffering. I felt there had to be someone who could give me the special kind of help I needed. But I had no idea who that person was.

Months went by. Memories of more heinous horrors kept surfacing in my mind. Nightmares brought back vivid details of the pain and fear. Dull, blurred, grayish-colored memories became sharp and distinct. It was impossible to ignore them. No longer could I keep pushing them back. They happened. They were all true, and I was being consumed by them.

My physical problems had rendered me disabled, and I was no longer able to work. This added to my emotional instability. I made an introductory appointment with a psychotherapist I had become casually acquainted with through my doctor's office. When my appointment day arrived, I had to fight off the urge to cancel. Before I was even seated in the therapist's office, I blurted out, "I've got to get help. I can't stand it any longer. I'll go crazy if somebody doesn't help me."

"What do you need help with, Lauren?" Betsy, the therapist, asked. "Is it your past?"

"No!" I answered without thinking. "I mean, yes . . . I don't know . . . I just need help . . . now . . . fast!" My "everything's under control" image, the image I had worked so hard to maintain, was gone. In panic I turned and headed for the door.

"Lauren, wait a minute." Betsy put her arm on my shoulder. "Please tell me what's wrong." I could hear the concern in her voice.

"You don't want to know," I said.

She read between the lines and gently responded, "You mean you're afraid to tell me, aren't you?"

I was trapped between two fears—a fear of coming unglued if I didn't tell and a fear of coming unglued if I did tell. This time the issue wasn't child abuse. The issue was the word I hadn't dared to speak to another soul—satanism!

Satan was engaged in an all-out war at that very moment. He was fighting for my silence.

"Lauren, let's talk tomorrow. I'll see you at 4 P.M." Betsy hurried out the door, giving me no time to answer with a "Yes" or "No."

I spent a sleepless night dreading the appointment, wondering if the result would be the same as with all the other times I had tried to find help. Childhood memories of the high school counselor, the policewoman, and the pastor told me it was futile. No one would want to hear my story. No one would believe me. There was no use in trying.

And yet, what if Betsy could help me? If there was even the slightest possibility that she really would believe me, shouldn't I give her a chance?

I kept my appointment the next day, but I didn't mention anything about satanism or ritualistic abuse. Betsy listened, knowing that I wasn't telling her my real problem. Finally she asked again, "Please, tell me what is wrong."

"You don't want to know," I answered again.

"Lauren!" The counselor's emphasis forced me to look up into her eyes. Without wavering, she decisively declared, "I don't care if you cut up a baby and threw it down the garbage disposal. It won't make me feel any different about you!"

Her words hit me like a flurry of punches. They left me numb to the core. She knew. No! She couldn't possibly know! I felt my face flushing, burning. This was incredible. Why had she chosen those words? I knew then that my biggest secret was going to have to come out, sooner or later.

It was only much later that Betsy told me she had purposely said the most shocking thing she could think of to reassure me that I could tell her anything without fear of how she would react to it. Her shock tactic worked. If she had the guts to say that, I reasoned, then just maybe she had the guts to listen to what I had to say.

The following months were incredibly difficult as I opened up the wounds of pornography and satanism. Not only was I reliving horror stories in the therapy session, but the horrors followed me home.

One afternoon, after a particularly unsettling session, I ran out of my house, jumped into the car, and drove at a speed much too fast for safety—mine or anyone else's. It was like I was trying to outrun my memories. A few minutes later I heard a siren. A police car was fast approaching me. I quickly pulled to a stop.

When the patrolman walked up to my window, I questioned, "Did I do something wrong, sir?"

Shaking his head and grinning, he chuckled, "You've got to be kidding! You don't know what you've done?"

I got the feeling that he thought I was trying to put one over on him. I wasn't. I honestly didn't know what I'd done. "No, sir. What did I do?" I asked politely.

"Why, you were only going 20 miles over the speed limit while driving through a major intersection against a red light. That's all you did!" he retorted. His amusement had now turned into extreme annoyance. "Thank God there weren't any pedestrians in the crosswalk. You could have killed someone."

Thank God, for sure! After the policeman handed me a ticket and walked back to his car, I laid my head on the steering wheel and wept. I remembered Victor's story about the woman who had died in a mysterious car crash. Satan was fighting in dead earnest for my soul. At the same time, God was surely watching out for me.

The Scripture came to my mind, "Satan has asked for you, that he may sift you as wheat. But I have prayed for you, that your faith should not fail" (Luke 22:31,32). I had been trying to fight the "good fight of faith" but I felt that I was losing the battle.

My hand trembled as I reached for the key to start the car. "Dear Jesus," I whispered, "don't let me kill anyone. Just get me back home."

Once safe inside my house, I dropped to my knees. I wanted to pound the floor in anger, but I was too exhausted. I was fighting Satan in my own strength, but I was no match for him. My strength surely didn't begin to equal his!

What was I doing wrong? I had prayed. I had read the Bible. I had gone to a social worker. And I was seeing a therapist. I had peeled off the facade of veneer that covered the real me. Yet here I was sitting on the floor, a critically wounded soldier felled by Satan's fiery darts. What was wrong?

Fighting Satan in my own strength had used up my energies. Too weary to even pray, I sat on the floor, quiet and still. And in that quiet moment I heard the Lord speak. There were no audible words this time, but I sensed His presence and message. It was unmistakable. In that moment He showed me that I needed special help. Not only had my physical and emotional self been abused, but God revealed that my spirit had also been abused. I needed healing from the abuse of my spirit. Yes, I had been freed from many memories of horror, but the continued torment and abuse by Satan himself had not yet been addressed.

The Intruder

The peaceful stillness of the moment was shattered by a voice. "Little one, it's too late. We're here to take you back with us. Won't you come?"

I knew the voice well. It was "Mother." For just a moment, I was tempted to respond. The sun had set and the room was in total darkness. I started to look for a visual manifestation of the spirit's presence when I felt a strong check in my heart.

Suddenly I cried out, "Jesus, what am I to do? I can't fight this by myself."

"Silly one, why do you pray to Him?" it interrupted. Then it laughed a shrill, sarcastic laugh. Its laughter grew louder and louder until I couldn't stand it. I covered my ears with my hands, but it was useless. I had to get away from it.

Too weak to stand, I crawled on my hands and knees to the bedroom and shut the door behind me. The laughter followed. "You can't get away from us," it laughed mockingly. "We're all around you. We're everywhere."

I knelt beside my bed and began to sob. My whole body was shaking. Clutching the bedsheets to hold myself upright, I cried out to God. I was desperate to find that special someone who could deal with this abuse of my spirit. If there was anyone who could help me find that someone, I knew it was God. Raising my head toward the heavens, I poured my heart out to Him. Years of pain, bitterness, and anger spilled out. For the first time in my life, I was completely honest with Him.

Up until now, I had been fearful of telling God exactly how I felt about my life. I was afraid of angering Him, or even causing Him to hate me. And God forbid that He should become so disappointed in me that He would leave me. Then I would have no one.

But tonight I was so desperate that I had to try to get His full attention in some way. If I told Him how I *really* felt, surely He would at least listen. And so it was in the midst of abject despair that I told Him my life wasn't fair. "Where have You been all the times that I cried out for Your protection?" I asked Him. "Sometimes I feel as if I love You and hate You at the same time. What have I done to deserve the life of hell that You have placed me in? If You won't help me, then I don't see much use in being Your child . . ."

Over the next hour I told God everything. Finally I was spent with exhaustion. There were no more tears. There was nothing left to say. Looking heavenward through swollen eyes, I said in simple, childlike words, "Father, I need Your help right now. If You hear me and You care for me like You say You do, please help me find somebody who can show me how to be freed from Satan's torment of my spirit. Amen."

At that point I was so physically and emotionally spent that I slumped to the floor and fell into a deep sleep. For the first time in months there were no nightmares, no dreams, no harsh memories. When I awoke the next morning, it was with renewed energy and hope. I had held nothing back from God. Surely He would answer. Soon!

The Wait

A few days later I was watching a program on a Christian television station. It was about a subject I had never found very interesting—Bible history and prophecy—so I wasn't paying much attention. I was half-asleep when I heard a woman speak. There was something about her voice that caught my attention. She was using terms like "occult" and "devil worship" as she described an encounter she had had with demon spirits. And most important of all, she believed it was real! "The abominations are real," she said, flat out.

From that sentence on, I soaked up every word she had to say. It was the first time I had heard someone describe (some of it in vivid detail) many of the same hellish events that I had witnessed.

The woman's final remarks in the interview absolutely gripped me. In kindness, yet with firmness, she said, "The one who tells you there's no way out for you isn't the Lord. If you're truly searching for a way out, ask the Lord to teach you how to pray against the evil one in Jesus' name."

Those were words of life and hope to a desperate soul. As the program ended, I declared, "That's the person I'm looking for. She's the special person!"

But I had only heard her first name—Johanna.

From that day on I purposed in my heart that someday I had to talk to her. If anyone would believe me, she would. However, I wasn't about to try to go searching for her. I had been turned down by so many others that I was afraid to make another effort. I wasn't about to risk another rejection. Also, Johanna talked about involvement with law enforcement agencies. Did she work with them? If so, would she have to turn me in? Besides, I didn't know if she was a counselor; I'd only seen her as a media spokesperson. So I couldn't be sure if she was God's person to help me. All I knew to do was to pray and ask God to somehow bring us together if that was His will. Only a miracle could make that happen, and if it did, I knew it would be from God.

Weeks and months went by. Perhaps I expected a phone call, a letter, some clue or link that would lead to our meeting. But there was none. No Johanna. I saw her two or three more times on television. Her message was the same. She spoke boldly about the occult and satanism. "These things are happening, people, but few believe them," she proclaimed.

"Sexual abuse, bestiality, infants sacrificed, children being forced to take part in murders . . ." This woman was not one to back down in what she believed to be the truth!

Each time I heard her make statements like "Satanists know how to cover their tracks," or "Somebody needs to stand up and say, 'This is what's going on.'" Again I lifted my prayer to the Lord that we might meet.

Meanwhile, I felt as if I were fighting a losing battle with Satan. I didn't know that little me actually had the authority in Jesus Christ to stand up to Satan by using prayer and the Bible. I didn't know that there was a very real and living power in the name of Jesus. I did know that Satan was real. I knew that he was big, bad, mean, and ugly. I knew that he had power, and, quite frankly, I had seen more satanists using his power than I had seen Christians using Jesus' power. What I didn't know was that Satan had been defeated at the cross, and that he only had the power over me that I *allowed* him to have.

If only I had known how to apply those spiritual truths to my life, I could have used them to receive freedom from bondage that I so craved. And if I had known that God had His hand on my life from day one and that He was guiding me to victory and freedom in His time, I wouldn't have been so frustrated and impatient.

Fortunately, I was no longer willing to sit back and accept my circumstances. I began to rebel against those who were harassing me to keep quiet. I spoke out against sexual abuse. I wrote letters to the editor of the local newspaper. I even dared to write a news article about pornographers, and I threatened to write more about them if my tormentors didn't leave me alone.

But there were limits to my progress. I tried to write a book about my past because Betsy said it would help to put my feelings down on paper. That was almost impossible. Much as she was helping me confront my memories, I knew now that the solutions were not in psychology. My problems were primarily spiritual, and they required a spiritual solution.

When was God going to send that special help? Where was Johanna? I would wait. I would hang in there, doing whatever

I could to help myself. A good friend of mine and I formed a support group for women who were victims and survivors of sexual abuse. That was progress. The Lord was showing me that I could take at least a part of my past and use it to help others. It didn't make the past any less painful, but it did help to know that some of the bad could now be used for good.

A Lady from the Heart

As a result of this support group, the Lord brought a beautiful person into my life. I had long admired Joyce Landorf and had been blessed by her books. Joyce had read an article about our support group for sexually abused women. Because of a deep concern she had for the countless women who were unburdening their souls to her about rape, incest, and other kinds of sexual abuse, Joyce and her production staff had been searching for the right way to present the subject on her radio program. Her producer approached me about the possibility of my doing a program with Joyce. As part of my healing process and my desire to help other victims, I said, "I'll be glad to do whatever I can."

The "whatever I can" turned into four programs. When I learned that one of them was to focus exclusively on my story, I gulped. It was too late to back out. Joyce was on her way to the studio. I couldn't change my story—I had already told them part of it. But it did seem like a good time for the Lord to come and take us all home!

I tried not to let my nervousness show as the narrator introduced the program: "Incest and sexual abuse. These cruel acts occur in more homes, even Christian homes, than most people realize. Sadly, sexual abuse commonly goes unreported and untreated because of the victim's shame and fear of exposure. This morning on 'From the Heart of Joyce Landorf,' a courageous woman will share the story of her personal trauma and her victory in Christ."

Why was I doing this? I wondered. What could I say to help the listeners of this radio program? Music was in the background now as the narrator invited people "to spend a personal moment with Joyce Landorf, author of over 20 bestselling

Christian books . . ." Just a few more moments. "Lord!" I prayed, "Please help me. Let me feel Your peace."

It seemed crazy for me to be on this show. I had many hidden secrets in my past that had yet to be resolved. Yet God had started a great work in my life. He had brought me out of the depths of Satan's clutches, and He was using me to help victims of sexual abuse find healing in Jesus Christ. For the first time I felt that my life was counting for something positive. Yes, I had a long way to go, but look how far I had come already.

Joyce and I were sitting at a table in a cramped sound room, a microphone between us. "Across from me is a woman who must, for a number of reasons, remain anonymous," said Joyce. "She is a very beautiful woman with an incredible past—one that in some ways is very hard for a Christian woman involved in normal family relationships with her husband and children and church to hear. It may be shocking to learn some of these things. But there is a tremendous need for my friend to be heard. We like to think that sexual abuse is something that happens to someone else in somebody else's neighborhood. When we assume that none of that goes on in our church or in our neighborhood, we are assuming far too much. That is not reality.

"Our guest today is founder of a support group for sexually abused women. Would you tell us about your organization?"

I took a deep breath and began. "I started this group because I didn't know of any other Christian-based organization dealing with this problem. There are many groups around the country trying to help victims of sexual abuse, but outside of human compassion and understanding, they have no real answers. I don't care how long you go to a therapist, or how many treatments you have, if you do not have the inner healing of the Lord Jesus Christ for any type of abuse— physical, sexual, emotional—you do not get total healing. That's the sole reason for our group—to introduce the Lord Jesus Christ as the basis for the beginning of their healing."

Joyce nodded knowingly as I spoke. She knew that many of her listeners were hurting—often from events that had occurred years ago—and that they had never had the courage to

face their pain. "After I speak, I take the emotional tempera-
ture of my audiences," Joyce said. "One out of every five is
telling me something like 'I was molested as a child; I am just
now beginning to face it and I'm torn apart.' Usually we don't
have time to discuss any details other than that this is this
woman's most closely guarded secret. As much as I want to
reach out and say I understand, I am limited in my response. I
was not sexually molested as a child, so it's hard for me to
identify."

My body stiffened as I knew what was coming next. Joyce
was about to ask me to tell my story. How was it that I
understood the pain? Why did I care about others who had
endured incest and sexual abuse as children?

Joyce recognized my fear, and before I began she softly
said, "This moment you are standing on a cliff, and you're
about to jump off and say to the rest of the world, to my
listening audience, 'This is what happened to me. I'm willing
to risk jumping off this cliff and telling you about it because I
want you to have hope. I want you to see God's healing in
your life.' Thank you for your courage and your vulnerability.
Why do you know so much about sexual abuse?"

The moment had arrived. For the first time I was about to
tell my story in public. Not all of it, for neither I nor my
audience could stand that, but enough to hopefully encourage others who were hurting like me. "I was an illegitimate
child," I began. "I was adopted into a supposedly good family. However, I did not go through an adoption agency. There
was no looking into the past of my adoptive parents. After I
was adopted, I began to be abused sexually."

"How old were you?" Joyce asked.

"I can't tell you about the very first years. I have no recollection of them at all. But from about the time I was four, I
begin to remember things. It has taken a long time to remember a lot of things. I think that's nature's way of just letting
you exist, a sort of protection. I was used as a child for pornographic purposes. I had many physical and emotional scars."

"There was physical abuse along with sexual abuse?" Joyce
prompted.

"There was a great deal of abuse of every kind you can
imagine. My therapist has said, 'I don't know how you ever

lived through it. I believe you because I hear the hurt in your voice and you couldn't have made it up. But I don't know how you made it.' I have only one answer. It's the Lord. There is no other reason why I'm here today."

"Even in spite of the anger and the pain and the hurt."

"At times the anger has been so intense in my mind and heart. I've had a lot of anger at God. 'Where were You, God, when this happened? You could have snapped Your fingers and it never would have happened.' Yet I have experienced the Lord Jesus Christ to be things to me that other people will never know."

"A richer, deeper way. A character of God that few will see," said Joyce tenderly.

"I thank Him now because I know Him in an intimate way. In suffering is the greatest place to learn how wonderful the Lord can be."

Both of us had tears streaming down our faces. Joyce seemed to be living my story with me. I knew she understood because she knew what it was to hurt. As the program neared its conclusion Joyce said, "I wish my listeners could see you. I wish they could feel the presence of God in this room. All the pain you went through, all that hurt—and this may be the moment when the Lord is going to share the plan, the good part of the plan, that through you God's healing love can go out to a very hurting world."

The music came on and the program was over. I had survived. And I felt good. God had sustained me through this. Someday He would enable me to tell more, for there were so many other girls and women like me, still hurting from their past, or trapped in pornography and satanic ritual abuse. But first God had more work to do in my life. I needed to talk to Johanna. She would help me find God's total release from the oppression of the evil one. Only then could I tell my full story. Only then would I be able to truly help other victims. Only then could I testify that God can heal, no matter how bad the hurt.

It was hard to say goodbye to Joyce and her staff. The Lord had used her in such a beautiful way to touch my life, just as she has touched the lives of so many others. She was in the very height of a personal crisis herself. Yet in the midst of that crisis she cared enough to reach out and touch me in mine.

The trip back home was traumatic. The closer I got, the more depressed I became. By the time I walked in the front door, I felt as if I were under a thick, dark cloud. I kept thinking about the plan, the good part that Joyce said was coming. I held onto that thought for dear life because I knew my struggle was far from over.

The following three to four weeks were total chaos. It probably was a blessing in disguise, for I had no time to think about my own problems. I was literally drowned in a sea of phone calls from victims across the United States and Canada who were responding to the radio programs I had done with Joyce. They were mostly from women, but even a handful of courageous men phoned to say that they had been molested as children or teenagers.

No matter where they were calling from or what sex they were, their cries were the same: "I can't share my secret with anyone else, and I feel so alone." From five o'clock in the morning until midnight each day, I listened to hundreds of hurting and desperate men and women. Each felt that his or her situation was unique, and that it was hopeless.

Sometimes when I answered, "Hello," all I heard on the other end of the line was silence or muffled sobs. After half a minute or so, I would say, "You've been abused sexually, haven't you?" Finally, after a few more seconds of silence, I would hear a quiet "Yes."

At first I wondered why these horribly hurting souls were sharing their secrets with me, a total stranger, when they hadn't dared to share them with anyone else. But then I realized, as I listened to more and more of them confide in me, that I really wasn't a stranger to them. For they knew that I had suffered the same hurts as they, and that our mutual sufferings instantly bound us together.

It was then that I began to sense what Joyce had meant when she said that perhaps now was the time that God would begin to use my hurt, my pain, and my shattering. Through me His healing love could go out to a hurting world.

However, in the ensuing months, good night's rests were few and far between. The nightmares were continuous. Shadows on the walls of my bedroom loomed larger than life, often becoming wildcats in the jungle poised to lunge at me. The threats with which I had been brainwashed, that had kept me captive in silence all these years, were now more likely to be carried out. For not only had I talked in private, but I had talked in public. My guiding spirit was now making its presence known audibly, and sometimes visually, more frequently.

Eighteen months had gone by since I had learned about Johanna. Each month brought new terrors. Eighteen months, but still no Johanna.

I realize now that God knew I wasn't ready. One more secret remained. My biggest secret. I would have to face it first.

❖ *10* ❖
With Tender Love

Let the little children come to Me,
and do not forbid them; for of such is
the kingdom of heaven.
—Matthew 19:14

Joey, Carly, and Lindy are safe—safe in the arms of Jesus. Keeping that reality ever before me, I will endeavor to share three precious lives with you.

Dear Jesus, where do I begin? I can count on the fingers of both hands the number of people who know that I am a mother. I don't even think of myself as a mother. I have so divorced that reality from my heart and mind that when I received a Mother's Day note this year from a very dear and close friend, it surprised me. It was the first Mother's Day remembrance I have ever received. In fact, if it had been a card instead of a handwritten note with personal words to me as a "special mother," I would have thought that she had sent it to me by mistake!

I always dreaded attending church on Mother's Days, not because I was a mother, but because of the way I had been treated by my mother. In fact, I was so bitter about her that after I ran away I never thought of her as my mother. When speaking about her, I referred to her only as "the woman who raised me."

Mother's Days came and Mother's Days went in meaningless insignificance. They simply didn't apply to me, until . . .

It happened one day during therapy in Betsy's office. I won't even try to explain the whats, whys, or hows of that session. I don't understand it. Certainly I had no intention of revealing my secret.

At first I heard crying. Then the crying turned to screams. I put my hands over my ears and tried to shut out their sounds. It was to no avail.

Then came the names—first Joey, then later Carly and Lindy. I never knew much about Carly or Lindy, except that they had been used in snuff films. Nothing else concerning them came to mind at that session.

But Joey? Within an hour's time Joey became a real, living, human being. A baby with a name and face. Oh dear God, *my baby*!

Bending over on the therapist's sofa, I slumped to the floor consumed in grief. My cries grew so loud that, fearing what others would think in surrounding offices, Betsy put her hand over my mouth to stifle the heart-wrenching wails.

The time had come for me to deal with the most sorrowful and painful part of my life. It was time to remember, time to admit, time to confront, and above all, time to forgive.

Whether I wanted to or not, I couldn't hold back the memories. They came pouring in through the open floodgates of my mind. I didn't want to admit them, for with admitting came an overwhelming feeling of guilt. Whether right or wrong, my conscience accused me: "You should have done something to stop it." I didn't want to face that. I wanted to jam the memories back into "never-never land."

And to forgive? I wasn't willing to consider that. No way would I ever forgive those who were responsible for the deaths—no, not the deaths—the outright *murder and sacrifices* of three precious innocent babies. NO WAY!

* * *

What do I tell? What do I not tell? How much can you take? How much can I take in sharing their pain with you? I think not much for either of us! To know that it does happen, to know that it did happen to my three little ones, is enough.

I have described how infants and children are sexually abused, tortured, and sacrificed, both for snuff films and ritualistic sacrifices. I think it is enough to know what you've already been told—that the more perverted the sexual abuse, the more heinous the torture, the louder the screams, the slower the death, the more parts of the body that are used for other ritualistic acts or worn underneath clothing, the more

Satan is pleased and bestows power on those who commit these acts of sacrifice to him. It is no less of a crime, no less diabolical, no more excusable or forgivable when the sacrifice is made for a snuff film. It is rotten, sinful, and evil to the core.

I must avoid a thousand and one details, the specifics of which would haunt you and give you sleepless nights. However, I and the countless other mothers who can identify with me don't have the luxury of avoiding the graphic horrors. We don't have the option of turning the page. We were captive to situations where we were forced to become pregnant.

Others became pregnant voluntarily, but at the time of delivery were forced to give up their newborns because they were inescapably involved in satanic covens that sacrificed humans as part of their ritual. Their babies were either snatched away against their wills, or because of their deceived state of mind they willingly surrendered their babies to be sacrificed.

I am not talking about primitive cultures in faraway lands. This is happening in North America. Dr. Al Carlisle, psychologist for the Utah State Men's Prison (and a noted authority and speaker on occult murders), told me in a taped phone interview, "In talking with a person who is a Black Magician or Black Prince in a satanic group that has engaged in sacrifices, he [the black magician] estimated that from forty to sixty *thousand* human sacrifices per year are made in the United States." Dr. Carlisle went on to say, "Even if that estimate is exaggerated and only half this number is correct, it indicates that we're simply not aware enough of what's happening."

Discussions by Dr. Carlisle with other authorities reveal that in a city the size of Denver, for example, there are probably 70 to 100 human sacrifices per year. Identical estimates were given by a person who has personally witnessed several human sacrifices. While these statistics are mind-boggling, they are perhaps not so unbelievable when we think of the tens of thousands of children that wind up missing every year.

Dr. Carlisle concluded his remarks by saying, "Even if the above-mentioned estimates of human sacrifices are higher than the actual figure, they indicate that the instances are far greater than what we have thought in the past, and both point to the fact that a serious problem exists."

If we can at least consider half or even a fourth of the estimate that forty to sixty thousand humans are sacrificed in North America yearly, then we must also consider the fact that there are scores of mothers who have borne the indescribable pain of having their children sacrificed, some of them right in front of their eyes!

If those of you who can thank God that you've been spared such an agony as this are bothered or sickened at the thought, I do not apologize. Rather, I call upon you to pray for these mothers. I ask you to pray for Almighty God to send someone to minister to them as they bear their hell of hells.

My Joey

My hell of hells has been the remembering of my Joey. I rarely got the chance to see him or to hold him. I knew that he was being abused and tortured for films. I knew that his screams during the torture were being recorded on tape to sell to the "slimes" who get their kicks from listening to babies scream in agony.

The few times I was allowed to see Joey, he looked worse each time. I prayed day and night for his misery to end—that God would take him quickly and painlessly. I knew there was no hope for him. Every day that Joey continued to live meant more agony for him. And worst of all, I knew his ultimate end.

I offered to take Joey's place—my life for his. I bargained that I would do anything—no act barred—if Joey's life would be spared. "Take my Joey and set him on a church step. Please!" I begged. "Put him in a box and leave him at a hospital or on someone's front door. Please!" I begged and cried until my voice, strained to the limit, broke, and was silenced.

It was no use. I wasn't the "perfect sacrifice." Joey was.

I wanted to put my arms around him, but they wouldn't let me. I wanted to tell him that his mommy wasn't doing this to him, and that his mommy wasn't able to protect him like a mommy should. I wanted to ask him to forgive me, but I never got the chance.

I will not, I cannot go into a complete accounting of Joey's sacrifice. I will not strip Joey of his dignity by allowing you to see him as I saw him. Suffice it to say that while offering him as a sacrifice, they chanted something about Satan accepting his heart as a pure and unblemished sacrifice. Then Joey's body was laid on a black robe. The coven members each held his candle to the edge of the robe. It was quickly engulfed in flames. Joey was no more.

As the flames began to consume the sacrifice, I yelled, "Satan, you didn't get Joey! Joey went to be with Jesus. He fooled you all. You may have gotten his heart, but you didn't get his soul!"

* * *

What happened to Joey is even now happening to babies, children, and teenagers across the country. Believe the un-believable! For God's sake, don't close your mind because it's too painful to face. My little ones and countless other innocent babies are destroyed in satanic rituals and snuff films. Many people refuse to accept the reality of this, not because they don't believe it *does* happen, but because they don't want to believe it *can* happen!

I beg you: Don't let Joey's life and death be for nothing. You can hide from the truth, but you can't change the truth. It's an ugly truth that needs to be stopped in the name of God and in the name of our children!

Recently I wrote a letter to my son on what would have been his birthday. It was my own personal way of coming to terms with his life and death. I've shared this letter with only a few dear and close friends.

As I've worked on this chapter, a desire has grown within me to leave a memorial to the countless little ones who while on this earth never got the chance to play, to laugh, or to be loved. So I share with you the letter I wrote to Joey as my way of remembering these courageous, precious, and beautiful children.

My Dear Joey,

Words cannot express my feelings on this your birthday.

If it had been in my power, you would have had the opportunity to grow up with love, security, warmth, and guidance. I know you would have grown into a young man, strong of character and gentle of heart.

I'm sorry for the pain you suffered. I hurt with you, my little one. I have to believe in my heart that in the special moments I had to touch you, even though they were few, you felt my love, a mommy's love.

My son, I will always love you in my heart. I carry you with me in a special place that only my Joey can fill.

Your mommy will never forget you. I pray that you, my special son, will never forget me.

I know that Jesus has been taking good care of you for me. I long and anxiously await the day when I take you from His arms and hold you in mine once again.

> With Tender Love,
> Your Mommy

* * *

You may ask how I deal with this memory. Not very well at times. It was not even possible at first. In reliving many of the horrors that I haven't dared to share with you about the ways Joey, Carly, and Lindy were sacrificed, I have all but given up the thought of getting through this chapter.

I knew I would have to go through pain and sorrow—but not this much! I knew my heart would ache—but not this much! I knew the tears would flow—but not this many!

Let me simply tell you how God has helped to ease the pain of this darkest portion of my life. One day, as I was struggling, trying to write this chapter, I laid my head down on my desk and closed my eyes to rest. In a beautiful and precious way the Lord Jesus turned the eyes of my mind toward heaven. There I saw Joey, Carly, and Lindy *as they are now*, safe in His arms. Their little faces beamed with merriment. Their eyes twinkled with excitement. Their wide grins reached from ear to ear.

Gone was the pain. Gone were the piercing screams of torment and agony. Gone were the scars that had covered their little bodies. Gone were all the signs of Satan's demonic injustices! I saw no lingering memories of horror in their innocent eyes of baby blue.

Yes, my little ones were home, waiting for the day when Jesus will place them back into their mommy's arms.

I called out. Oh, I knew they couldn't really hear me, but I called out anyway—for my sake, I guess, more than for theirs: "I'm coming. I'm coming. It won't be long now, my little ones."

I don't know just when it will be. But I can wait now. For I know they're free from the memories of Satan's insane evils.

Joey, Carly, and Lindy are safe in the arms of Jesus . . . for all time and for all eternity.

❖ 11 ❖
Miracles Do Happen

Finally it happened—a breakthrough!

A parent of an abused child contacted me about using the story of my life to help other victims. "I'm not ready to do that," I said. "I can't allow my story to be known until a certain thing happens."

"And what is that thing?" he inquired.

I really didn't want to tell him, because I knew it wouldn't mean anything to him. In fact, he would probably figure it was a cop-out. Nevertheless I answered, "I have to find a certain person and get help from her before I can allow the public access to my story."

Obviously his next question was, "Who is the person you're looking for?"

Very casually I replied, "I'm looking for a woman named Johanna. I keep seeing her on TV, but I don't know who she is or how to get hold of her."

In a flash he whipped out a business card from his wallet, turned it over, and showed me a handwritten name and phone number. "I think this is the person you're looking for."

There it was—the name "Johanna Michaelsen" and her home phone number.

I didn't sleep at all that night. When morning came I wanted to dial the number at six o'clock, but I forced myself to wait until about ten. My hands were shaking so badly that I could hardly push the right buttons with my fingers.

"Hello." I recognized the voice. THAT voice.

A million thoughts raced through my mind. "What if she thinks I'm a crank caller?" "How do I explain who I am and why I'm calling?" "What if she hangs up on me?"

Gathering every ounce of courage, I told her my name and briefly described the very basics of my situation. Then I took a deep breath, paused for a moment, and blurted out, "Would it be possible to talk with you?"

I wanted to hang up because I knew she was going to say "No," and I didn't want to hear it. Where would I go from here? This was my last hope. I had to force myself to listen to her answer.

"Yes, my husband, Randolph, and I would be happy to talk with you. How about this Thursday morning at 11 o'clock?"

My heart was pounding. Did I hear right? Did she say "Yes?" After 18 months, was I finally going to be talking to this woman just two days from now?

Somehow I managed to calm down enough to answer, "Yes, I'll be there. Thank you."

The Meeting

The two days between the phone call and the meeting went by slowly, but finally Thursday morning came. As Johanna described to me in a later conversation, "The air was so thick with a feeling of depression that you could have cut it with a knife." I'm sure that was true, for I had come to her with a do-or-die desperation. I sincerely believed that if Johanna couldn't help me, help would never come. I would forever suffer under Satan's oppression, never knowing true spiritual freedom.

It didn't take long for a lifetime of hurts and horrors to start tumbling out, things that I had never dared to share with anyone else. The pain of sharing was so great that I began to tremble and sob. I kept looking into Johanna's eyes for a sign of disbelief. I never saw it. I kept listening to her voice for any hint of distrust. I never heard it. I only heard words of understanding and comfort. I knew then that I was being believed and accepted.

One hour passed, then two hours, then three hours. More and more came pouring out. The dam had broken, the resistance was gone, and the pain from countless years of holding back surged forth from the depths of my soul.

The fourth hour passed. The fifth hour passed. More pain. More horrors. I waited for criticism. I waited for disbelief. I waited for rejection. They never came. I only received understanding, acceptance, comfort, and love. I was ministered to in gentleness, patience, and kindness. When the pain would become too great for me to express, Johanna would just say softly, "I know, I know."

The sixth hour came and went. More sharing. More listening. More prayer. More ministering. The meeting ended finally—after seven hours! Little did I know that those seven hours were but the beginning of a long journey for the three of us.

The Battle Begins

In a way that could only have been the Lord's doing, I spent the next month at Randolph's and Johanna's home. Because of my past and my distrust of people, I never voluntarily stayed overnight at anyone's house. Seldom did I even visit someone for more than an hour, and then I had to get out and go back to my home. Even my friends had difficulty understanding how I could stay at someone else's home, especially with people I didn't even know. I believe that the Lord took all fear of this new situation from me, because He knew that it would be during this time that my fight for freedom would be fought.

For the first few days I really did little but watch Johanna and Randolph. I watched the way they lived. I listened to how they talked. I looked for inconsistencies in their Christian walk. I found none. I really expected them to change their minds about helping me. They didn't.

The second day of my stay, I did nothing but cry the entire day. From the moment I awakened that morning until the moment I finally fell asleep in the wee hours of the following morning, I cried. These were not just a few tears; they were total hysterics. I sobbed and agonized. I held onto Johanna, and laid my head on her shoulder and cried at the top of my voice, right next to her ear. Her blouse was soaked with my tears. I would quiet down for five or ten minutes, then start sobbing again.

Johanna had every right to become impatient. I gave her plenty of reason to say, "Okay, Lauren, that's enough. Let's get it together." But her sole response was that of patience, kindness, and understanding as she continually prayed that the Lord would strengthen us for this battle.

Randolph was gone for much of that tearful morning. When he arrived home early in the afternoon, he found Johanna holding me in her arms on the sofa as I sobbed. I'm sure he had heard my crying from the moment he opened his car door in the garage. He walked over to the sofa and sat down beside me. I let go of Johanna, put my head on his shoulder, and continued to cry. "I've got something for you," he said, opening a bag he had brought into the house. "It will make you feel better."

He pulled out a small square box and handed it to me. I let go of him long enough to open the box. Inside was a coffee mug. On the front were some cute little animals and in bright colors the words "Smile . . . God loves you!"

I held the cup close to me and looked up at Randolph, unable to speak. He smiled and said gently, "This is to always tell you that God loves you, and we love you—for always."

Every morning since that day I have used that mug. And every time I use it I'm reminded of the abounding, measureless love that these two precious servants of the Lord showed me. They really meant it. I waited. I watched. I listened. If anything, their commitment to me only strengthened as those first days passed and I finally relaxed. I could see, not just by their *words*, but by their *actions*, that these two people were for real. I was ready to go to work.

However, I soon learned that, at least initially, I wasn't able to do much of anything but be a passive bystander in this fight for my freedom. I had quit attending church more than a year before, and my faith was down to almost zero. I was in tremendous emotional turmoil, and Satan was putting up a tremendous fight to keep me in bondage. For the first three weeks I felt as if I were living in a hell that was almost as painful as the hell I had come from. In fact, Satan did his best to make it seem that the fight wasn't worth it. He fought against me harder than he had at any other time in my life. In retrospect, I realize that this was really a good sign, for he knew that he no longer had me neatly tucked away in his grasp. I was fighting for my freedom. His strong opposition was only an indication that he knew he was in danger of losing.

The Bully Principle

Actually, I was afraid of Satan. I cowered to him. I let him kick me all over the place. Every time Johanna would say something like "Don't let Satan do that to you," a thousand memories of past horrors inflicted by him and his followers would flash through my mind. I would protest, "Johanna, you don't know what he can do. There's no way I can fight him. He's too strong."

The bottom line was that I was afraid to challenge Satan for fear that he just might decide to order Mother, my spirit guide, to do away with me—permanently. I wanted to stay off the front line of battle. Maybe then he wouldn't notice me, and someone else could fight the battle for me.

After one of our typical exchanges, Johanna thoughtfully said, "You know, Lauren, I think it's time that you learn about 'the Bully Principle.' You don't have to let Satan kick you around. You can stand up to him, look him square in his old ugly face, and laugh at him. He's just a big bully anyway. That's all he is—a bully!" She stamped her foot on the floor to emphasize the word "bully."

Believe me, I had never thought of Satan as a bully. I knew about the usual bully in school, who delights in being cruel to a smaller or weaker person. The bully never picks on a person his own size for fear of losing. He often teases, intimidates, and threatens without ever intending to carry out those threats. But to call Satan a bully? Never!

"How can you call Satan a bully?" I asked. "You know what I've told you about him."

Johanna smiled and sat me down. She never got ruffled when I showed surprise or a lack of understanding. "Look at what Satan is doing to you now. He's taunting you with every threat in his repertoire. I have to admit, he's putting on a pretty convincing act. But that's exactly what it is—an act, a show, a pretense—just an empty threat. You have Jesus Christ living in you, and Jesus is greater than Satan. All Satan can do is make you *think* he is all-powerful."

I thought about what she was saying. I *do* have Jesus in me. Satan *is* on the outside. Suddenly my face lit up and I smiled. "You're right! All Satan can do to me is stand on the outside and throw rocks at me, just like the bully at school does."

That was a major insight. Immediately I felt stronger. When I began to really see that Jesus was alive inside me, and that Satan was only looking at me from the outside, it was as if Satan began to shrink in size right before my eyes.

Then Johanna told me the secret behind the Bully Principle. "When Satan comes creeping in and whispers such bully tactics as 'You're not going to make it' or 'You'll never win' or 'You might as well give up,' you can either say, 'You're right, it's no use' . . ."

Knowing that this was not the right response, I shook my head.

"That's right," she encouraged. "What you want to say to him is 'I recognize you, Satan, for what you are—a defeated foe at the cross of Jesus Christ. I will not bow down to you. I will not cower. I will not give in. I will use the power that Jesus Christ has given me through His Word and through prayer to stand firm against you.' "

Johanna smiled and asked, "Do you know what will happen when you talk to Satan like that? He'll just slink off like the bully he is."

From then on, every time Johanna saw even the smallest fear in me she would say, "Remember the Bully Principle!"

There was no way that I was going to let Satan bully me into quitting. There was no way that I was going to let Satan have any more power in my life. Not when I had come this far! He had bullied me around long enough. I determined to stand my ground!

When the warfare became the heaviest and I felt the weakest (that's when Satan likes to play the bully role), I would say with every ounce of strength within me, "Greater is He who is in me than he who is in the world."[1] "If God is for us, who can be against us?"[2] "We are more than conquerors through Him who loved us."[3] Again and again I would quote those Scriptures.

Johanna also taught me how to be very specific when using the Word of God. When Satan would try to tell me that I was guilty, I would quote the Scripture—always out loud— "There is therefore now no condemnation to those who are in Christ Jesus."[4]

When Satan would taunt me with fear and threaten to drive me crazy I would say to him, "The Word of God says, 'God has not given us a spirit of fear, but of power and of love and of a sound mind.' "[5]

Another tactic that Satan used every night when I went to bed was the threat to torment me with nightmares. I would come back at him with this Scripture: "I will both lie down in peace and sleep, for You alone, Lord, make me dwell in safety."[6]

I learned a really neat fact: Satan didn't seem to want to hang around when I was quoting the Word of God. He truly is a bully! Sure, he could stand face-to-face with me in the heat of the battle as long as I was defenseless, but as soon as I appropriated the sword of God's Word, that mean, powerful guy became nothing but a bully. Usually he would turn tail and run.

Night Skirmishes

Anyone who has done hand-to-hand combat with Satan knows what I had to learn the hard way: The worst times of battle come during the long, dark, night hours. Satan fights his best at night. He loves darkness. He is the very ruler of darkness.

During the first month I dreaded going to sleep. Satan knew that I was learning to stand up to his attacks while I was awake and alert. Ah, but those night hours, when one is asleep and the mind is not alert to the enemy's approach— that's when he's at his best. I began to have the most tormenting nightmares, reliving every pain of the past. There was not a moment's peace to be found while I was sleeping. Every moment was filled with terror. Johanna put a small handbell on the nightstand in order to call her if I needed her. I never needed to use the bell, for my screams awakened her almost nightly.

Satan may have been a bully during the daytime, but when darkness fell he became the master of deception. I was unable to fight his deception because the nightmares were so real; it was difficult to separate reality from imagination. At times he was so deceiving that I was certain I was still being abused by the evil persons in my past.

Oftentimes, and for a period of time it was every night, I would awaken to hear Johanna praying beside me, rebuking and binding those spirits that Satan had sent to terrorize me. I became very familiar with her prayers. She would pray in the most authoritative voice I had ever heard: "Satan, I come against you in the name of Jesus Christ. I come against any evil spirit you send to do your bidding. I command your workers of iniquity to take your hands off my sister and depart from her. I bind and rebuke any curse of harm that you have sent upon her. Lord Jesus, I ask for the covering and the shielding of Your blood over her mind and body. In Jesus' name, Amen."

But Satan was relentless. He and the spirits who had been sent to do his bidding would not back off after the first prayer. They did not want to leave a person over whom they had had free rein to torment and terrorize for years upon years. Oftentimes he would hang in there with a fierceness that would intimidate even the mature Christian warrior.

Satan attacked me in diverse ways. I often felt as if I were being choked to death—I actually felt hands on my throat and found myself gasping for air. I often heard the fiendish laughter of evil spirits, and occasionally I felt their presence around me. Sometimes the spirits would make the sounds of babies crying in torment—the crying sounds that I had heard in reality as I witnessed the torture of a baby used in a satanic ritual. One night Johanna found me crawling into the bedroom closet in an attempt to get away from the mimicking sounds which the evil spirits were making of crying babies.

Perhaps many of you are thinking that I was mentally unbalanced, that I was just imagining these horrors. That would be a natural reaction, considering the horrors I had endured for so many years. I can only assure you, along with the corroboration of Johanna and others, that I was not suffering from delusions. It's true that the nightmares were a reliving of things that were in the past. But the evil spirits who revealed themselves to me in those night battles of spiritual warfare were real.

In Mike Warnke's book *The Satan Seller* you can read of similar activities. He describes how evil spirits actually do physical harm to people. He tells of an evening where a woman, a messenger of Satan, literally materialized out of nowhere right in front of him in his living room. She gave the message to him and then dematerialized in like manner.[7]

It would be much easier to leave out these accounts, but if I did, Satan would win yet another victory. Satan is real. He does real things. Until we recognize this, we can't fight against him and his demonic emissaries. And so I dare to tell you of the actual forces I had to contend with in my battle for freedom and healing.

As the nights went by and battle upon battle was fought, I became strong enough to fight along with Johanna. I repeated the words she prayed. Finally, when she felt that I was strong enough to pray on my own, she said, "You be watchman over your own spirit and soul. When you see the evil one sneaking up, you address him in the name of Jesus Christ. You sound the alarm and pray, 'No! I spot you, and I see you for what you are. I reject you. I renounce you. I rebuke you. And I shatter and break your curses. I will allow no spirit that is not from God to remain around me. I am not subject to you, for Jesus has set me free. The Lord Jesus Christ is my Master, and I obey Him only. Go! I command you to leave in the name of our Lord and Savior, Jesus Christ!' "

When I began to fight on my own and use the power of prayer I felt for the first time in my life that *I* was in control, not Satan. At the end of every battle, Satan had to flee. And he did!

It was then that the Lord ministered to me. Often too exhausted to move, Johanna would help me to sit up in bed. I would rest my head on her shoulder as she read words of comfort, encouragement, and strength from the Word of God.

I will lie down and sleep in peace, for you alone, O Lord, make me dwell in safety (Psalm 4:8 NIV).

> We are pressed on every side by troubles, but not crushed and broken. We are perplexed because we don't know why things happen as they do, but we don't give up and quit. We are hunted down, but God never abandons us. We get knocked down, but we get up again and keep going (2 Corinthians 4:8,9 TLB).

> That is why we never give up. . . . We do not look at what we can see right now, the troubles all around us. . . . The troubles will soon be over, but the joys to come will last forever (2 Corinthians 4:16,18 TLB).

> The Lord is my light and my salvation—whom shall I fear? The Lord is the stronghold of my life—of whom shall I be afraid? When evil men advance against me to devour my flesh, when my enemies and my foes attack me, they will stumble and fall. Though an army besiege me, my heart will not fear; though war break out against me, even then will I be confident (Psalm 27:1-3 NIV).

It was those "songs in the night" that brought healing to our wearied minds and bodies. Johanna would read and read. Oftentimes, if they were Scriptures I knew, I would say them softly with her. It was a precious time—a time of being loved with the love of Jesus Christ.

The night battles usually ended with something that was totally incongruent with combat. Something was sure to strike us both as being funny. We would laugh and laugh until we ended up saying, "No more, no more!" The Lord surely must have a sense of humor. That laughter, usually after five o'clock, relieved us of the strain and exhaustion of a long night's battle. We were laughing. Dawn was breaking. Another victory had been won!

Jesus Takes the Bad

There was still one major hurdle standing in the way of my total healing. Memories of the past were still causing great pain and bitterness. When a child is abused physically, she is also injured emotionally. The physical wounds may be treated, but all too often the emotional wounds are ignored.

There is a common misconception that children are too young to know what *really* happened and that they will forget about the incident or incidents as they grow up. Those closest to an abused child often adopt the attitude that there is no reason to treat the way she *feels* about what has happened. And, as is all too common, many children internalize their feelings, giving the impression that they have somehow survived the trauma with their emotional stability intact.

Nothing could be further from the truth. Physical wounds heal over time as a natural course of nature. Emotional wounds do not. As the physical scars begin to heal and fade, the emotional scars grow bigger and bigger. It is no longer the physical trauma that is hurting, but the lingering memories and feelings about the trauma. If the adult victim of earlier abuse does not deal with those feelings, her life will be adversely affected.

Until I got into therapy, I internalized my grief. Depression and tears were my constant companions. I grieved. I cried. I hurt. And I felt sorry for myself. When I started therapy and began to bring those internalized pains into the light, my depression turned to anger. The more I talked about my past, the angrier I became. That's a healthy step forward. However, it isn't healthy to remain there. After the anger came bitterness. Then hatred, and rage.

There were times when I tried to relate past horrors to Johanna, only to find myself becoming so angry that my face would turn beet-red. My fists would clench until my knuckles turned white. I would try to express my anger, but it was so intense that I couldn't speak, and I felt as if I were going to explode.

I hated everyone who had abused me. I even began to hate those whom I felt had let me down by not somehow seeing the horrors behind my tears. I know now that some of that anger and hatred was misdirected, but at the time I was too consumed with bitterness to see it.

I knew that the Lord understood. But I also knew that it was displeasing to Him, and I would not find the peace I was looking for until I got rid of that anger and hatred. But how? The more I tried, the worse things became.

Johanna recognized what was happening. She saw that the more I remembered, the angrier I became. Yet she never condemned me. She never made me feel that I had no right to be bitter or angry. She just continued to show me the love of Jesus through it all.

That was very important to me. She accepted me the way I was. She loved me for me. Time after time she would tell me, "I love you. Nothing will ever change that—nothing you've done or nothing anyone else has done to you. We love you! Period!"

One of the biggest things that helped me to accept Johanna and Randolph's love was that they never made me feel as if they were doing me a favor, or that I owed them something in return. In fact, Johanna made me feel as if she needed me. Time after time she would open her arms wide and say, "I need a big hug." Or she would say, "I'm so glad the Lord brought you into my life." And even in the very midst of such heavy crisis, she or I would make a remark that struck both of us as being extremely funny, and we would laugh. After the hysterics died down she would say, "Thanks—I needed that."

Then it was always back to the grueling work of fighting Satan. Johanna and I talked about my growing anger and hatred. I knew those feelings weren't punishing the people who had caused my pain; they were only hurting me. I admitted it, which was step number one.

The next step was the hardest thing I had to do in receiving healing from the pain of my memories. I had to give every physical and emotional scar to Jesus. I was not to bear them any longer. You might think that this would be easy, but letting go of the past turned out to be a bitter fight. For if I gave it all to Jesus, there would be no more excuse for my self-pity. I would likewise have to make a choice not to take back any of the hurts. It was, in effect, a final choice to step out of the past, to put an end to my grieving and live in the freedom that was mine for the taking. The time for making excuses was over. Feeling-sorry time was over. It was time to live. It was time to receive the healing the Lord was offering. But I still had to overcome this one final hurdle.

It was evening. I was sitting on the sofa in the living room, wrestling with my anger and hatred and bitterness. Johanna sat down beside me. I'm sure that my pain was etched on my face. By now we had gone through so much together that she was very sensitive to my feelings and always knew when I was hurting. In fact we had become so close that we had begun to call each other "Sister."

For several minutes she was silent. Finally she asked, "Are you ready to give your scars to Jesus . . . all of them?"

I wanted to run from her question, but as I looked into her face I knew that she was in dead earnest. There was no escaping. The hour had come for me to put an end to my past. With fear and hesitation I answered softly, "Yes."

Johanna slipped off the sofa and sat on the floor in front of me. I began to sense that she knew something I was not aware of. She was fully prepared for the struggle that was to follow. I wasn't. I only knew that I was committed to stay in the battle until victory was won. Nothing was going to deter me. "Lord, give my sister the strength she needs to get through this step," Johanna prayed. Little did I know just how much strength I would need.

My body bore many scars. Some were from early childhood and had nearly faded away from the passing of time. A few were so bold and vivid that they had defied my attempts to disguise them. Each one was inflicted for a different reason. Each one carried a painful memory. And each one had to be named, one by one, and given to Jesus.

Ever so patiently and carefully, Johanna helped me identify each scar. At times it seemed to take forever to name a scar that brought back intensely painful memories. Sometimes there was a deafening silence between her identification of a scar and my ability to name it. Then slowly, with Johanna's help, I prayed.

"Jesus, I give to You the mark on my forehead that was branded on me by Victor, identifying his control over me. Because You own me, Lord, and I am Your child, I ask that You receive this scar. I give the meaning of this scar to You, and I give the emotional pain of this scar to You.

"Jesus, I give to You the long slashmark on my right arm.

"Jesus, I give to You the mental scars of having to stand naked and be photographed as a little girl.

"Jesus, I give to You the pain of the murders of my little ones."

On and on the naming, the giving, and the letting-go went. Over those places that were just too much to name specifically, Johanna would simply hold her hand over me and pray for the entire area.

Perhaps an hour or more went by. The struggle was so intense that after I had finally named the last physical and emotional scar, I began to tremble uncontrollably. I had worked so hard that my clothing was soaked wet with perspiration. Even my hair was wet. Johanna's husband wrapped a blanket around me.

I knew it was over. We had both fought hard. Looking into Johanna's face, I said, "You knew before we started that this battle was going to be one of the hardest things I've ever done, didn't you?"

Johanna nodded.

"How did you know?"

With a smile of memories long past, she answered, "I've been there before."

As I sat on the sofa trembling, Johanna put her arm around me and drew me close to her side. "I want to tell you something I saw as we were praying. I know it will encourage you," she said softly. "I saw Jesus standing with His nail-scarred hands outstretched toward you. In His hands was a golden bowl."

I began to sense that I was hearing something very special—something that was meant just for me.

Johanna continued, "Every time you named a scar, Jesus took it and put it into the bowl. When it was full, He stretched out His arms and showed you the scars in His hands."

"Did Jesus really accept the scars I gave to Him?" I asked hesitantly.

"Oh yes, He did. And as He held them close to Himself, He looked at you with tears of compassion."

A warm feeling came over me. I felt a oneness with Jesus.

The bitterness I had held against Him was gone. For the first time in my life I felt His healing balm cover every scar and every memory. That memory of Jesus holding my scars unto His bosom was a vital step in the healing of my memories.

Both Johanna and I were deeply moved. We sat in quiet reverence for several minutes. "You know, Sister," Johanna finally spoke, "no longer are you to look on your scars as badges of shame. Jesus wants you to see them as badges of courage!"

I thought for a moment. Then I replied confidently, "Yes, badges of courage!"

"Honey, when you're tempted to go back to your old ways of thinking, pray this prayer: 'Lord Jesus, I will set my mind on You. Not on the horror and the pain of the past, but on You as You bring peace and restoration.' "

I had learned yet another way to win over the enemy. I immediately prayed that prayer, and I've used it over and over when I've been tempted to dwell on old memories and feelings.

Special People

Neither Johanna nor I had shared much with other people about what was going on. However, Johanna had related some of the situation with her sister, Kim, and had asked her to pray. Kimmie would call every morning to see how things were going. She told Johanna during one of those calls that the Lord was awakening her every morning at the same time to pray for us.

When Johanna asked her what that time was, Kimmie replied, "Three A.M. It's always at three A.M."

I was both amazed and blessed at her answer, for our most strenuous warfare was always fought between three and four o'clock in the morning.

One morning Kimmie told me that as she was on her knees praying for me the night before, she felt urged by the Lord to give me the first chapter of Philippians as words of comfort and encouragement. As I anxiously read that passage, one verse stood out. I read and reread it:

I know that through your prayers and the help given me by the Spirit of Jesus Christ, what has happened to me will turn out for my deliverance (Philippians 1:19 NIV).

I knew then that the Lord had not only directed me to Johanna, but was blessing Johanna and myself with other special people who were backing us in prayer while we waged the battle on the front lines.

Still, I remained very selective about revealing the hidden parts of my life to any but those few people I considered "safe." Johanna and Randolph, who by now had become a real sister and brother to me, were safe. Johanna's sister and brother-in-law were safe. After all, they went along with the territory. They had taken me into their hearts and home just like my brother and sister had done—believing me, accepting me, and loving me. In addition, there were a few special folks at Johanna's church—handpicked by the Lord, each one of them. So I knew they were safe!

I had drawn a line of demarcation around these "safe" people. I was certain that there was no need to include any more people in the sharing process. Surely no one else needed to know—until a man came into my life who said, "The world needs to know. Tell it to the world!"

The man was Ken Wooden. Johanna had met and interviewed Ken not many months earlier on a television program she was hosting with Hal Lindsey. Ken had done an outstanding job of revealing facts about sexual abuse and satanic ritual abuse on the program. During the month I spent with Johanna, we were often on the phone to Ken for advice about certain things that I was having difficulty dealing with about my past.

Ken decided to fly out to meet with us so that we could all sit down and communicate more effectively. I was already hesitant to talk to this man whom I had never met. Suddenly he was sitting in Johanna's living room, advising me to tell my story to the world.

This was a shock to end all shocks. I could hardly believe that I had dared to share my "behind-closed-doors" life with the handful of persons whom the Lord had set apart to minister to me. Now I was to share that life with the world? NO WAY! After all, I wasn't a fool.

It didn't take me long to find out that Ken Wooden knew what he was talking about. He is dedicated to destroying the myths and exposing the realities about criminal abuses—physical, sexual, and ritualistic—that exploit the children of our society. He is founder of The National Coalition for Children's Justice, and is the author of a booklet and video called "Child Lures—A Family Guide for Prevention of Youth Exploitation." As an investigative reporter, he helped produce segments on satanism for ABC's *20/20* news program and the injustices suffered by children in preschool molestation cases for CBS's *60 Minutes*. The Lord had sent the right man for the right time.

My problem was the threats my victimizers held over me. They still had me pretty much where they wanted me—quiet and behind closed doors. Sure, I had felt fairly safe in letting my secrets out to the select few who were ministering to me. After all, hadn't the Lord sent me to them and them to me? And only He knew how desperately I needed help. But I never intended for those secrets to go any further. I surely hadn't dreamed of telling the whole world, of going public, of writing a book.

Ken said, ever so calmly, "Your safety is in letting the world know what you've been through." I thought he was crazy. But he proceeded to explain his reasoning. "If you keep quiet, Lauren, they have you right where they want you—subservient, frightened, and confused." In the next sentence he carefully emphasized each word: "If you let them know that you're telling the world, they won't dare touch you!" Then he grinned like a cat that had just caught the mouse and remarked, "You know how they are, don't you? Those creeps are just like cockroaches. When the light's turned on, they run!"

As soon as Ken said that, I began to see how wrong I had been in keeping quiet, and how right he was in admonishing me to tell the world. Following his advice, Johanna, Hal Lindsey, Ken, and I went on a nationally televised Christian program just a few days later. Scared to death and barely able to find the breath to speak, *I told the world*.

When my portion of the interview was over, Hal Lindsey looked into the camera and sternly rebuked the creeps who had been harassing me: "By the way, satanists, if you think you're going to have a victory by killing her—if anything happens to her—we're onto you! There's enough information in different places that you'll never stamp out what she knows. So don't even try! The Lord Jesus Christ will see to it that you're nailed!"

I can't begin to express how I felt at that moment. Hal's warning cut straight through to the heart of the matter. No messing around. No skirting the issue. No treating it lightly. Hal said it. Hal meant it. And everyone knew it! For the first time in my life I felt protected. An incredibly heavy burden was lifted—a burden of secrecy, of hiding, of fear, and of aloneness.

From that moment on, most of the harassment stopped. I received fewer phone threats—threats to blackmail me using pornographic photos of me, and threats to physically silence me. There were no more threatening notes pinned to my front door when I opened it in the morning. Only one time, not many weeks later, did I find something when I opened the door. It was a dead pigeon with a long pin stuck through its heart. But after that act of ugliness I was left alone. Ken had proven himself right—it was better to tell the world than to remain hidden in the cloak of secrecy.

There will still be battles to fight and victories to win. But no victory will be as sweet as the hard-fought victory that freed me from the torment of the evil one!

❖ *12* ❖
Free at Last!

Throughout the years I've often been asked how I handle the past. My muscles would tighten, my heart would skip a beat, and my fists would clench. The bitterness that I had never been able to deal with would simply overwhelm me.

Then when I would respond, I would try to give an answer that sounded good—not what I really felt.

The first time I was forced to address that question after I found my freedom was at a women's retreat. I had been asked to give a short testimony of what the Lord had done in my life. I knew I would have to say something about the past, and I wasn't looking forward to it.

When the moment arrived and I was walking up to the podium, my mind was troubled about what I would say. "Will they see through the front I'll have to put on for them?" I wondered. "Will they hear the bitterness in my voice?" The thoughts were like tiny creatures playing tag with each other. By the time I reached the front of the room, I felt thoroughly frustrated and defeated. I lowered my head for several seconds and stared at the podium. The silence was deafening. Finally I knew I couldn't wait any longer. "Well, here goes," I thought. "I might as well get this over with."

As I looked up, an incredible thing happened. The most beautiful peace flooded my mind, as if the Lord was covering my thoughts of the past with a warm, cuddly blanket. I felt my eyes become moist, and within seconds, tears were flowing. I opened my mouth, but I couldn't say anything. So I stood, gazing at the women, and for the first time I noticed that tears were on their faces too.

In the next few seconds, the Lord spoke to my heart as clearly as if He had appeared in person and spoken audibly. "I have allowed the circumstances in your life *for a greater good, a higher purpose*," He said, "that My plan for your life might be fulfilled. I want to take that which was evil in your past and

167

turn it into something that can be used for good and My glory."

That overwhelmed me. I could only close my eyes and pray, "Lord, if You can use my past for good, then I wouldn't have to be bitter about it. My past would have a purpose. Lord, please do it!"

It was done. Right there! Instantly! When I opened my eyes, I began to smile. I felt new. I felt fresh. For the first time in my life I opened my mouth and began to speak about my past without bitterness. My past was going to be used by the Lord Jesus—not for evil, but for good. His good!

"Folks, I'm here to tell you that it doesn't matter what has happened in your past." What freedom! I had never been able to speak like this before. "It doesn't matter any longer, because Jesus has turned it into something that will bring glory to His name."

I spoke for three or four minutes. There was no front, no pretending, no bitterness—just an incredible peace in knowing that the evil didn't have to remain evil. Jesus had snatched that from Satan's hands to use for good.

When I finished, I returned to my seat and bowed my head. "Dear loving heavenly Father," I whispered, "thank You for the circumstances You have allowed in my life. May the strength and wisdom You've given to me in the very midst of those trials be used to bring hope to others. Amen."

I raised my head with a new purpose in life. Satan had meant to harm me. Yes, most assuredly so! He meant those unending years of darkness for evil. *But God had a different plan for my life. God had a better idea.* And I purposed in my heart that I would allow Him to fulfill that plan.

Not a Bed of Roses

Just because I have the assurance now that my past can be used for God's good doesn't mean that my life is a bed of roses. The first time I wrote these lines, I wanted everything—myself, others, circumstances, memories—to look wonderful. I wanted to paint a rosy picture of life after freedom. But life isn't just a bed of roses. I still find thorns along the way.

This was a dilemma. I wanted to show people the joyous difference that took place in my life after I allowed the Lord to deal with my past. I wanted people to hear the rejoicing of a soul set free. And yet I still experience the pain of remembering. I still have nightmares. Sure, they're less frequent, but they're there. And in sharing my testimony with others, I sometimes still go through a hell of sorts. I realize that as time passes, and I tell and retell my story, it will become easier. But for now, the reliving my past for others is still painful.

The question I faced was, "Should I make my life sound like it's a bed of roses, or should I show my pain? And if I show that I still feel pain from my past, even though it's so much less now, will people think that I haven't been healed and freed?"

About 18 months after I found my freedom with Johanna, I gave a small portion of my life story on a video documentary on sexual abuse and pornography. As the director interviewed me, I was especially careful not to reveal my real feelings about the role that pornography plays in sexual abuse and how it had affected me. All I wanted to show on camera was that the Lord can and does heal completely, and that I was an example of His healing and freeing powers.

When the filming was completed, I asked the director how he felt it had gone. Quite truthfully, I was very pleased with the manner in which I had conducted myself throughout the interview. But the director said, somewhat reluctantly, "You said all the right words, but I wish you could have let the audience feel what you're feeling. They need to know how sexual abuse and pornography have affected you—not only as a child, but you as an adult trying to cope with the past."

"But if I really let my feelings out, on a gut level, I'd be sure to cry," I protested. Even as I spoke, tears began to fill my eyes and trickle down my face. Quickly wiping them away, I whispered, "If I cry, the audience will know that I still hurt."

"Of course you still hurt!" the director said. "You're going through the healing process. It isn't that the Lord can't heal; it's just that healing takes time. It's not true that at the snap of a finger a lifetime of pain disappears. The truth is that the Lord has begun a miraculous work of healing in your life. But it's a day-to-day process."

As I rocked back and forth in my rocking chair, I began to see that the director was right—it was okay to show that I still hurt. In fact, it was the only honest thing to do. If I pretended that life was nothing but a bed of roses, then how would other victims feel who were still going through pain?

So, tired as I was, and as tired as the film crew was, we agreed to shoot the entire interview again. This time I opened up honestly. The tears flowed. The pain showed. But this time when the filming was finished, we all felt that the love and healing of Jesus Christ was more apparent through the honesty of pain and tears.

So now when someone asks, "Do you still cry?" or "Do you still hurt?" I answer without apology, "Yes, but I have the Lord Jesus Christ to share it with. As the days go by, He's taking me through the healing process and I'm getting better. You can count on it!"

I'm so thankful that I decided to show the reality of my newfound freedom. Rather than turning victims away, I find that they are relieved to know that it's a daily struggle.

Recently I received a letter from a young woman who had been ritualistically abused as a child. Her parents were satanists and had subjected her to untold horrors. It was even difficult for me to read page after page of the ways her parents had abused her, all in the name of Satan. I'll never become hardened to his tactics of evil and darkness.

This young woman, whom I'll call Anne, had been in therapy for well over a year. Both she and her therapist were Christians. They used the Scriptures and prayer in the therapy sessions. Anne was active in her church with volunteer work. She attended weekly prayer meetings. And yet there were times when Satan battled her in such fierce ways that she was tempted to give up.

The last paragraph of Anne's letter ended with this heart-rending cry: "What am I doing wrong, Lauren? The battle never ends. I can't go on any longer."

Anne's plight is not an isolated case. Her experiences as a survivor of Satan's underground are not unique. I hear the sounds of weariness, of frustration, of even wanting to call it quits in almost every letter I receive from victims. But there is good news!

Since receiving Anne's letter, I've corresponded with her and talked to her on the phone. As I shared some of the pain that I still feel—pain which I used to consider a curse and a sign that I wasn't healed—it became a blessing that God used to encourage her to press on. It helped her to know that her struggles were normal.

Anne is doing better now. She's going to make it, as are countless others who have felt the sting of the enemy but are now standing in the power of the Lord.

I've tried to be very honest about some of the problems I still face since I've been freed from the enemy's hold. No doubt there will be some lingering pain of memories that Satan won't allow to disappear out of your own life once you've entered into your newfound freedom. In fact, as I've shown from my own life, the battle may become quite intense for a period of time until Satan is convinced that you really mean business. However, I want to emphasize loud and clear that even though life isn't just a bed of roses, it isn't all thorns either. In fact, *the roses far outnumber the thorns*!

If I listed all the thorns of my past, they would seem endless, though I'm sure there must have been a few roses I missed along the way. The horrors were so all-consuming that I saw and felt nothing else. The thorns simply choked out any roses that may have tried to bloom.

Today, if I listed the thorns that are in my life, there would be some. But they're becoming less and less as I learn to stand firm in resisting the enemy. I know there will always be some thorns in my life as long as I'm on this earth. The exciting news I have to share is that the roses in my life are multiplying faster than I can count them. For that I praise Jesus. The roses are beautiful! They're brilliantly colored! And they're all God's creations!

Freedom . . . What a Difference!

What a difference! What a change! Night turned to day, tears turned to laughter, and I truly found God's gifts of life:

> BEAUTY for ashes,
> JOY instead of mourning,

PRAISE instead of heaviness
(from Isaiah 61:3).

God took the thorns of ashes, mourning, and heaviness and replaced them with roses of beauty, joy, and praise. Then He added other roses to my life. He blessed me with the rose of smiling, the rose of sparkling eyes, the rose of lighthearted-ness, and the rose of humor. I could go on and on. My rose garden is overflowing!

I think that the rose I enjoy most is the rose of laughter. A friend warmly exclaimed to me a few days ago, "I think you were born to laugh, Lauren. You do it better than anyone else I know."

Yes, I can laugh now. But I still cry, too. There are times when I still cry over the pain of the past. And I cry over the victims who are still trapped in Satan's underground and the little ones who continue to be abused and murdered as sacrifices to Satan. But now the tears and memories have a positive purpose. The tears are not shed for nothing. The memories are not recalled without hope. No longer am I suffering only for myself. That's the difference.

I now cry for others. I now remember for others. When a victim of Satan's underground calls me and asks for help, I can listen—not as one who is there too and wants to be helped as much as they. Instead, I can listen and talk and pray and cry and remember as one who can say, "My friend, I have an answer for you. I know it works because it worked for me." Then I can share with the person where I've been and what God has done for me. That's how God is taking the evil of my past and using it for good. It makes all the difference when I can say, *"I know. I've been there too."*

My tears and my remembering are no longer weights around my neck. They're tools of hope to other victims of Satan's underground who need to hear it from one who has been there. Jesus Christ did not free me to live unto myself; He freed me to live for Him. He freed me to be living proof of the hope that can be found in the darkest situation. And I can help ever so much better now because I'm honest with victims. I let them see and hear and feel my pain. If I had nothing with which they could identify, they would write me off in an instant. I remember for them so that God can use it for their healing.

And so I laugh. I sleep without endless nightmares. I walk the streets without fearing what or who is around the corner. I can answer my front door without a paralyzing fear coming over me. I don't have to be so terrified of my friends finding out about my past. I am a little worried about that, but as a dear friend told me over dinner one evening, "Your real friends will stick with you no matter what they find out about your past." Another friend put it this way, "I'm with you for the duration, luv."

Best of all, I can come to Jesus, not with the bitterness and anger I used to have but in peace, in love, and in joy, knowing that He has accepted me just as I am. That is freedom, freedom to be the real person I am in Jesus without feeling as if I were a puppet in the hands of the enemy—wanting to go one direction but feeling pulled in the opposite direction. I have been freed from the power of Satan to the greater power of Jesus Christ. There is no freedom so complete as the freedom I've found in Him!

What Now?

I can't fully answer the question "What now?" It's probably best that I can't foresee all that is in the future. I do know that from the moment I said "Yes" to the Lord about sharing the other side of my life, I haven't been able to keep up with all that He's been doing for me. Every morning when I awaken I say, "Well, Lord, what do You have in store for today?" I feel as if my head is spinning as I try to see all His good works.

My physical condition is an absolute miracle. If anyone had told me that from the time I said "Yes" to the Lord until now I would not have to be hospitalized, neither I nor my doctor would have believed him. I would either have laughed at him or become angry at him for making such a cruel joke.

Within an eight-year period I had been admitted to the hospital over 40 times. From the very day I obeyed the Lord and went public with the truths I had been hiding I have not occupied one hospital bed. This is a miracle that only God can perform!

I must also give credit to my doctors who worked so faithfully to get me through several life-threatening episodes and enabled me to live as normal a life as possible. Yes, the pain is still there, often haunting me day and night. But I'm a functioning human being now. I know that the Lord is enabling me from day to day to be faithful to that which He has called me. He will not call His children to do business for Him without furnishing them with the abilities necessary to carry out that business. Believe me, the Lord Jesus has performed many miracles in my life to prepare me for the business to which He has called me.

It is very tempting, in the dark of night when all is still and I feel like a frightened, lone watchman standing on the mountaintop, to want to shut the door to God's calling. However, in that same stillness my thoughts always go back to Rhonda and Cicely and Marsha and the young teenage girl who wouldn't tell us her name, and I know there is no turning back. It is for thousands of children like them that I press on.

I know the road ahead will be rough, but not the "rough" of previous years. My prayer is, "Lord, may I remain willing for You to use the 'rough' of my yesteryears and the 'rough' of my future in telling about it in order to bring hope to others." In myself I am nothing. I'm a sinner saved only by God's grace. Not by my works, which are few. Not by my strength, which is weak. Not by my goodness, which doesn't exist. Only by His grace, His strength, His goodness, and His mercy am I strong!

The best way to express how I feel is to repeat the words of the apostle Paul when he wrote, "I am glad to boast about how weak I am; I am glad to be a living demonstration of Christ's power, instead of showing off my own power and abilities (2 Corinthians 12:9 TLB).

So it's all right that I feel inadequate, that I feel incapable, that I feel weak and powerless, for my strength is in Christ. As long as I rely on His power, He will enable me to do what He has called me to do.

When I was agonizing over the decision to write *Satan's Underground*, Johanna offered me the following words of encouragement: "Sister, the Lord has chosen you to help bring light to those who have been in darkness, freedom to those who have been in bondage, and peace to those who have never known that it existed for them." My daily prayer is that nothing will deter me from that calling.

I have found that in ministering the peace that my sister was talking about, God has not only used the hurts and pains of my situation to help victims of Satan's underground, but He has graciously used it to bring a message of hope to persons who feel trapped in any kind of hopeless situation. God is using the particulars of my own personal hell to say to all people that there is hope in the darkness of anyone's hell, no matter what that hell is.

There is one thing that has troubled me when sharing the story of my life. That's when those who hear it and are in a painful situation of their own compare their pain with mine and conclude that they should be handling their own pain better. "After all," I've heard so many hurting people confide, "you went through so much more than I did. I shouldn't be hurting so badly. I should be handling my situation better."

Not true! Your pain is your pain. Your hurt is your hurt. Your darkness is your darkness. Your feelings of aloneness, of helplessness, of hopelessness are just as real as mine were. They are just as devastating to you as mine were to me.

Impossible Situations

I say to women who are being battered by their husbands, I say to people who are living with an alcoholic spouse or parent, I say to those who are living with a drug addict, I say to parents who have a son or daughter who has just let out his or her secret that he or she is homosexual or lesbian, I say to teenagers who know that their mother or father is having an illicit relationship or are getting a divorce—I say to all of you, whatever your pain, THERE IS HOPE!

I say to the batterer, the alcoholic, the drug addict, the homosexual or lesbian, the person who is living in immorality, the girl or woman who is considering abortion or has had an abortion, I say to all who are hurting because of an undesired lifestyle—THERE IS HOPE!

And I say to persons who are living in the pain and hope-lessness of attitudes that keep them defeated, whether it be bitterness over past hurts or dwelling on past successes that keep you discontented with present mediocrity or failures, I say to persons who are struggling with anger, hate, or jeal-ousy that makes daily life a misery, I say to all of you in the midst of painful attitudes—THERE IS HOPE!

How blessed I was when Danielle, a friend of a friend of mine, called a few days ago. Danielle is a battered wife who had just confided to my friend that she was thinking about suicide as the only way out of her nightmare. "I called you because my friend told me about you and said that you knew what it was like to live in an impossible situation," she said in a broken voice, obviously trying to hide her crying. "I can't take any more. I've prayed for so long that there's nothing left to pray. And nothing has changed."

Then in such a hushed voice that I could barely hear her, Danielle let out the thought that most of us who have been in impossible situations have thought at one time or another: "I just want to end it all."

A silent prayer rushed through my mind: "Thank You, Father, that I am at last free so I can share my story of hope with Danielle."

After relating a little of my story and how God freed me, I said, "Danielle, there are three things I can promise you. I want you to write them down. Number one is that Jesus is with you. You're not alone. Number two is that Jesus will be everything you need Him to be to you in the very midst of your pain. And number three is that God will bring you out in His time."

"How can you be so sure, Lauren?" I could hear the plea in her voice. She wanted an answer that would satisfy her.

Praise God that because of the past which God mercifully and miraculously brought me through I could add the words that always made a difference: "Danielle, I know it's true. I can be sure because I've been where you are—in pain, in misery, alone, and feeling helpless and hopeless. And God did those three things for me."

Danielle ended up going to a shelter for battered women in her town, and is now on her way to new freedom in Jesus

Christ. And I am sitting here at my desk feeling overwhelmed at the goodness of a God who would take a story like mine and use it to help others who are hurting.

Most of us have hurt badly in one way or another. Many are still hurting. I think we can all find healing in the words of this song:

Wounded Soldier

I am a wounded soldier,
　　but I will not leave the fight,
Because the Great Physician
　　is healing me.
So I'm standing in the battle
　　in the armor of the light,
Because His mighty power
　　is real in me.
I am loved, I am accepted
　　by the Savior of my soul.
I am loved, I am accepted
　　and my wounds will be
　　made whole.*

A Letter to Victims

Dear Victim,

Since I first began thinking about what I would include in this book, I knew I wanted to write a personal letter just to you. If it weren't for you—the thousands of you who are out there alone, hurting, and desperately looking for a way out—I wouldn't be writing this book.

Of course, it is also my desire to inform the general public about what is going on. And I know that for myself, in writing about the hurts of my past, there has been a therapeutic healing, a sort of cleansing of mind, heart, and soul. But you have been foremost in my mind as I have struggled to lay bare my soul, revealing all those secret pains I never thought I would share with anyone.

My main concern is you, the wounded one. *Your freedom is the cry of my heart.* If through this book some victims of Satan's underground find their way to freedom through Jesus Christ, then all the pain and struggles I went through in "telling it like it is" will have been worth it.

I can say this in all sincerity, my dear ones, for I well remember how I longed for just one person with whom I could identify—just one person who would not only *believe* what I was going through but, just as importantly, one person who would *understand* what I was going through.

Then I think of you who are longing to identify with someone who knows and understands the hell you're living in. The old Indian proverb says it well: "Don't criticize me until you've walked a mile in my moccasins." Friend, I've walked in your shoes. I've lived through your hell. I can honestly look at you straight in the eye and say, "I know what you're going through, and I know what you're feeling."

Sharing my life scared me to death! Not only were there certain parts of my past that I did not want to reveal, but I knew that if I was obedient to the Lord in revealing them, I would also have to relive them step by step, detail by detail, horror by horror.

I procrastinated. I made up reasons why I shouldn't have to do it. I begged God to let me off the hook. I rebelled when He didn't. I felt sorry for myself. Finally, when I was still enough to listen, God spoke to my heart and said, "That's enough, Lauren! Let's get on with it."

Finally I surrendered my will, as stubborn as it had been, to the will of my Master and Lord, Jesus Christ. It didn't come easy. It was like pulling teeth that weren't ready to be pulled. But the surrender to His will was an absolute must, for He and I both knew that only through the process of sharing would I ever be able to reach you, the victimized and walking wounded of Satan's underground. And so I've shared my life with you.

In hopes that your freedom will be more easily gained than mine, know that there are those who will believe you. I know that many of the horrors you've gone through are unbelievable. I know the things you've done, and whether you were forced to do them or you chose to do them, *I do not judge you!* There are others out there who will also believe you and accept you *just the way you are.*

So if you are searching for a way out of the hell you've been living in, pray to Jesus—just talk to Him; He'll hear you—and ask Him to lead you to someone who will minister the hope and freedom of Jesus Christ to you. It is terribly important that you have someone to whom you can talk, someone to whom you can unburden the agonies of your heart, someone who will encourage you and stand by you as you go through the healing process.

I beg you, dear victim, don't give up. I know your struggle and agony. But as you read in the chapter before this, freedom is more than worth the struggle. And with someone by your side who will encourage you and love you and pray for you, you can make it! And if the Lord doesn't readily give you someone, He still will sustain you. He will be your all and all until that time He leads you to someone.

I'd also like to talk a little bit about how to deal with the guilt you're feeling. Even though I was a victim, I felt such crushing guilt that it nearly killed me. I felt condemned by thoughts like "I should have fought back harder," "I should have tried to run away more often," "When I got older, why did I still go with them?" and "Why did I allow it even as a young adult?" I couldn't even begin to understand it all, much less give acceptable answers. And the same questions I was asking of myself were being asked by others, which made me feel doubly guilty.

The fact is that my way of life was all I had known since day one. I didn't know any other responses. It's difficult, even now, for me to understand how brainwashing works, and how repeated ritualistic abuse affects people in such a way that they allow things they don't want. Even after I found my freedom, these issues were driving me crazy. And they will do the same to you if you let them.

I found the answer. It deals with all these issues, so that finally, at long last, I have found total peace from guilt. It's simply called "Asking for forgiveness."

I can hear you crying, "Me? Ask for forgiveness? After all those creeps did to me? Never!"

I smile, but only because I responded the same way. Not once, but time and time again. I literally cringed at the thought of me asking for forgiveness. It was totally absurd. "Why in the world should *I* ask for forgiveness when it was *they* who need to be forgiven?" I argued. "*I'm* not in the wrong. *They* are!"

It really rubbed me the wrong way (and that's putting it mildly!) when a pastor whom I deeply respected and loved suggested that I ask for forgiveness for the things in my past. Did I ever bristle! I was offended to the core of my being, or perhaps I should say "to the core of my self-righteousness."

I vehemently argued that I didn't need to ask for forgiveness. "I haven't done anything wrong!" I declared. "They were the ones at fault. I'm not going to repent for what they did." Then I used my well-worn sentence: "I'm the victim, not the criminal!" I left his office feeling quite misunderstood and unjustly condemned.

Even now, I feel that I was certainly misunderstood and condemned. However, the feeling of guilt and the questions like "Why didn't I fight harder?" and even "Why didn't I just kill myself?" raced for first place in my mind.

Then one day, not long ago, I fell prostrate on the living room floor and wept, agonizing with the thought of asking the Lord to forgive me of the past. Finally I gave in. I just had to find peace of mind and heart. I could no longer listen to the questions that made me feel guilty.

"Oh dear Jesus," I cried out, "I don't care who's to blame. It doesn't matter anymore. I don't want to hide behind the word 'victim' any longer." Even as I said that one sentence, I began to feel a burden lift from my heart.

Crying out from the deepest part of my soul, I asked the Lord to forgive. "Lord, for everyone who has abused me, I forgive them. And especially for everything I have done that has been sinful and displeasing in Your sight, please forgive me."

Finally I asked the Lord to forgive me of things I had only blamed on everyone else. My dear friends, I cannot begin to describe the incredible peace that flooded my soul. For the first time in my life I felt that there was nothing that anyone could hold against me.

I couldn't blame others any longer, for they were forgiven. And best of all, no one could blame me. I didn't have to feel guilty, for I had been forgiven.

This is the final thing I would like to share with you—you who are victims of Satan's underground. I share it in love. Don't hide behind the word "victim" like I did for so long. I realize only too well that anyone who becomes trapped in the hands of Satan soon becomes his victim. But don't allow your victimization to stand in the way of receiving the total freedom, healing, and peace that the Lord wants to give you.

I was stubborn. I held out for my rights as a victim. But it was only to my detriment. It doesn't matter how much of a victim I was, and it doesn't matter how much of a victim you are; we all stand in need of God's forgiveness. And God is most willing to give us His forgiveness.

Friend, if you want real peace from the past—free from the haunts, free from the guilt, free from the burdens—then forgive those who have done wrong unto you, and ask the

Lord to forgive the wrongs that you have done. Your past will be covered by the shed blood of Jesus Christ, and the Lord Jesus will never hold you accountable for it. *That is real peace.*

Before I close my letter, please let me say again that there are people who want to help you, who genuinely care about you, who will believe you and who will accept you *just the way you are.*

Remember that there is nothing you've done, voluntarily or involuntarily, that Jesus Christ can't or won't forgive. There is no sin so great, no guilt so heavy, that Jesus can't take care of it. There is hope for you through the love, forgiveness, and healing of Jesus Christ. In Him lies your freedom and peace.

I'm earnestly praying for you that you will accept that freedom and peace through Jesus Christ.

I love you!

Lauren

❖ 14 ❖
The Divine Prescription

Who are the victims of Satan's underground? If that question was asked of you, how would you answer? Perhaps those children forced to pose for pornographic publications and films. Or people suffering the physical and emotional damage of sexual abuse and perversion. Or the unwilling participants in satanic rituals.

Most assuredly, you are right. We who have been subjected to such horrendous abuses are without a doubt the victims of Satan's underground.

There are, however, vast groups of victims who are not so blatantly obvious, people who have been and are now being deceived. Because the numbers in these groups are increasing at an alarming rate, and because the deception is so cunning that it is often barely detectable, each of you is at risk! Your physical, emotional, and spiritual well-being are at stake. In some cases, your very life may be at risk!

Perhaps you think I am exaggerating. Please bear with me for a few moments. You may be surprised to discover that you really are a victim.

Are you a TEENAGER . . .
who has become spellbound by games like "Dungeons and Dragons" where evil is a dominant theme? Do you wear satanic-oriented jewelry like the pentagram because it's the "in thing" to wear? Do you flash the sign of Satan with your index and little fingers because all your friends do it? Do you listen to heavy-metal music that condones and even encourages suicide, the torture and murder of babies, and Satan worship because that kind of music is "where it's at"? WATCH OUT . . . YOU ARE BEING DECEIVED!

Are you a COLLEGE STUDENT . . .
who is interested in learning about and experiencing deeper insights into life? Are you searching to find out what and who

you really are through involvement with activities like ESP, meditation, astral projection, and guided imagery? Are you trying out each of the so-called "religious" movements to increase your awareness? Have you opened your mind to spirit guides who will hopefully point you in the right direction? WATCH OUT . . . YOU ARE BEING DECEIVED!

Are you a HOUSEWIFE . . .

who has become bored with the housework-and-children routine? At a friend's invitation, did you decide to attend what sounded like a fun gathering of other women just like yourself? Did the gathering start out with an "innocent" introduction to the Ouija board? Did you find that no other game could come close to matching the unexplainably spell-binding powers you saw in the Ouija board? Were you then introduced to the art of reading tarot cards (again, seemingly innocent)? Were the powers of the pyramid, of crystals, and of colors explained as ways of enhancing your up-till-now dull, humdrum life as a housewife? Were you fascinated and eager to learn more? WATCH OUT . . . YOU ARE BEING DECEIVED!

Are you an ADULT MALE . . .

who has tried the traditional church and has seen only wimpy weakness—more death than life? Did you hear that there were other gatherings where "real" power was there for the asking? In your search for evidence of supernatural power, did you find yourself attending ritualistic-like ceremonies where "other gods" were called upon or where Satan was represented as merely "another god" whose power could give you the good things in life you so desire to attain? Have you seen that power? (And you will, for it is real!) WATCH OUT . . . YOU ARE BEING DECEIVED!

Are you a PROFESSIONAL PERSON . . .

who wants to gain an edge over your peers in climbing the corporate ladder? Do you want to gain that competitive edge in the world's marketplace? Have you succumbed to convincing slogans for seminars or motivational tapes such as "Discover

Your Own Potential," "Discover Your Own Divine Self," "Be Your Highest Self," or "How to Master the Impossible"? Have you joined metaphysical groups, dabbled in the occult, or enrolled in human-potential or possibility-thinking classes? WATCH OUT . . . YOU ARE BEING DECEIVED!

Are you ANYONE . . .

who has found yourself intrigued with "New Age" teachings like "I am God" or "I am a god" or "I can create my own reality"? Are you intrigued with the New Age phenomena of out-of-body experiences, UFO's and space traveling, and the transmigration of souls? Are you tempted to seek spiritual counsel from channelers, astral guides, or other extraterrestrial guides? Are you reading materials that are asking you to make a complete surrender and trust of your mind—but you're not sure to whom or to what? WATCH OUT . . . YOU ARE BEING DECEIVED!

Did you find yourself included in one of the preceding groups of victims—those who have been and are being deceived by the evil one?

Sadly, many of you will have to answer in the affirmative. And by far the overwhelming majority of you never thought of yourselves as victims. You were only following a fad when you flashed the sign of Satan. You were merely trying to broaden your horizons when you opened your mind to guided imagery and visualization techniques. You were just getting out of the house to have fun when you joined your friends to play the Ouija board. You were earnestly looking for a religion that had power when you attended groups that called on "other gods." You were only improving your professional skills when you enrolled in that high-powered, self-improvement seminar.

Of course you didn't think of yourself as a victim. That's where the deception begins. In each of these areas, you are being *directed toward* the power of self, the power of nature, the power of another god or other gods, or the power of Satan, and you are being *pulled away from* the power of God. *You are becoming a victim of Satan's deceptions.*

Satan has no conscience. Scripture describes Satan as the father of lies. His sole purpose is to control you. He will do whatever it takes to control you. Satan does not mind *how* he takes control; he only cares that he *does* take control. It is wise to remember that "your adversary the devil walks about like a roaring lion, seeking whom he may devour" (1 Peter 5:8).

One of Satan's main deceptions is making the worship of anything or anyone else besides Jesus Christ appear harmless. In reality, the worship of anything or anyone other than Jesus Christ is ultimately the worship of Satan. The bottom line is: "You shall have no other gods before me" (Exodus 20:3).

This book has attempted to portray Satan in his true character—*evil*. But many are falling prey to his image of deception—an *angel of light*.

Scripture states that Satan can and does appear as an angel of light. Satan is a master at making the worship of himself appear to be right and good, truthful and honest. His list of deceptions is endless. It is no wonder that thousands of well-intentioned people are being caught up unawares in the greatest master-deception of all.

Are you feeling trapped? Do you feel yourself drawn toward unseen forces you can't identify? Have you tried to get out, but can't? I know the feeling. It can get pretty scary, and for some of you it can totally consume you with guilt, because you feel that you should have known better.

Are you saying to yourself, "What do I do now? If it's really true that I've been deceived, that I've fallen prey to the deceptions of Satan, what am I to do?"

Don't make the mistake of allowing yourself to feel like a fool for falling for Satan's tricks. And don't fall into another all-too-common trap that Satan sets—making his victims feel that they are the guilty party, that they are to blame, and that they will always be pushovers for his deceptions. If you fall for that lie—and it is a lie—Satan will keep you right where he wants you: under his thumb.

You are not a pushover, a softie, or a sucker. You are a *victim* of Satan. He does not play by the rules. He plays dirty. He stacks the deck. So if you willingly or unwillingly play his game, you cannot win—ever!

Satan is the great imposter, the great masquerader, the grand deceiver. If the "real" Satan were asked to stand up, you would have a hard time believing it was he. He would be the wolf in sheep's clothing.

Satan is the one who marked you to be a victim of his underground. Satan is the one who ever so patiently and cunningly stalked you. Then, when the time was right, he sprang the trap and you became a victim of the greatest "con man" who has ever lived or ever will live.

The good news is that there is hope for you, no matter why or how you became a victim! The good news is that whether you're presently involved in any of the areas I've shared, or whether you've managed to separate yourself from actual involvement but are still tortured by memories that haunt you night and day, there is complete deliverance and healing available for you!

Your only answer, your only hope, your only real freedom is in Jesus Christ. I've shared with you how I found Him to be my answer. Now I long to share with you in a simple and practical way how you can find Him to be *your* answer.

Remember, Satan will try his best to deceive you into thinking that: 1) you're into this too deeply to be saved; 2) it won't work; or 3) it's too hard. None of the preceding are true. Your freedom is yours for the asking—period! Satan is a poor loser, and he will try to fill your mind with all kinds of lies to keep you from receiving your freedom. When you begin to hear his lies, recognize them as just that—lies! Don't allow him to keep you from receiving the freedom that God has so lovingly provided for you.

* * *

First of all, let me assure you that you don't need anyone else's help to become a child of God. This is a decision between you and God and no one else. It is true that if you've been a victim of Satan's underground over a period of time, or you've been heavily involved in occultic or satanic activities, or you've been a long-term victim of any type of evil abuse, you may find that once you have accepted Jesus Christ as Lord and Savior, you may need others, just as I did, to do spiritual battle with you. But please know that you need only two people to become a child of God—you and Jesus.

Second, you don't need to be in any special place when you ask Jesus Christ to come into your life. Where are you reading this right now? Wherever you are is fine. The Lord Jesus hears the cry of a hurting heart no matter where that cry is coming from.

Last of all, you must know that there is nothing you've done, whether voluntarily or involuntarily—and just as importantly, there is nothing that has been done to you—that has made you too bad, too dirty, too shameful, or too guilty to be accepted by Jesus. He is a loving Savior. He didn't come to earth to die on a cross for perfect people. He died for people like you and me whose lives have been torn apart and need the saving and healing touch of a loving God.

Let me share one verse with you that has helped me and countless other victims know beyond a doubt that they have a right to come to Jesus just as they are.

> God says He will accept and acquit us—declare us "not guilty"—if we trust Jesus Christ to take away our sins. And we all can be saved in this same way, by coming to Christ, no matter who we are or what we have been like. Yes, all have sinned; all fall short of God's glorious ideal; yet now God declares us "not guilty" of offending him if we trust in Jesus Christ, who in his kindness freely takes away our sins (Romans 3:22-24 TLB).

NOT GUILTY! Those words will lift that unbearable load of guilt from your heart. They are words of hope and freedom. *Jesus Christ will pronounce you "not guilty" no matter who you are or what you have done!*

Many of you are carrying a false sense of guilt and shame. By this I mean that some of you, like myself, have been forced involuntarily into certain activities. I was a victim, and yet I felt as guilty as my victimizers were. That was just what Satan wanted. I was needlessly carrying around that horrible load of guilt and shame, and it was ever so real. I needed that unbearable weight lifted from me. Whether I deserved it or not didn't matter. It was there!

The only condition that Jesus gives to us in order to be free of guilt is that we accept Him into our lives.

I can't write anything more important than to let you know that this salvation is yours just for the asking. It is yours just for the receiving. And it is yours just as you are!

How freeing that truth was when I finally realized it! I no longer had to go begging to the altar every Sunday. I no longer had to try to pray hard enough, hoping that it would ease my pain. Jesus Christ had done it all for me.

Jesus Christ said, "The one who comes to me I will by no means cast out" (John 6:37). That's it! Period! He loves you. He died for you. He's done all He can for you. Now He's waiting for you to come to Him. And when you do come to Him, He has promised that He will not turn you away.

There is no magic, no trickery, no mysticism, no witchcraft involved in coming to Jesus. There are no occultic powers, no satanic powers, no spells, no chants, no mantras, no visualization techniques, no guided imagery processes. Above all, *there is no self-power involved*. The only power needed is the power that comes from Jesus Christ, the one and only true power.

We mentioned the weights that burden our hearts and minds—the guilt and shame, the pain and heartache, and the ugliness of sin. Jesus will cleanse you from all of these things as you confess them to Him. His Word promises, "If we confess our sins, He is faithful and just to forgive us our sins and to cleanse us from all unrighteousness" (1 John 1:9).

Confession opens up your heart to a cleansing. It's like cleaning house, not only of your sins, but also of your memories of horror and abuse. Jesus not only wants to forgive and cleanse you of your sins, but He wants to heal those memories that have haunted and tormented you for so long. He wants to take all that is bad and replace it with all that is good.

Remember, the price for your salvation has already been paid. All that is left for you to do is to receive it. The most costly and precious gift you could ever have, the gift of eternal life through Jesus Christ, is yours if you will but receive it.

Will you come to Jesus now, just as you are? All you need to do is talk to Him. Tell Him how you feel. Ask Him to come into your life and be your Lord and Savior. He'll do the rest! If you want to, you can take time out right now to talk to Him. He's listening.

If you try to pray, and you feel something resisting you, find someone who can pray with you. You can be sure that Satan doesn't want you to talk to Jesus. He may be opposing your effort to pray, making you feel like it's useless to even try. Someone else praying with you can be a big help.

Did you do it? Did you ask Jesus to come into your life? If so, you have become a child of God, and you will never be anything less than His child! Your salvation is secured—past, present, and future!

Now that you have Jesus Christ living within you, you have all the power you need to overcome Satan. You need no other power. You need no other god. You need no other spirit. Jesus Christ is your all in all. He is your everything! Colossians 2:10 says that "you have *everything* when you have Christ" (TLB). YOU ARE COMPLETE IN HIM!

As a child of God, it is important to stay away from former practices. Satan may tempt you to go back to your old ways. The temptation doesn't mean you're doing something wrong; it simply means that Satan doesn't like losing you.

You may find it necessary to renounce your former practices. The Word talks about this: "We have renounced secret and shameful ways" (2 Corinthians 4:2 NIV). To renounce means to give up, to abandon. It won't do much good to confess your secret and shameful ways if you keep on dabbling in them.

Johanna Michaelsen talks about renouncing in her revealing book *The Beautiful Side of Evil.*

> For example, believers with occultic backgrounds which have never been renounced are manifesting medium-istic gifts which go undiscerned. . . . Some of these believers are often still involved in such things as astrol-ogy and palm reading, and usually completely unaware

of the spiritual dangers involved. Somewhere, down the line, sooner or later, they will experience an emptiness in their walk with God—a strange reluctance to read and trust His Word. A black, lingering depression settles over them, plaguing them with doubts about God and their salvation.[1]

You need to reject all secret and shameful practices and activities. Stop reading occultic, witchcraft-related, or satanic literature. Cease chanting special mantras that have been given to you. End all contact with spirit guides. Do not play any more with the Ouija board and tarot cards. No longer place your faith in special colors, pyramid powers, etc. There must be a 100 percent separation from "other-power" connections. It is critical to your continued freedom that you have no contact with any power that does not come from Jesus Christ and Jesus Christ alone.

There is an excellent passage in the book of Acts that tells how the Ephesian Christians, after being moved by God's message of truth, dealt with their evil practices and occultic objects: "Many of the believers who had been practicing black magic confessed their deeds and brought their incantation books and charms and burned them at a public bonfire" (Acts 19:18,19 TLB). We too are to clean our houses, ceasing to practice occultic deeds and doing away with all occultic objects.

Our Divine Armor

Once you have made Christ the Lord and Master of your life, it does not mean that Satan will put his proverbial tail between his legs and take flight. Satan is a sly old fox. He will most likely hang around to see if you really mean business. He will take his punches and jabs just to see how strong you are in your new life.

There are no instructions more vital to your continued freedom and victory than the words found in Ephesians 6:10-17. These verses identify the divine armor of God. Every piece of armor is absolutely essential for your protection and victory. There is one catch—it does not magically jump in place by saying "abracadabra."

> Put on all of God's armor so that you will be able to stand safe against all strategies and tricks of Satan (Ephesians 6:11 TLB).

You must put it on. *You* must take the initiative. No piece of armor, no matter how divinely crafted, will do you one ounce of good if it's left at home while you've gone into the front lines to do battle.

Each piece is listed in this passage. Become familiar with each one. They are your friends. Without them you stand naked and unprotected before Satan.

Verse 14: Having your loins girded with TRUTH . . .
What truth?
That the Lord your God loves you with an everlasting love.
That He will not leave you or forsake you.
That He is victorious over all the schemes of the devil.

Verse 14: Putting on the BREASTPLATE OF RIGHTEOUSNESS . . .
What righteousness?
That you are clothed with the righteousness of God.
That you stand before Him a child of God—spotless, blameless, and pure in His sight.

Verse 15: Having your feet shod with the GOSPEL OF PEACE . . .
What peace?
That God is not angry with you.
That He wants to replace the memories of your horrors with His ever-abiding love.

Verse 16: Taking up the SHIELD OF FAITH . . .
What faith?

With which you will be able to extinguish
the flaming arrows of Satan.

With which you will be able to guard yourself from every trick of Satan to try to
deceive you.

That enables you to say "Jesus Christ has
triumphed over the evil one. In His victory I
stand victor!"

Verse 17: Taking the HELMET OF SALVATION . . .
What salvation?

That same salvation which says you were
freed from sin and death.

That same salvation which rescued you
from the prey of the evil one.

Verse 17: Taking the SWORD OF THE SPIRIT . . .
What Sword of the Spirit?

The Word of God, which you can use to
come against the lies of Satan.

The Word of God, which gives direction
and purpose to your life.

This is your "Designed by God" armor. *Wear it daily.* If you
do, no matter how fierce the battle becomes, you will remain
standing strong. That is a promise!

In addition to reading Ephesians 6:10-17 and mentally putting on each piece of armor, daily prayer is a must. Verse 18
says, PRAYING ALWAYS . . .

That prayer which should be your daily communication
with the heavenly Father.

That prayer which enables you to unburden yourself
of even the most secret and hidden hurts in your life.

That prayer which keeps you strong in the midst of
spiritual battles.

We are all in a spiritual war—not just the victims of Satan's
underground, but every child of God. Armor protects us from
the enemy. Prayer assaults the enemy.

The following prayer is not magic. The words in themselves have no special powers. In fact, you may use whatever

words are most comfortable to you, for prayer should be an honest expression of your heart. As you pray to the heavenly Father, He will see your intent, attitude, and commitment.

> Almighty God,
> I come to You in the name of Your Son, Jesus Christ.
> I ask that You remove anything in my life that is displeasing to You.
> I bind the strongholds of Satan, and I shatter any plans that Satan has formed against me.
> I give You my mind and ask You to fill it with power, with love, and with soundness.
> I give You my will and ask You to make it obedient to You.
> I give You my body and ask You to clean out any residue of evil that remains.
> Above all, Father, I give You my life, my whole being.
> May Jesus Christ be Savior, Lord, and Master, as I worship and serve only You, now and forever.
> Amen.

* * *

I'd like to give you a prescription. I call it my packet of prescription verses—Scripture passages that I personally use whenever I'm in need.

These are verses that have been helpful to me, not only in the heat of the battle, but also in my everyday life. Daily skirmishes are sure to follow the victory of the big battles.

The person who has just gained freedom must not be alarmed when he or she experiences continued attacks of the enemy. You can be assured that this is the norm, not the exception. As you continue in your walk with Jesus, you are just as susceptible to attacks from the enemy as you were when you were a newborn child in Christ. The good news is that your spiritual armor will never wear out. It will be your sure protection for the rest of your life.

REMEMBER: This is not panic time; this is assurance time!

Prescription Verses

If you're doubting your salvation:

"God says He will accept and acquit us—declare us 'not guilty'—if we trust Jesus Christ to take away our sins" (Romans 3:22-24 TLB). You are NOT GUILTY! "He guarantees right up to the end that you will be counted free from all sin and guilt on that day when He returns" (1 Corinthians 1:8 TLB). Your salvation is assured—FOREVER!

"I give them eternal life, and they shall never perish; no one can snatch them out of my hand" (John 10:28 NIV). Jesus' power to protect your salvation is greater than all the combined forces of earth and hell!

"There is therefore now no condemnation to those who are in Christ Jesus" (Romans 8:1). Satan's accusations are a lie!

Is Satan bugging you?
"Resist the devil and he will flee from you" (James 4:7).

"Do not give the devil a foothold" (Ephesians 4:27 NIV). Stand up to him. Give him no room, no place, no ground. Crowd him out!

"He who is in you is greater than he who is in the world" (1 John 4:4). Satan can be no bigger in your life than you allow him to be!

"If God is for us, who can be against us?" (Romans 8:31). Your victory is assured!

"The Lord is faithful; he will make you strong and guard you from satanic attacks of every kind (2 Thessalonians 3:3 TLB). You are safe in Jesus!

Do you still feel subject to Satan's power?
"The reason the Son of God appeared was to destroy the devil's works" (1 John 3:8 NIV).

"He has rescued us from the dominion of darkness and brought us into the kingdom of the Son he loves" (Colossians 1:13 NIV).

"Having disarmed the powers and authorities, he made a public spectacle of them, triumphing over them by the cross" (Colossians 2:15 NIV). Satan's power and authority were taken away at the cross. His works were destroyed. He is a defeated foe in your life!

Do you doubt any of God's promises to you?
"He carries out and fulfills all of God's promises, no matter how many of them there are" (2 Corinthians 1:20 TLB).

"Heaven and earth will disappear, but my words remain forever" (Matthew 24:35 TLB). Believe them, claim them, and prove them.

I'm not doing so well. What do I do now?
"It is for freedom that Christ has set us free. Stand firm, then, and do not let yourselves be burdened again by a yoke of slavery" (Galatians 5:1 NIV).

"Forget the former things; do not dwell on the past. See, I am doing a new thing!" (Isaiah 43:18,19 NIV). Stand firm in your God-given freedom. Don't look back. Don't dwell on those things which were. Let your new life in Jesus Christ consume you!

Finally, there is one verse that I quote every time the evil one shows his ugly face. I've found it to be one of my strongest pieces of artillery against the wiles of the devil. It's John 14:30 (AMP) and it makes four distinct declarations of truth about Satan:
1. He has no claim on me.
2. He has nothing in common with me.
3. There is nothing in me that belongs to him.
4. He has no power over me.

The more you repeat these truths, the stronger you will feel in Jesus Christ. Some people eat an apple a day to keep the doctor away, but I state these truths every day to keep Satan away. It works! And it will work for you, too.

Take courage and rejoice! You have all of God's power to overcome the enemy. You need no longer fear him. He is defeated!

❖ 15 ❖
The Big Picture

CHICAGO, Illinois: "The arrest last week of a 14-year-old Du Page County youth who allegedly threatened to kill two younger boys as a sacrifice to the devil is the latest evidence of what some authorities believe is a growing incidence of Satan worship by young people in the Chicago area.

". . . a Westmont junior high student was accused by police of confronting two younger boys in a field, leading them to where he had dug a shallow grave and threatening to kill them with knives and sticks 'as a sacrifice to Satan.' "

". . . Devil worship was said to be involved in a series of mutilation killings in Cook and Du Page Counties in 1981 and 1982, in which 4 men abducted and murdered up to 18 young women. One of the men confessed to police that severed parts of the women's bodies were used in sexual and cannibalistic rituals devoted to Satan."[1]

LOS ANGELES, California: Four people were arrested in connection with the alleged ritual abuse of 15 children in a close-knit neighborhood in Pico Rivera. Charges were dismissed in municipal court because of lack of evidence. Nevertheless, two years later three children in one family still suffer deep emotional trauma. All were abused sexually. One boy said he witnessed the sacrifice of Mexican babies. He also witnessed the sacrifice of a German shepherd dog and was made to drink its blood. He was lowered into a grave in a coffin with a dead body. All of the children were told that their home would be burned down and their parents killed if they talked.

WEST POINT, New York: At least 30 children were allegedly abused at the West Point Academy Day Care Center. Dr. and Mrs. Grote left their 2½-year-old daughter at the center while they taught Sunday school. The girl told her parents that she was taken to a local high school and pornographically photographed. Later she informed them that she had been dressed as a bride and married to the devil in a ceremony. At that same ritual a dog was sacrificed. The Grotes pressed for a full investigation, and in the resulting publicity Dr. Grote was asked to resign his commission at the academy.

As recently as 1982, stories like these were virtually unheard of. At first these cases were too awful, too incredible, too bizarre to be believable. But now hardly a day passes that there isn't a newspaper article or television report about satanism and/or ritual abuse. In particular, there have been a rash of cases in preschools. Over 800 allegations have been reported in Los Angeles County alone, involving 64 schools and 27 neighborhoods.

Most horrifying are the report of actual crucifixions. We don't hear much about them because they're too unbelievable to talk about. They are unthinkable—unimaginable. Yet they happen. Children and adult survivors of ritualistic abuse are courageously beginning to describe what they saw—human beings crucified. Parents and therapists are listening to yet another horror of Satan's evil that makes up the bigger picture of ritualistic abuse.

We would like to deny this. We would like to chalk it all up to the overactive imagination of little boys and girls. But we can't. "A 2½-year-old, if she doesn't have some sort of exposure to that sort of thing, can't make it up," said Dr. Grote, a physician, while on the Geraldo Rivera show. "They don't have the imagination capacity at that age to make something like this up. It's so horrible that I couldn't make up the stuff she was telling us."

Children are telling about what decomposed bodies look like and smell like, what colors they are, how soft or hard they are. They are describing internal organs of people and animals. Except for medical personnel, most mature adults don't know these facts. A child couldn't possibly know this unless he had seen these things.

Satanists help the process by confusing the children. For example, they will tell children they are being taken to "The Castle." In fact, this castle may be several buildings. When detectives question the children, each may say, "I was taken to the castle," but when questioned on where this castle is and what it looked like, each child gives a different description. So the children are thought to be lying because they give conflicting testimony.

The abusers also confuse children by varying their disguises. Several children will say they were abused by "Tom," but when they are asked to describe this person, one child says he has blond hair, another brown hair and a mustache. In fact, both descriptions fit because the man changed his appearance. Also, the children's recollection of crimes is often muddled because they witnessed the acts while in a drugged state.

Convicted serial killer Henry Lee Lucas in an extensive interview explained that his crimes were inspired by his involvement in a satanic cult. "No one wants to believe the cult story," he said. "The TV people cut it out. The writers don't write about it." He was asked why it was so difficult for the police to obtain documented evidence in order to gain convictions. "They're just like me. We are trained not to leave evidence."[2]

What we have are diabolically evil groups of people perpetrating carefully planned crimes against a segment of society that is easily bullied into silence. And when the children do speak, their stories are so incredible that they are just not believed.

But their stories are true. Former satanists who have escaped are telling similar stories. One young man was a high priest in satanism until he became a born-again Christian. On the Oprah Winfrey Show he said, "I started when I was at the age of five. I started out in what is known as the earth mother religion. Eventually I was told that it was Satan we were worshiping." He told about how four times a year his group performed human sacrifices. "The victims are easily picked up. They are wandering teenagers looking for a good time, runaways, skid-row bums, paper boys. . . ."

On November 19, 1987, Geraldo Rivera interviewed a former satanic priestess who identified herself only as Elaine. "At 17, I saw my first sacrifice—a live baby," she said on the CBS network television program. "They carved the heart out of this child. I was told that if I said anything, I would be killed in such a manner or worse. These people mean what they say. They absolutely, totally control the children and the young, the teenagers, in absolute total fear. You fear for the rest of your life that they're going to kill Mom and Dad or brothers and sisters. They mean it, and you know they mean it. It's real."

This kind of activity has accelerated greatly in recent years. In 1981 the Witches International Coven Council (WICCA) listed several goals at their convention in Mexico. This list was intercepted and confiscated by law-enforcement officials. Among their objectives are:

- To bring about personal debts, causing discord and disharmony within families
- To remove or educate the "new-age youth" by:
  a) infiltrating boys'/girls' clubs and big sister/ brother programs
  b) infiltrating schools, having prayers removed, having teachers teach about drugs, sex, freedoms
  c) instigating and promoting rebellion against parents and all authority
- To have laws changed to benefit our ways, such as:
  a) removing children from the home environment and placing them in our foster homes
  b) mandatory placement of children in our day-care centers
  c) open drug and pornography market to everyone[3]

These goals are being systematically pursued, and one of the primary avenues is through preschools. Apparently satanists are actively training and seeking employment in preschools throughout the country, and using this as a base for recruiting and programming children for satanism. What these children see, hear, and endure is practically beyond belief: people in robes; sexual abuse; drugged lemonade; animal sacrifices; human sacrifices.

If this is true, why don't the police make arrests? Why aren't these abusers thrown in jail? The fact is that investigators are finding it extremely difficult to obtain evidence that will stand up in court.

Perhaps a classic illustration of the problems encountered in these cases occurred in Bakersfield, California, between 1984 and 1986. It all started on June 26, 1984, when a five-year-old girl told her mother that she had been molested. An investigation began and two men—one a minister—were arrested. In the following months several other children and five more arrests were made. Eventually the case grew to include allegations of mass murder, cannibalism, and kidnapping. There were 80 suspects, 60 alleged victims, and the reported murder of 29 infants during satanic rituals. Twenty-one children were taken from their parents and placed in foster homes for their protection.

Kern County sheriff Larry Kleier stated publicly that he was " 'absolutely convinced' that at least nine children witnessed the deaths of other children during satanic rituals involving sexual molestation," according to the *Bakersfield Californian*.[4] But others were not convinced. Ultimately the case fell apart because the children kept mentioning satanism in connection with their alleged abuse, and no corroborating evidence could be found to substantiate their allegations. The district attorney finally dropped the case in a plea-bargain with the defendants.

California State Attorney General John Van de Kamp did an investigation of the case and concluded in an 80-page report: "The strongly held belief in the unquestionable truth of the victims' statements led some sheriff's deputies to neglect the search for additional evidence. This failure to substantiate the children's claims became more pronounced when allegations of satanic rituals and homicides emerged. The more bizarre the allegation—and the lack of evidence to support it—the more the children's credibility suffered."[5]

The tragedy is that many ritualistically abused children will probably continue to suffer abuse because they were not believed. Children in totally different areas of the country, separated by thousands of miles, are telling the same stories and repeating many of the same gruesome details. While it is possible that some of these children are lying, it is inconceivable that so many could make up such stories that agree in so many ways. We cannot write these children off just because their stories are unbelievable. That is Satan's job—to make them unbelievable. He wants us to dismiss them.

In reading about these children and what they have had to say about the horrors of ritualistic abuse, many psychologists and therapists are realizing that precious little information is available to help them in treating their severely disturbed clients. Many counselors are also taking a closer look at some of the adult clients in their practice. With sexual abuse victims, they're often exploring the possibilities of ritualistic abuse in the client's childhood and teenage years. Many psychologists and therapists have been startled to find that as they opened up this avenue, they had more than one adult client with repressed memories of sexual and other abuses involving some type of ritualistic activity.

Ritualistic abuse victims are not something new. The fact is that we're just now learning how to identify them. With the explosion of new cases all over the country, it is essential that we be able to identify victims and minister to them. Many therapists and parents of ritualistically abused children have called me saying, "I've tried all I know to do, and it isn't working. We're getting nowhere. What do I do now?"

It is my hope that the information in the next two chapters will at least give a few answers to that question and render a clearer understanding of a subject area that is relatively unfamiliar to many people. I am not writing this from a therapist's or ex-satanist's viewpoint. I am not a practicing therapist, and I never was a satanist. I am writing through an ex-victim's and a survivor's eyes.

It is my prayer that this material might help many more victims escape from the clutches of Satan's underground.

❖ 16 ❖
The Ritualistically
Abused Child

Children who have been ritualistically abused and are not treated will suffer the consequences of that abuse far into their adult life. Mental-health professionals, ministers, and laymen alike are making a sincere attempt to help these children, but many of them feel inadequate for the task.

Parents of ritualistically abused children are not only frustrated, but many I've talked to are panicked. They are frequently living with a child who has exhibited a 180-degree change in personality and behavior. The child may be talking about killing the parents or perhaps has even attempted to do so. The child may be exhibiting violent behavior toward the family pet. The child may suddenly be doing devil dances. Attempts by the parent to understand and help their child, though very sincere, have been futile.

The ritualistically abused child is bound in his or her own secret world of torment and will remain captive in that world until someone with the right knowledge guides the child to freedom. Hopefully, the following information will help to partially fill in the gap that exists in understanding the ritualistically abused child.

Reporting Abuse

Guiding your child through the court system can be a nightmare of long duration, and one that may not produce a satisfactory outcome. However, ethically, morally, and legally it is essential that you report the suspected or known abuse.

According to the penal codes of virtually every state in our country, the child-endangerment laws prohibit anyone from willfully permitting any child to suffer, whether physically or mentally. In many states you may not have to report the abuse, but if you fail to do so you are placing yourself in a compromising situation at best, and perhaps in a dangerous legal bind. In virtually all states, child-care custodians, medical practitioners, psychiatrists, psychologists, social workers, marriage/family/child therapists, and employees of child protective agencies are mandated by law to report any known or reasonably suspected abuse of a child.

Even though the court system can be an endless, tiring, and frustrating process—and you may feel like you've lost your child to the courts for the duration of the investigation and trial (if there is one)—it is essential that people pay the price to make these cases of ritualistic abuse known. Consider the positives. First of all, your child will know that his parents are visibly interested in his protection and well-being. The world is full of grown-up children who have deep-rooted emotional scars because they feel betrayed by their parents, who chose not to take assertive action in protecting them and working to effect a conviction of their abusers. *In the eyes of the child, to do nothing, to remain silent, is to condone the behavior of the abuser.*

Second, even though the outcome may not be completely satisfactory, at least the present abuse of your child, and perhaps other children, will be stopped. Abusers seldom abuse just one time. In the case of ritualistic abuse, scores of other children are most likely involved. Your action will probably help many children besides your own.

Tragically, there is a high percentage of alleged ritualistic abuse cases among young children (through first grade) in group situations such as preschools, day-care centers, and summer camps. The explanation for this is simple: Children of younger ages are easier to abuse and are more easily intimidated, threatened, and brainwashed into keeping silent. The abusers know that there is little chance of a child under five years of age being considered a credible witness. Also, if young children have been abused ritualistically, they may have been targeted to be conditioned children who will be involved in satanism for the rest of their lives.

Ethically and morally, it would be difficult to live with the knowledge or suspicions of ritual abuse and not report it. Facing the emotional dilemmas produced by silence far outweigh the dilemmas produced by reporting the abuse. By not reporting ritualistic abuse, we give a green light to abusers. They win. We lose. More important, our children lose.

We must send a message to the perpetrators of ritualistic crimes that we will not stand idly by, giving them license to practice their heinous deeds of evil. And we must show our children that we are here to do everything in our power to protect them from such evils.

Silence is our worst enemy.

Keeping Life Normal

The ritualistically abused child often gets lost in the shuffle as the parents' anger is understandably directed at the victimizers. That can take all your time and energy while your child is standing silently on the sidelines, in desperate need of your full attention. There will never be a time when your child needs you more.

Some legal systems are getting better at limiting the questioning of the victim, not making the child sit on the witness stand for hours or even days while retelling horrifying accounts of abuse. However, even under the best of controlled situations it is bad for the child.

As much as possible, keep your child out of the limelight of interviews, cameras, and radio and television coverage. To add unnecessary media attention to your child's already-altered routine is a burden that he or she does not need. And for most children, such attention only serves to reinforce the abuse trauma.

You must decide what is best for your child. There is nothing more important than your child's welfare. In everything that is being considered in connection with your child (to the extent that you have a voice in the decisions) ask yourself the question "Will this action help my child or will it only cause further trauma?" Regardless of what happens in the courts, you can bring healing and restoration to the shattered life of your child.

Traditional Therapy

Most therapists readily admit that their knowledge of ritualistic abuse is inadequate. That inadequacy is not the fault of the therapists. Training and reference materials dealing with this subject have been virtually nonexistent. Almost the only source for information is the children themselves, but because the children are extremely reluctant to talk about their experiences, it is difficult to learn enough to fit the pieces of the puzzle together.

The children are afraid they won't be believed. They're often not aware of some of the abuse to which they were subjected. Many of them have been drugged and/or put in a hypnotic or trancelike state before they were abused. Many are still under the influences of mind control via curses and/or brainwashing. Last of all, as a means of protecting themselves from the resulting emotional trauma, the children repress memories of the abuse from their consciousness.

It is understandably difficult for the therapist to make progress with the ritualistically abused child when so many negative factors are at work. As a result, many therapists choose one of two ways to deal with the child.

One approach is to try to counteract the negative influences of the ritual by reenacting parts of it using opposite practices. For example: Using white magic (lighting white candles) to counteract the black magic (lighting black candles), or calling on forces of good to negate the forces of evil.

The other alternative for some therapists is to avoid dealing with the ritualistic experiences of the child altogether. That is an understandable choice, and in many cases perhaps the wisest choice. To delve into the areas of ritualistic abuse without a knowledge of the subject can be devastating to the victim. However, as the therapists themselves agree, ignoring the problem is only a temporary solution at best. Somewhere down the line the problem must be addressed if the child is to find relief. The only real answer is to gain as much information from as many sources as possible. Hopefully, the information presented here will be one of the sources that will help to eventually bring together all the pieces of the puzzle.

Understanding Ritualistic Abuse

Ritualistic abuse has one main thread running through it—CONTROL. The victim is brought under control through various practices, of which the more common ones will be listed and described in this chapter. Many of these practices have been used on children who were ritualistically abused at preschools, day-care centers, and summer camps. Similar testimonies of abuse are being reported from coast to coast.

These abuses control the children by preventing them from talking about their experiences, by keeping them captive to the indoctrination they have received through mind control and brainwashing, and by maintaining a connection to satanism for the rest of their lives. Children who have been ritualistically abused are controlled by forces other than self, parent, or teacher. They are controlled by unseen forces—satanic forces.

One of the main problems in dealing with this subject is an unbelief in supernatural forces. If one does not believe that evil or satanic forces exist, it is impossible to deal with ritualistic abuse. Several people in the mental-health profession, all of whom I highly respect, have told me that they do not believe in the supernatural (specifically, demonic spirits). If satanic ritualistic abuse is the product of supernatural and evil forces or spirits—and it is—then the people dealing with ritualistically abused children must take such forces into account.

I believe that as more facts about ritualistic abuse are uncovered, the reality of such forces and powers will be exposed, leading to a better understanding and a greater number of professionals who believe.

The following descriptions are examples of common ways that children are ritualistically abused, indoctrinated, and controlled.

1. THE THREE MAIN VALUES OF THE CHILD'S BELIEF SYSTEM ARE DESTROYED.

God: God is mocked at rituals. Children are forced to desecrate religious items by urinating on the Holy Bible and spitting on an upside-down cross. They are also sexually abused with religious items, such as sexual penetration by a small cross or else torn pages of the Bible rubbed against sexual areas, or they are sexually abused by victimizers who are wearing clerical robes.

Country: Patriotism is destroyed through practices such as sexual penetration with the wooden handle of a small U.S. flag while patriotic music is played in the background. The victimizer is sometimes dressed in a military uniform to increase the child's association of patriotism with ugliness.

Family: The child is told that "they" (the abusers) are the child's new family. The child may be asked to draw a picture of his or her natural family and urinate or defecate on it. Some children have been ritualistically married to another child victim or to an adult member of the satanic coven. Some have then been sexually abused by the "married partner," and if a girl, may have been told that she is going to have a baby.

2. BRAINWASHING KEEPS THE CHILD SUBSERVIENT.

Participation: Self-participation by the child victim is one of the most effective means of keeping that child continually connected to the abuse setting. If the child is forced to harm or kill an animal, or forced into sexual activity with another child, an adult, or an animal, he or she then ceases to feel like a victim. The child is made to take on the role of a victimizer. The child believes that he or she is just as bad and evil as the abuser, thus assuming an incredible burden of guilt either by association or by participation. Once the child feels guilty and to blame, he or she becomes an integral part of the abuse act.

Repetition of phrases: Truth phrases are designed to keep a child from telling. Examples are: "My spirit guide is watching me." "My spirit friend will report me if I tell." "No one will believe me." "I am bad." "I am evil." Truth phrases help to take away parental control. Examples are: "I am all I need." "I need no one else." "I obey only myself."

Trigger words: The use of trigger words, known only by the abuser and the child, recall events of terror or specific threats made by the abusers. The mention of words such as "meat locker," "Popsicle," "pressure cooker," "the oven," "hot box," or "the circle" can bring terror to a ritualistically abused child. Trigger words may be simply taught to the child or put into the child's subconscious mind while drugged or in a hypnotic, trancelike state.

Pictures or drawings: Just as truth phrases and trigger words have hidden meanings known only to the abuser and the child, pictures and drawings are used to remind the child of abusive episodes and threats of what will happen if they tell. This is an especially common practice in preschool and day-care centers where ritualistic abuse has occurred.

A picture or a drawing of an animal with large eyes or ears often means that the eyes see the child and the ears hear the child. A picture of a rabbit or a turtle may remind the child of a small animal that he either saw killed or one which he was forced to stick a pin or knife into. A drawing with a sentence or a poem beneath it may contain trigger words. A picture of someone in a costume or uniform may remind the child of his abuser who wore an identical costume or uniform.

3. RITUALISTIC SEXUAL ABUSE IS COMMON.

Where performed: Ritualistic abuse has allegedly occurred in all kinds of places: church sanctuaries, church basements, home basements, cemeteries, funeral parlors, preschools, day-care centers, secluded hillside areas, caves, etc.

Types of abuse: Ritualistically abused children have endured about as many types of sexual abuse as you could list, and then some. Very few of these have much to do with strict symbolic religious beliefs, and none are harmless. Most of these methods cater to perverted demonic lusts and are done to gain the approval of Satan.

The most frightening reason that children are ritualistically abused is for brainwashing and indoctrination purposes. The children are introduced into the ways of satanism and are then kept in satanism for the rest of their lives by guiding and controlling demonic spirits.

Forcing a child to have symbolic sexual relations with God is considered one of the strongest mockeries against God and one that pleases Satan the most. Religious or satanic artifacts are often rubbed against the child's sexual areas. Drawings of God with sexual organs or drawings of the child's parents' sexual organs may either be forced into the child's mouth or rubbed against the child's sexual parts. Teenagers who have been brought to a ritual by parents who are coven members, or teenagers who are there through seduction or force, are often forced to have sexual relations with each other, are group-raped by coven members, or are forced to have sexual contact with younger children.

4. "SPIRIT ABUSE" IS AN ELUSIVE AND LITTLE-UNDERSTOOD ELEMENT OF RITUALISTIC ABUSE.

When a child is forced to have symbolic sexual relations with God, not only is there a certain amount of physical abuse (whether moderate or severe), but there is also an abuse of the child's spirit by satanic spirits. Sexual abuse injures the body, mind, and emotions. Satanic ritualistic abuse injures the body, mind, emotions, *and spirit—that part of the child which deals with religious or spiritual values.*

First of all the abuse debases, corrupts, and perverts the child's religious values. The highest form of life becomes the lowest and most vile. Beliefs that were honorable and good become dishonorable and evil. That is why many parents say that their ritualistically abused children suddenly take on an anti-God attitude. They hate God, refuse to pray, or pray only to Satan, and then tell their parents that they now serve Satan or that Satan is their father.

Sexual abuse of preschoolers is often and mistakenly thought to be the "normal" or usual acts of body caressing, oral sex, and vaginal or anal fondling and/or entry. Not so! This type of ritualistic abuse *always* results in sexual perversion of the child, caused by the entry of perverted evil spirits into the child's life. Satanic sexual ritualistic abuse of preschoolers and other young children is the most serious, devastating, and long-lasting form of sexual abuse.

Spirit abuse of a child is particularly insidious because it is an extremely deceptive form of abuse. The child is not aware of the abuse of his spirit. It leaves no visible marks of identification. (However, many of the signs of what to look for are listed later in this chapter.) Spirit abuse cannot be detected by a doctor's physical examination. It is understandable, then, that when one cannot see it and the child isn't aware of it, it remains untreated.

What to Do

A very tragic picture has been portrayed of what happens to a child that is sexually abused. It is important to note that *every child who has been ritualistically abused has also been sexually abused as part of the abuse*. It is a frightening picture indeed.

However, it is not a helpless or hopeless situation. Parents, please know that *there is help and there is hope*! Satan's evil spirits are subject to people who know Jesus Christ as their Savior, Lord, and Master. People who have Jesus Christ living within them have the authority to command those evil spirits to leave. In other words, to get out!

If you as the parent are a Christian, you can pray and command the spirits to get out of your child. Or you can take your child to someone who is a Christian and knows how to pray. This isn't an option. If you want your child healed from the effects of ritualistic abuse, *freeing him or her from spirits is something you must do*. (How to pray for your child is covered later in this chapter.)

Spirit guides or spirit friends: The ritualistically abused child is often given a spirit guide or a spirit friend. The child is told and believes that the so-called "good" spirit is his or her secret friend and will give guidance, security, and well-being throughout life. Part of that is true. The child will be guided— but not for good—and the child will only be secure as long as he obeys the orders of that spirit. The spirit guide or spirit friend is an evil spirit that will maintain a deceptive hold on the child's involvement with satanism and satanic influences.

Usually, if the child is found talking to the spirit guide, the parent or therapist understandably passes it off as the normal behavior of a child talking to an imaginary friend. In reality, if the child has been ritualistically abused, he is more than likely talking to his given spirit guide or spirit friend. That spirit is neither imaginary nor a friend. Its sole purpose is to control the child.

As we just discussed in the section on spirit abuse, the same principles of prayer must be used to get rid of the spirit friend or spirit guide. *All spirits of evil are treated in the same way—through the power of prayer.* You command the spirit to leave your child in the name of Jesus. You ask that the Lord Jesus fill your child with a spirit of love and of power and of a sound mind. God will be faithful to do what you ask Him to do.

Evil spirits: Children who have been ritualistically abused are often the targets of evil spirits that cause both physical and mental distress. Symptoms of physical distress show up in children's complaint of sudden headaches or cramps or even the expression of a feeling that they are dying. The sexual parts of the child may burn. Many children have expressed the feeling that they arc being scratched or clawed inside, and in some cases they have actually had unexplainable bleeding from the vagina or anus. Sometimes children scratch or pull at themselves in an effort to make the bad feelings go away.

Symptoms of mental distress show up in depression, oppression, and possession. Suicidal tendencies, more often in pubescent or postpubescent years, are on the rise. There is growing documentation by psychiatrists and law-enforcement personnel attributing attempted and successful suicides to satanic involvement and/or ritualistic abuse. Murder tendencies and capabilities by ritualistically abused children as young as four years of age have been diagnosed by psychiatrists.

Evil spirits are real, and their influence and control over ritualistically abused children are real. It makes more sense to accept their existence and deal with the ritualistically abused child accordingly than to deny their existence and either ignore the child's symptoms or treat them with methods that aren't effective.

5. SATANIC CURSES ARE INVOKED.

Curses are invoked for any number of purposes. A curse can be invoked to cause a child to feel safe when he or she is really in danger. A curse can summon spirit beings to inflict illness, disease, and even death. A curse of suicide or murder can cause the person to respond accordingly. A curse can inflict a spirit of sexual perversion within a child. A curse can cause rebellion, confusion, fear, hatred, rage, torment, bondage, etc. These curses are capable of controlling a child for the rest of his life. Like evil spirits, the effects of curses cannot be treated by traditional methods.

The circle is used as a satanic symbol. Many ritualistically abused children cringe at the mention of the circle. Whereas the circle for adult coven members often means a place of protection, a place of sacredness, and a place where powers descend, to many ritualistically abused children the circle produces terror.

Children have often been placed within a circle which has been drawn on the ground or floor. Sometimes a *pentagram*, an upside-down five-pointed star (another satanic symbol), is drawn within the circle. The child is abused within the boundaries of the circle. Curses are invoked upon the child within the circle. The child is told that nothing done within the circle can ever be exposed outside the circle.

Only as the child keeps all events within the circle is he or she safe. If the child retreats outside the circle (for example, to tell someone what has been done), something very bad will happen to him. Inside the circle is safety. Outside the circle is danger. This is called "The Power of the Circle."

Often when children of ritualistic abuse try to tell their parents or their therapist of things that happened within the circle, they immediately see the circle in their mind and are either afraid or unable to reveal anything more. "The Power of the Circle" (the curses invoked on them while standing in the circle) is at work on the child.

The curses of *isolation* and *enclosure* keep the child from breaking free of its powers. The child feels totally isolated within the circle. Just as the circle isolates the child, it also encloses the child, for it has no beginning and no end. There is no way out. Nothing can cross the line of the circle, because it has no broken places. That is why care is taken to keep the line of the circle unbroken. Nothing done within the circle can ever find its way out. The child is mentally isolated and enclosed within its boundaries.

Contrary to what this information sounds like, it is not spooky "hocus-pocus" talk. It is not fanaticism nor is it "off the deep end." These powers, curses, and evil spirits are real. They are the work of Satan. They must be understood and sensibly dealt with.

Identifying Victims

"Ritual abuse is slowly, systematically, and deeply ingrained in a child's psychic," writes Ken Wooden. "Consequently, an object, a person, a location, something in a book or on TV, may cause the victim to spontaneously wrest the experiences of ritual abuse from the recesses of his/her mind."[1] Immediate action is mandatory for best therapeutic results.

The following are symptoms or manifestations of ritualistic abuse. However, do not automatically assume that your child has been ritualistically abused just because he or she displays one or two of these behaviors. If you do notice a *sudden change* in your child's personality, accompanied by several of the following behavioral traits, there is a strong possibility that your child has been abused in some way, and quite possibly has been ritualistically abused.

What Parents Should Watch for in Their Children

Behavioral Changes

1. Talking to unseen persons. Insisting they are real. It is certainly common for children to make up imaginary characters to whom they will talk and with whom they will play. Usually the child will be happy to tell others who his or her imaginary friend is. However, if your child comes up with an "imaginary" person and he or she refuses to talk about it, and exhibits a more serious or even fearful attitude toward this person, it is possible that

the child is talking to a spirit guide or spirit friend. Such a spirit would be given to the child by satanists during a time of ritualistic abuse.

2. Preoccupation with sex. Often using new words for sexual activities or body parts.

3. Doing devil dances, spirit dances, or other heretofore-unfamiliar types of dances, songs, chants, and/or prayers. If you ask your child what he is doing, he will more than likely inform you that he is dancing or singing or praying to the devil. This is a major warning sign if the child heretofore has not exhibited such behavior, seems totally preoccupied with doing it, and refuses to stop even under the warning of punishment.

4. Fear of or unusual preoccupation with the number "6" or multiples thereof. This is sometimes manifested by the child's terror of his sixth birthday. Such a fear might exist because a child has been told that he will die on his sixth birthday.

5. Verbal or written words that are strange (not known or understandable to you) or verbal or written words that are backward. This is certainly not referring to children with dyslexia or other learning problems. These will be words or phrases that will suddenly become a vital and permanent part of the child's vocabulary. They will not be sporadically spoken on a whim, nor will the child leave these words and go on to other made-up words as children often do. The backward words may have a Christian meaning. If the child has been ritualistically abused, words of the Bible have been taught to the child in a backward manner so as to degrade or mock the Word of God.

6. Sudden, radical, unexplainable mood change. For example, a child that has normally been rather reserved suddenly becomes hyperactive and starts tearing the house apart or having violent, unexplainable temper tantrums.

7. Sudden, irrational fear of being left alone for even a few minutes.

8. Fear of colors, especially red, black, or purple.

9. Sudden, unexplainable fear of small spaces. Some children enjoy playing in small places. But if they suddenly become terrified of confined areas, it may be that they have been abused and/or shut in coffins, cemetery or field grave holes, closets, etc.

10. Sudden fear of bathing or extreme and heretofore-unexhibited preoccupation with cleanliness.

11. Sudden desire for frequent change of underwear.

12. Sudden change in normal toileting practices. Almost all ritualistically abused children have been forced to eat feces and drink urine as part of the degrading process. If your child exhibits a sudden fascination with or abhorrence to urine and feces by drinking the urine or putting feces into his or her mouth or spreading it over the body or the bathroom, it is an indication that he or she may have been abused with urine and feces.

13. Sudden, violent, hostile aggression against parents or siblings. We are not talking about normal childhood anger that is to be expected among preschool-age children, but an obvious attempt to actually kill a family member with a weapon such as a knife, or a violent threat to commit such an act.

I have no desire to create mass hysteria among parents. Children will be children. They often change habits, patterns, behaviors, speech, and play practices. However, if a parent notices several of the above-stated changes in the child's behavior, it would be wise to investigate further into the cause. In addition, parents can look for further clues in the following areas.

1. Pictures or Objects. If the child says that he or she brought these home from school or found them somewhere, watch for symbolisms or signs of satanism in pictures with:
   • pentagrams
   • crescent moon with five stars in the curve of the moon and dominant colors of black, red, and purple

Watch for pictures with:

- disproportionately large eyes or ears (The child may tell you, "The eyes are watching me," or "The ears are listening to me.")
- houses of construction paper with doors that open (Ask the child what happens when the door is opened.)
- animals like a rabbit, especially if a child is unusually adamant about the picture staying in a prominent location (It may represent mutilation or sacrifice, and the child was ordered to leave it on the refrigerator or other prominent place as a reminder of what could happen to a family member or pet if the child reveals his or her abuse.)

2. A sudden fear of religious objects or persons. These would include—
   - crosses, statues, candles, etc.
   - communion bowls, cups, wine, bread, etc.
   - clergymen, especially when dressed in clerical robes

3. Sudden, irrational fear of certain places. These may be places where the ritualistic abuse was performed, or they may be places that are similar-looking that remind the child of the actual abuse site. They may also be places where the child was taken and shown bodies or parts of bodies of "people who didn't obey" or "people who talked." Such scare tactics frighten the child into obedience and silence. (Usually when a parent asks a child why he is frightened, the child will tell, or it will be obvious that this is simply the normal fear of a new setting. But if he has been ritualistically abused, that fear will not go away, and he may be too scared to explain his fear to you.)

The Teenage Years

It is not unusual for teenagers to exhibit rebelliousness, have a total belief in self, to question or reject their religious beliefs, and to even express suicidal tendencies. That in itself does not necessarily indicate previous ritualistic abuse. However, if your teenager exhibits extreme evidence of these signs, think back on his or her preschool years. If you recognize several of the red flags of ritualistic abuse that we have just covered, there is a possibility that he or she was ritualistically abused as a child.

The Role of the Parents

Children who are victims of ritualistic abuse should be given therapy. However, parents can also play a vital role in the healing of their ritualistically abused child. If the child is very young, the parent will certainly be the dominant person, and possibly the only person, who will have direct contact in ministry to him or her. Young children have a natural trust for their parents. (That is, so long as their parents are not the abusers!) Also, parents spend the most time with their children, as opposed to the therapist, who at best has only an hour or two a week with the child. The parent can minister to the child in the familiar home setting.

If the child is older or is a teenager, the parent can assume an important part of the ministry, coupled with the counseling of a therapist, psychologist, or minister who is knowledgeable and trained in the area of ritualistic abuse.

If it has been determined that your child is a victim of ritualistic abuse, be certain that whoever ministers to your child in the area of the powers of darkness is a Christian. Remember that part of the ministry will have no effect if the person ministering does not have Jesus Christ dwelling within him. You are dealing with principalities, powers, and rulers of darkness. The usual methods of therapy cannot cancel the effects of evil spirit beings, curses, and other powers of darkness. Satan recognizes the person who is not a Christian. He does not have to obey the commands of one who does not possess spiritual powers. The powers of Satan can only be overcome by the power of Jesus Christ.

With this in mind, the Christian parent who can apply the most basic principles of spiritual warfare may be the one who is in the best position to minister to the ritualistically abused child.

Breaking the Powers of Darkness

The first step in the healing process is for a child to be freed from the powers of evil that he or she has been under through the ritualistic aspects of the abuse. These powers must be broken for the child to experience that freedom. The children cannot do it for themselves. As a Christian, you can exercise the authority God has given you to break the powers of curses and the influences of evil spirits that are harassing and damaging your children. The personality and behavioral changes that are listed earlier in this chapter are the direct result of evil influences, spirits, and curses that the child was subjected to. Breaking their hold on the child is the first step in bringing about a total healing.

In no way does the breaking of the powers have to frighten the child. It is not a magic act. No weird spells have to be cast. There is no need to talk in a loud voice. There is no need to assume that the dramatic and sometimes "off-the-wall" movie versions of exorcism are going to occur. In fact, you can exercise your authority over the powers of darkness calmly and quietly while the child is asleep.

As a child of God, you have the right to pray a prayer such as the one below over your child:

"Heavenly Father, I bring my child, _____, to You. In the name of Jesus Christ, and in the authority and power that You have invested in me, I bind the powers of darkness, and I break the powers of curses that _____ has been subjected to. I place _____ in Your hands, and I ask that Your guardian angels surround and protect him from all future attacks of Satan. Thank You, Lord, for bringing _____ into the freedom and love of Jesus Christ."

Other behavioral symptoms of ritualistic abuse may continue to appear after you have prayed for your child. If they do, *don't give up!* You may need to pray a prayer such as this many times.

Continued signs of ritualistic abuse do not mean that you're doing something wrong. Your child is being healed, but healing is a process, and more often than not it takes time. Be encouraged with the Scripture, "Ask and it will be given to you, seek and you will find, knock and it will be opened to you" (Luke 11:9,10).

These are Jesus' words of encouragement in response to a person's *persistence.* Your continued persistence in prayer for the healing of your child will be rewarded.

Besides this most important step, there are several other things that a parent can do in guiding his child to wholeness. Each case of ritualistic abuse is different. No one knows your child better than you. You may find ways to help your child that are not included in the following suggested general helps.

1. *Discuss fears.* Common fears associated with ritualistic abuse are reflected in statements such as these:
    "I am damaged."
    "I am bad."
    "They'll come and take me away when I'm sleeping."
    "They'll kill you (the parent) if I tell."
    "Is Satan my father now?"
    "It's all my fault."
   Children often have a fear of medical procedures such as blood tests, injections, and pills. They associate such procedures with:
    • the taking and drinking of blood at rituals
    • injections or oral drugs given to the children to sedate them during the ritualistic abuse
    • memories of witnessing the dismembering of body parts or the opening of bodies—animal or human

2. *Pray.* Allow, but don't push or force, your child to name the memories that are frightening and to give each one to Jesus. Reassure your child that Jesus has taken them and that they no longer have the power to frighten the mind or sadden the heart.

3. *Read the Word of God.* Read the Word of God together with your child. Record verses of love, of peace, and of safety on a cassette tape. Play them as you listen together or while your child is sleeping. Encourage your child to say them out loud along with the tape. As your child does this, he or she will begin to memorize them. Encourage your child to say them when fear knocks at the door of his heart.

4. *Use the Armor Game.* Using Ephesians 6:14-17, teach your child what the armor of God is, and that it is for his protection. Then make a fun game out of it and teach him

how to put on the whole armor of God. Have him memorize each piece and where it goes on his body. If he or she is too young to remember each piece, draw a picture of each piece and make a checklist for him to mark off. Have the child name each piece and go through the physical motions of putting it on. Kids love to play act. They'll enjoy picking up the helmet of salvation and putting it on their head. They'll get a kick out of putting on the breastplate of righteousness and buckling it around their chest. What's more, your child will leave the house for school or play feeling safe and secure.

5. *Make your house a "safe house."* If your child has expressed a fear that "they" (the abusers) are going to come and get him, or if your child is having frequent nightmares from which he is awakening frightened, be sure that there are locks on all doors and windows of your house. Then walk your child through the house, showing him or her that your house is a safe house.

6. *Display a photo of the entire family.* Many ritualistically abused children have been told that their family doesn't love them any longer, that their abusers are their new family now, or that their mommy and daddy and/or brothers and sisters will be killed if they talk. A photo of the entire family, including the family pets, placed at the child's bedside will reassure him that the family is intact.

A Word of Encouragement

Rest assured that your child can be healed of all damages from ritualistic abuse, and can live a completely normal life once again.

Remember the Scripture "He who is in you is greater than he who is in the world" (1 John 4:4). Use that power for the healing of your child.

After the effects of ritualistic abuse are dealt with through the ministry of spiritual warfare, many of the traditional counseling techniques can be beneficial to the child victim of ritualistic practices and abuse.

One last point. In an effort to prevent the lives of innocent babies from becoming needless statistics of ritualistic abuse and sacrifice, I must add the following warning:

WARNING: Unwed mothers who are pregnant and want to place their babies up for adoption should phone or visit their city or county Human Services Department to confirm the legitimacy and license of any adoption agency or placement home, and/or any personnel to whom they are thinking of signing over their newborn infant.

The Adult Victim of Ritualistic Involvement

Some of the information presented in the preceding chapter is also applicable to the ritualistically abused adult. Many adults are only now remembering that they were ritualistically abused as children. Others are being recognized as victims of childhood ritualistic abuse and are just beginning treatment for that abuse. Still others need help as either voluntary or involuntary victims of satanism and ritualistic involvement as adults. Please keep in mind that this information should be tailored to each victim and situation.

Rituals

The stated order of occultic and satanic rituals is as follows:

Invocation
Petition
Sacrifice (offering)
Thanksgiving

Sounds like your average church service, doesn't it? Or at the very least like an innocent, harmless ritual. Not so! All ritualistic practices worship another god. The Word of God plainly states, "You shall have no other gods before Me" (Exodus 20:3).

These invocations, petitions, sacrifices, and thanksgivings are made to:

gods of beauty and nature
gods of a good person or prophet
or to Satan himself, who promises the worshiper—
    healthy lust
    material well-being
    security

Mind Control

In any religion or form of worship, followers should be allowed to think for themselves. In every religion that has a god other than Jesus Christ, adherents are not allowed to think for themselves. Their minds are deceived, then controlled, and sometimes owned. This happens through:

repetitious chants or mantras
spirit entities (beings) that are petitioned to enter one's mind
evil curses that are invoked upon the person

Repetitious chanting narrows the mind's thought processes, refocusing it into one direction only. If a person repeats one or two words or a sentence long enough, giving intense focus to those words, they will become true to him no matter how false, deceptive, or bizarre those words may be.* Repetitious chanting of mantras opens the mind to suggestions and thoughts that a person would not ordinarily entertain. It is just another form of brainwashing. Whether it is through chants, through petitioned spirit entities, or through invoked curses, the mind is controlled by someone or something other than the person himself.

Ritualistic Abuse

It is a common practice and an important part of satanic rituals for victims to be offered on the altar for activities that are, more often than not, abusive in nature. Whether or not satanists admit it, sex and sexual perversion (the latter being the more prevalent because it supposedly pleases Satan more) are an integral part of most ritualistic ceremonies. While the satanists may claim that these sexual acts are merely a part of the religious ritual, many of these activities serve mainly to satisfy the lusts of the flesh.

Other abusive practices involve the spilling of blood and

---

*I was given the sentence "Satan is my father" to repeat over and over for 30 minutes at a time, three times a day. Another sentence I had to chant endlessly was "I obey Satan only." My one salvation from those chants becoming truths was that, although I said them out loud, in my heart I silently repeated, "Jesus is my Father" and "I obey Jesus only." Even then, I sometimes felt that Satan was becoming my father.

the dismembering of various smaller body parts—most often a finger or toe or parts of them. These abuses are either allowed voluntarily or are forced involuntarily. Either way, the participant becomes a victim to Satan through deception, mind control, and/or force. The offering of one's body for such perverted and abusive practices is easily performed because the victim is usually under the influence of:

- trances which have been hypnotically induced through repetitious chanting
- drugs
- threats of retribution that instill fear of future harassment and abuse
- deceptive beliefs that offering one's body for abusive practices insures one's safety and position in the coven.

Somewhere in the realm of abusive ritualistic practices the sacrificing of human lives, whether symbolically or in reality, must be included. To most of us it is inconceivable that humans could or would do such a heinous act for any reason or under any influence. It is imperative to understand that, first of all, most of the sacrifices involve involuntary or deceived victims. Second, to much of the occult and satanic world there is a belief that either the principles of good and evil are equal or else that evil does not exist. If one adheres to that belief system, then anything and everything goes. To assume that evil does not exist certainly accommodates any and all lifestyles and practices.

If a person believes that he is predestined to offer a sacrifice to Satan, that person is relieved of all responsibility for his actions. If a person believes, as satanism teaches, that sin gives spiritual, mental, and physical pleasure, and that the seven deadly sins of greed, pride, envy, anger, gluttony, lust, and sloth are sacred, then it is no wonder that crimes of such heinous proportions can be committed without remorse!

For example, to witches and satanists, Halloween is a religious holiday called "The Celebration of Death." I can only look on it as a celebration of murder, or more to the point, as an excuse for murder. I was witness to the sacrifice of small animals, larger animals, a goat's head with large horns, and an infant on successive weeks leading up to Halloween night, when the mother of the previously sacrificed infant, or a pregnant woman and an infant, were sacrificed. As a Christian, I cannot conceive of a person doing these things without remorse. But satanists believe there is no evil, and so they can perform such atrocities without feeling guilty.

As a witness to the unseen side of Halloween, I cannot celebrate it in the traditional way with ghosts, skeletons, haunted houses, and jack-o'-lanterns. I urge all Christians to find an alternative way of spending this day.

Satanic Mockery

Victims who have been in Satan's underground have seen, mocked, and degraded everything that is good, everything that is pure, everything that is true, everything that is just, everything that is virtuous, and especially everything that is holy.

The Word of God is read backward.
The Lord's Prayer is prayed backward.
The cross is hung upside down.
The high priest spits on the cross and cries out
  "Hail, Satan!"
The "sacred" altar is used for perversion, abuse, and
  sacrifice.

Summary

This has been just a brief introduction to occultic and satanic beliefs, practices, and rituals. Try to imagine how a victim feels. He or she was deceived into coming under such demonic influences. He has been controlled and abused for months or perhaps even years. Confusion, fear, oppression, guilt, shame, anger, hatred, and a host of other destructive forces are at work, viciously preying on the victim's mind.

It is extremely difficult for adult victims of ritualistic involvement to break free. They need much help and understanding if they are to do so.

Foundational Counseling and Ministry Techniques

Affirmative Suggestions

1. Accept victims just as they are. Intense hostility, fear, distrust, insecurity, heavy oppression, and even initial denial are common emotional characteristics.
2. Be flexible. The length of involvement in the occult, satanism, and/or ritualistic abuse, the degree of involvement, and the amount of physical, mental, and spiritual abuse make each ministry situation different.
3. Assure the victim that he or she can say anything. And be prepared to hear anything.
4. Assure the victim of strict confidentiality. Then keep it. A broken confidentiality can be devastating, especially in matters of this nature.
5. Allow the victim to recall the past at his own rate. The Lord will bring individual memories to light as the victim is able to deal with them. He will never overwhelm the victim.
6. As the Lord brings painful memories to mind, have the victim:
   • Name the situation
   • If needed, ask for forgiveness
   • Give the memory to the Lord
   • Relinquish anger, hatred, and hurt
   • Ask the Lord for His peace for each memory given to Him
7. Continually assure the victim that victory is certain through Jesus Christ.
8. Encourage the victim to fight spiritual warfare on his own as his growth in spiritual truths matures.

Methods or Attitudes to Avoid

1. Do not try to deprogram. Such techniques are often emotionally abusive and too mentally draining and overwhelming.

2. Do not force regression therapy. A victim's experiences are often too numerous and horrifying to use directive techniques deliberately aimed at forcibly recalling and reliving them.
3. Do not use guilt and/or punishment tactics to pay for actions. The victim needs separation, forgiveness, and restoration, not reinforcement.
4. Do not push victims faster than they can go. Remember, the victims are often dealing with traumatic memories and powers of darkness that have long controlled them.
5. Do not expect victims to be carbon copies of each other. Each victim has had different experiences, and each reacts differently to them.
6. Do not reflect any degree of negativity toward a victim or toward anything you're told.

Understanding Satanic Curses

Curses are invocations to bring evil, harm, torment, and control. They convince a victim to respond to the purposes for which they were invoked.

Curses Can Affect an Adult Outwardly

This is true even though the adult is not controlled or possessed internally. They are invoked:
1. To punish a rebellious worshiper.
2. To bring physical harm to an enemy of Satan who is perceived as a threat to the coven. An enemy of Satan is usually a Christian, or at least one who speaks out against satanism.
3. To bring harm to someone who is simply not liked by a coven member.

Curses Can Control One's Thoughts and Actions

1. Curses invoked at a ritual can be set in motion weeks, months, or even years later (such as suicide or murder).

2. Curses are a method of keeping the victim in line.
3. Adults who were ritualistically abused as children, even though they have been away from those activities for years, often feel a sense of unexplainable foreboding and/or mental control by spirit entities.
4. Victims can remain this way indefinitely unless the spirit abuse is dealt with by using the principles of spiritual warfare.

Understanding Satanic Oaths Taken By an Adult Satanist

An oath is a contract made with Satan or an evil spirit for the purpose of gaining power from their assistance or control. A satanic oath may require only verbal affirmation, or it may require a sacrifice to seal the oath, such as the severing of a finger part. It is often taken while standing within an unbroken circle, or it may be taken while standing within certain areas of a drawn pentagram.

Oaths join the worshiper to Satan. If the oath is broken, curses to bring evil consequences on the adult may be invoked. The worshiper may be forced to make even more dangerous pledges to Satan to regain that favor or control.

Brainwashing and Mind Control

Brainwashing occurs when one way of thinking is replaced by another, either by visibly forcible means or by secretively deceptive means. Mind control is a product of brainwashing.

Brainwashing and mind control take place through:

1. Manipulation by evil spirits. When a person opens his mind for spirits that are not of God, former traditional beliefs, moral standards, and values are replaced with Satan's perverted systems of thought. Sadly, most followers remain naive in thinking that they are still in control of their thoughts.
2. Acceptance of satanic doctrine through use of physical force. If a person has been marked by satanists for

use in the service of Satan, and if that person rebels, the use of systematic ritual abuse is a sure way to wear down the ability and desire to rebel. Such repeated abusive practices result in an inability of the mind to resist indoctrination.

All followers of satanism are victims of brainwashing and mind control. Once the mind is opened, Satan is sure to enter.

Brainwashing and mind control leave the victims:

- helpless to think for themselves
- totally ingrained in satanic thought processes
- separated from normal and wholesome thought processes
- unable to rid themselves of deceptively evil ways of thinking

The Way Out

The Power of Curses Must Be Broken

Be as specific as possible in naming the curses. If that is not possible, name the feelings or symptoms produced by them. Once the curses are broken, believe that they have no power over you!

Oaths Must Be Renounced

Again, be as specific as possible. Know that Satan cannot hold you to an oath once it is renounced, even though it was voluntarily taken.

Be persistent! Satan is reluctant to obey, and he does not give up easily. Show him that you mean business. Be aware of Satan's tricks to deceive you. Remember that Satan is a defeated foe. Victory is assured through Jesus Christ!

Adult Victims Must Be Helped

The victim may still be under Satan's influence and possibly under his control. He or she may not be able to fight at first, so you may have to do the fighting instead. The victim may have sincerely tried to pray but is so bound that he or she is unable to do so.

Under Satan's influence, the victim may even resist you at times. Try to not become impatient with that resistance.

One of your weapons, without which you are powerless, is the WORD OF GOD, which gives you authority in Jesus Christ and protection for the battle against Satan.

Your second weapon is PRAYER. Prayer is your communication with the Lord, without which you cannot fight the battle. Prayer is the context within which you exercise your authority. Prayer is the avenue through which you are upheld mentally, physically, and spiritually.

The good news is that the battle can be won through Jesus Christ! Through a knowledge of ritualistic practices and the application of spiritual-warfare principles, the adult victim of ritualistic involvement and abuse can be healed and freed, once and forever!

❖ *Epilogue* ❖
Still They Cry

"Will someone listen to me?"

The victims still cry, but few people hear or answer.

When all is said and written about satanism and ritualistic practices, about waging spiritual warfare, about breaking curses, about renouncing oaths, and about severing ties to occultism and satanism, the basic need is still the same: Victims need someone who will listen to them.

The victim who is coming out of Satan's underground doesn't need all-night prayer meetings, lists of do's and don't's, and "thou shalt not" sermons. To put it bluntly, victims don't need to be overwhelmed and inundated with "religiosities."

Although my first meeting with Johanna and Randolph lasted several hours, and they could have used those hours to wage intense spiritual warfare, they chose instead to do nothing but listen to me. That is exactly what I needed right then. The last thing I wanted or needed was to be preached to, and I surely wasn't ready for spiritual battle. I just wanted to be heard and understood.

If you're a layperson who wants to help victims, but you don't feel prepared or perhaps even called to get into spiritual warfare with them, that's okay. Not everyone is given the same ministry in the body of Christ. The one thing you can do is to minister the love of Jesus Christ by listening and showing that you care. Other ministries may follow, but none is more important than the ministry of love.

The apostle Paul wrote in Romans 13:8, "Owe no one anything except to love one another." It is a charitable heart, not works, to which a wounded victim of Satan's underground responds first. All of the works we've talked about won't amount to a hill of beans if they're not prefaced with love!

More and more victims are coming to our churches for help. Unfortunately, instead of being accepted and loved, many are turned away. Some of the reasons are understandable, but few if any are acceptable. Victims have horrendous stories to tell. Their experiences are shocking at best and unbelievable at worst. The satanists have accomplished their intent in making the practices and abuses so heinous that if the victims do speak out, they aren't believed. To not believe them gives undue credit to Satan and denies the victims any hope of being helped.

Some churches have turned victims away because they have a difficult time accepting people whose experiences are so shocking, repulsive, and foreign to them. Church-sheltered Christians who have lived their lives between the four walls of the church often remain strangers to the world around them.

Some Christians do an about-face and walk the opposite direction when the subject of satanism is brought up. Some shudder when the word "Satan" or "satanism" is even mentioned. It's no wonder that most victims of Satan's underground never tell their stories! It's no wonder that they choose to stay in their hell of silence rather than seek help.

The doors of some churches are closed to more people than we either realize or care to admit. What type of person fits into your church? Would Christ's congregation, those whom He spent His life ministering to, be welcome in your church today? If we can't show Christ's love to a hurting world, who will? You can be sure that Satan's doors will always be open!

The other ministry that I would earnestly implore all Christians to engage in is that of prayer, specifically praying that the light of the Lord Jesus would shine into the darkness of Satan's evils.

I've seen the power of prayer in action. One night I witnessed a bright light suddenly appear out of nowhere in the midst of a ritual where a human sacrifice was going to take place. Several victims have told me similar stories. In each instance the coven members verbally recognized the light as God's light, and they hurriedly shut down their rituals and fled the area.

The conclusion is this: Satan works in darkness. When the light of Jesus shines upon his works, he has to close up shop!

I urge Christians to pray, especially between the hours of six o'clock in the evening and midnight—midnight being the preferred time of death for human sacrifices. I urge you to pray that the Lord Jesus would shine His light upon every ritual where a human life is to be sacrificed. I've seen it work. Others have seen it work. And if every other attempt to put an end to such demonic atrocities has fallen short, prayer may be the only answer.

Pray without ceasing. Make this request a part of your daily prayer. And if the Holy Spirit wakens you in the middle of the night with a burden to pray about this, don't question it. Just pray! Human sacrifice may take place at any time.

I need to make one other important point. I want to make it absolutely clear that I was involuntarily connected to an extremely abusive group of satanists. Satanist groups are as diverse in their activities as are churches of various denominations. Not all satanists and covens practice the extremely heinous acts that I witnessed. However, even though it is fairly obvious, I also want to make it clear that all satanists serve and worship Satan, the prince of darkness.

* * *

Still the little children cry,
   from their beds where their daddies did something dirty and bad to them in the middle of the night . . .
   from their schoolrooms where grownups dressed in costumes did things to them they'll never tell anybody—not even Mommy and Daddy . . .
   from a yucky room where there was no place to hide, and they had to take off all their clothes for relatives—maybe even strangers—who took naked pictures of them.
          "Will someone listen to me?"

Still the teenagers cry,
   from the bus stations where they arrived looking for the good life . . .
   from the street corners of skid row or the red light district where they hang out . . .

from the cold, cement basement floors of condemned buildings where they tried to get a couple of hours of sleep at night . . .

from dingy, fleabag hotel rooms where they prostituted their bodies to earn a few dollars.

>*"Will someone listen to me?"*

Still the adults cry,

from their therapist's office as they begin to painfully put bits and pieces of memories together about repressed childhood abuses . . .

from only God knows where as they agonize over ritualistic acts of insanely demonic evils that they either witnessed or were forced to take a part in.

Still they cry,

>*"Will someone listen to me?"*

Notes

Chapter 3

1. According to Dr. Shirley O'Brien, human development specialist at the University of Arizona. From "As It Was in the Days of Noah" (Southwest Radio Church, 1986), p. 40.
2. "Child Pornography and Prostitution: Background and Legal Analysis" (Department of Justice, 1987; Child Pornography © American Bar Association; Child Prostitution © Covenant House), p. 25.
3. Simmons 1980 Market Research Bureau; provided by the Institute for Media Education.
4. O'Brien, "Noah," p. 39.
5. Judith A. Reisman, "Content Analysis of Children, Crime and Violence in *Playboy*, *Penthouse*, and *Hustler*," Executive Summary, p. 8.
6. O'Brien, "Noah," p. 39.

Chapter 11

1. From 1 John 4:4.
2. Romans 8:31.
3. Romans 8:37.
4. Romans 8:1.
5. 2 Timothy 1:7.
6. Psalm 4:8.
7. Mike Warnke, *The Satan Seller* (Logos International, 1972), p. 87.

Chapter 14

1. Johanna Michaelsen, *The Beautiful Side of Evil* (Harvest House Publishers, 1982), p. 183.

Chapter 15

1. Eric Zorn, "Satan Worship Called Dangerous, Growing," in *The Chicago Tribune*, Sunday, Apr. 27, 1986.
2. Joel Norris and Jerry Allen Potter, "The Devil Made Me Do It," in *Penthouse*, Dec. 1985, p. 178.
3. John Frattarola, "America's Best Kept Secret," in *Passport*, special edition, 1986, p. 5.
4. *The Bakersfield Californian*, Tuesday, Sep. 30, 1986, p. 5.
5. "Report on the Kern County Child Abuse Investigation," Office of the Attorney General, State of California, p. 71.

Chapter 16

1. Kenneth Wooden, *Questionnaire on the Occult* (The Wooden Publishing House, 1984), p. 1.

Recommended Reading

Bubeck, Mark I., *The Adversary* (Chicago: Moody Press, 1975).

Bubeck, Mark I., *Overcoming the Adversary* (Chicago: Moody Press, 1984).

Frank, Jan, *A Door of Hope* (San Bernardino: Here's Life Publishers, 1987).

Hollingsworth, Jan, *Unspeakable Acts* (New York: Cogdon and Weed, 1986). (This book is written from a secular point of view, but it provides excellent reading about a successful trial of multiple child sexual abuse at a day-care center.)

Koch, Kurt E., *The Devil's Alphabet* (Grand Rapids: Kregel Publications, 1971).

Koch, Kurt E., *Occult Bondage and Deliverance* (Grand Rapids: Kregel Publications, 1971).

Lindsey, Hal, *Satan Is Alive and Well on Planet Earth* (Grand Rapids: The Zondervan Corporation, 1972).

Marrs, Texe, *Dark Secrets of the New Age* (Westchester: Crossway Books, 1987).

Matrisciana, Caryl, *Gods of the New Age* (Eugene: Harvest House Publishers, 1985).

Michaelsen, Johanna, *The Beautiful Side of Evil* (Eugene: Harvest House Publishers, 1982).

Michaelsen, Johanna, *Like Lambs to the Slaughter* (Eugene: Harvest House Publishers, 1988).

Peters, David B., *A Betrayal of Innocence* (Waco: Word, 1986).

Warnke, Mike, *The Satan Seller* (Plainfield: Logos International, 1972).

Wildmon, Don, *Case Against Pornography* (Wheaton: Victor Books, 1986).

Other Good
Harvest House Reading

THE BEAUTIFUL SIDE OF EVIL
by *Johanna Michaelsen*

Hal Lindsey's sister-in-law shares her extraordinary story about her involvement in the occult and how she learned to distinguish between the beautiful side of evil and the true way of the Lord.

LIKE LAMBS TO THE SLAUGHTER—Your Child and the Occult
by *Johanna Michaelsen*

Dungeons and Dragons, Saturday morning cartoons, Star Wars, E.T., yoga, spirit guides, guided imagery and visualization, storybooks on witchcraft and the occult. Are these merely innocent fun-filled activities, games, and toys designed to expand your child's creativity and intelligence—or is there a deliberate, calculated effort to raise a generation of psychics, shamans, mystics, and "channelers"? This book explores basics of the New Age Movement as it relates to children and exposes the deadly effects of the subtle occult practices so prevalent among our youth today.

STORMIE
by *Stormie Omartian*

The childhood of singer/songwriter Stormie Omartian, marred by physical and emotional abuse, led into teen and adult years filled with tragedy. Searching for an end to the inner turmoil which constantly confronted her, Stormie found herself on the verge of suicide. In this poignant story there is help and hope for anyone who doubts the value of his or her own life. It gloriously reveals a God who can bring life out of death if we are willing to surrender to His ways.

GODS OF THE NEW AGE
by *Caryl Matrisciana*

There is a worldwide conspiracy threatening today's society. In a fascinating look at Hinduism and its well-disguised western counterpart, The New Age Movement, Caryl Matrisciana prepares us to be spiritually discerning in the days ahead. Must reading for every believer.

OUT ON A BROKEN LIMB
by *F. LaGard Smith*

Millions of people have been exposed to the teachings of reincarnation, Eastern mysticism, and the New Age Movement through actress Shirley MacLaine's autobiography *Out on a Limb*. F. LaGard Smith explores the biblical meaning of life and afterlife in this answer to the MacLaine book.

Dear Reader:

We would appreciate hearing from you regarding this Harvest House nonfiction book. It will enable us to continue to give you the best in Christian publishing.

1. What most influenced you to purchase *Satan's Underground*?
   - ☐ Author
   - ☐ Subject matter
   - ☐ Backcover copy
   - ☐ Recommendations
   - ☐ Cover/Title
   - ☐ _____

2. Where did you purchase this book?
   - ☐ Christian bookstore
   - ☐ General bookstore
   - ☐ Other
   - ☐ Grocery store
   - ☐ Department store

3. Your overall rating of this book:
   - ☐ Excellent ☐ Very good ☐ Good ☐ Fair ☐ Poor

4. How likely would you be to purchase other books by this author?
   - ☐ Very likely
   - ☐ Somewhat likely
   - ☐ Not very likely
   - ☐ Not at all

5. What types of books most interest you?
   (check all that apply)
   - ☐ Women's Books
   - ☐ Marriage Books
   - ☐ Current Issues
   - ☐ Self Help/Psychology
   - ☐ Bible Studies
   - ☐ Fiction
   - ☐ Biographies
   - ☐ Children's Books
   - ☐ Youth Books
   - ☐ Other _____

6. Please check the box next to your age group.
   - ☐ Under 18
   - ☐ 18-24
   - ☐ 25-34
   - ☐ 35-44
   - ☐ 45-54
   - ☐ 55 and over

Mail to: Editorial Director
Harvest House Publishers
1075 Arrowsmith
Eugene, OR 97402

Name _____

Address _____

City _____ State _____ Zip _____

Thank you for helping us to help you in future publications!